The FOOTSTOOL of GOD

EARTH IN SCRIPTURE AND PROPHECY

Rodney Turner

Grandin Book Company
Orem, Utah

Dedication

To our children

Michael, Evan, Stephen, Jeffrey, Tracy and Rebecca

First published in 1983 by
Grandin Book Company
Orem, Utah 84057

ISBN 0-910523-03-7

Printed in the United States of America

Contents

iv

Introduction

Although the eventual demise of the planet earth is prophesied by some religious—and most scientific—sages, death is no more Earth's final fate than it is that of its myriad offspring. Because of the atonement and resurrection of Jesus Christ, death has been rendered an event rather than a destiny. Consequently, Earth and man are far more than passing incidents in the course of cosmic happenings; their relationship is both purposeful and everlasting.

This is the story of that relationship as told in prophecy and Holy Writ—both ancient and modern. It is a story without an ending, since all that has happened, and all that God has revealed concerning what will yet happen, is but a prologue to Earth's immortal career.

Yet what a prologue it is! From creation, to fall, to baptism, to sundering apart, to renewal, to death and triumphant resurrection—the biography of the earth is a romance of the highest order. For, unlike those romances in which God is not a participant, Earth's romance will not end in death, but in everlasting life.

What applies to Earth also applies to her worthy offspring—especially man. There is a symbiotic tie between Earth and man which binds each to each in the divine scheme of things. This relationship will only grow stronger and more splendid as time merges into eternity.

Because this precious knowledge has been vouchsafed us by the Creator via revelation, scripture, not science, constitutes the primary source of the concepts expressed in this work.

No attempt has been made herein to suggest a synthesis of religious and scientific opinion concerning the origin, nature, and destiny of the earth. Our present level of knowledge in both areas simply will not admit of a valid resolution of the discrepancies between the two. Eventually, whatever human error has crept into either viewpoint will be sloughed off, and, in their purity, the two will become one truth. But, for now, each must be understood and judged on its own merits and in its own context. To force a synthesis of their disparate views of creation, in pursuit of an illusion of harmony, adulterates both religion and science and only delays their ultimate authentic union.

They cannot be honestly reconciled at present; it is wrong to pretend that they can. For example, the earth's immortality enjoys no more scientific credence than does the immortality of man. Prevailing scientific opinion maintains that this planet and its life forms are products of natural, evolutionary development which began, and will end, in chaos. It is futile to argue the point; the revelations of God point us in one direction and prevailing scientific opinion, based upon empirical research, in another.

Admittedly, the truths found in science and in religion are harmonious, since all truth—whatever its nature or source—constitutes a noncontradictory, unified whole. (See JD, 20:74.)

Truth is not something dreamed, imagined, assumed, conjectured, rationalized, or theorized—*it is reality*. (See Jacob 4:13; D&C 93:24.) And when any portion of that reality is discovered by the scientist or the religionist, it will always be in perfect harmony with the *totality* of truth as it is possessed by an omniscient God.

The searching minds down through the ages who have been instrumental in bringing forth bonafide spiritual or secular knowledge constitute the authentic revelators of true religion and true science.

The scriptural conservative seeks to preserve the integrity of those truths found in Holy Writ. While he recognizes the presence of some myth and symbolism therein,[1] he feels obliged to interpret the vast majority of scripture from the standpoint of the objective (exoteric) connotations normally associated with the language. If God intends some subjective (esoteric) meaning, it is for him to make it know by additional revelation through his prophets. Hence, the scriptural conservative is inclined to agree with Joseph Smith that "the scriptures say what they mean and mean what they say." (TPJS, p. 264.)

Orson Pratt also opposed the "spiritualizing" of scriptures:

> We do not read the Scripures as most of the inhabitants of the earth do, thinking that they must be spiritualized. There are scarcely any of the prophecies but what this generation, as well as some of the past generations, interpret as meaning something altogether different from the reading of them. They look upon inspired men as saying one thing and meaning another, and the only way to ascertain what meaning they really wish to convey is to get an uninspired man to give some

---

[1] Certain stories, passages, and books of Holy Writ are obviously of a symbolic or allegorical nature since they do not pretend to reflect reality as it pertains to the consistent ways of God or to the natural order known to man. The creation of man and the visions in Daniel, Ezekiel and Revelation are examples of this.

other meaning entirely different from the literal construction
of the words of the inspired writer. (JD, 20:8, 9.)

He then went on to say that when the Latter-day Saints received the Holy
Ghost they learned that scripture was to be understood "in the same light,
and in the same sense" as they would understand any uninspired docu-
ment.

Further, when those scriptures pertaining to God's creative enterprises are "spiritualized" into myth and symbolism (so as to render them
innocuous) both he and his word are gratuitously demeaned.[2]

While human reason and experience are legitimate tools in the search
for truth, they are not the only tools, nor even the best tools.[3] In this fallen
world we are counseled to seek learning by study for the precise reason
that we are not capacitated to receive it entirely by faith.[4] Few men have
been pure enought to obtain extensive knowledge by direct revelation
from God.

Consequently, knowledge must be obtained primarily through our
own minds (via study or reason) and secondarily through the mind of God
(via faith or revelation). This is as it should be in this sphere of man's
development; it is not wrong. But what *is* wrong is that some men will exalt
learning obtained by study by denigrating those truths that an omniscient
God has revealed by faith! True knowledge and wisdom have but one
source. Muddy the stream though we may, the Fountainhead remains
pure.

Since the final word will be spoken by the Creator himself, the
dogmatic defense of any theory—scientific or religious—which purports
to provide that word can only be pride-begotten foolishness. Jesus Christ
is the one who will reveal the whole truth concerning the origin and
purpose of the heavens, the earth, and all things in them. (See D&C
101:32-34)

The Footstool of God was written with a conscious awareness that fallible
men do not produce infallible books. Still, it is hoped that the reader will

---

[2]The cliche, "The Bible is not a textbook on science," has become the
rallying cry of those who wish to disregard its information on geology and
anthropology.

[3]Joseph Smith said: "The best way to obtain truth and wisdom is not
to ask it from books, but to go to God in prayer, and obtain divine
teaching." (*HC*, 4:425.)

[4]See D&C 88:118; 109:7. Note that learning by study or human
reason is secondary to learning by faith.

not make me an offender for a word lest, in doing so, the essential story of the origin and destiny of this wondrous planet be rejected. Be assured that in due time the definitive biography of "the mother of men" will be forthcoming from her Creator.

Revelations given through the Prophet Joseph Smith have served both to confirm and expand upon the biblical treatment of the earth. Therefore, scripture—ancient and modern—was the primary source for this work.

It was augmented by relevant statements of leading authorities in The Church of Jesus Christ of Latter-day Saints with full appreciation of the fact that not all of their pronouncements carry equal weight. Some of them are admittedly speculative in nature and do not reflect the official position of the Church. Indeed, the Church has no official position on a number of the concepts discussed herein. This does not mean that these concepts are false; it only means that they do not come within the pale of established doctrine—dogma. In time, we shall doubtless learn that a number of these speculative ideas were correct, others will fall by the wayside. Time continues to be the measure of all things.

The writer has included some representative statements of respected scriptorians solely for purposes of information. Others have been quoted because they served to flesh out key passages of scripture and had the ring of truth about them. The subjectivity of the writer in doing this is readily admitted.

Especial attention has been given to the teachings of Brigham Young, second president of the LDS Church, and to Orson Pratt, a leading nineteenth-century apostle-theologian. The views of these early authorities are representative of virtually all that was later taught on this subject.

While both of these men were thoroughly convinced of the validity of Holy Writ, their respective approaches to it were somewhat different. Orson Pratt was inclined to considerable speculation on matters of eschatology and prophecy. Brigham Young, on the other hand, was less inclined to draw upon the written word for his views; he had confidence in his prophetic calling and the personal revelation it afforded him. Then too, he was, as he phrased it, "an apostle of Joseph Smith" and regarded the Prophet as his spiritual mentor. Speaking to this point, he said:

> On the things of God, on the building up of his kingdom, on the doctrines Joseph taught, or on anything that pertains to the priesthood, I will not lay my memory aside to prefer any man's living. I know how I received the knowledge that I have got. I have seen the time when I first saw Joseph that I had but one prayer and I offered that all the time. And that was that I

might be permitted to hear Joseph speak on doctrine and see
his mind reach out untrammelled to grasp the deep things of
God. But in consequence of the wickedness of the children of
men and the consequent inability they possessed to receive
heavenly things, he could not impart what was made known to
him of the Lord. I was with him several years before I pre-
tended to open my mouth to speak at all, but I would constantly
watch him, and if possible learn doctrine and principle beyond
that which he expressed . . .An angel never watched him closer
than I did, and that is what has given me the knowledge I have
today. I treasure it up and ask the Father in the name of Jesus
to help my memory when information is wanted and I have
never been at a loss to know what to do concerning the Kingdom of God. (Discourse of Brigham Young, October 7, 1863,
Church Archives, Salt Lake City, Utah.)

Brigham Young's non-theoretical approach to doctrinal matters,
coupled with his intimate knowledge of the teachings of Joseph Smith,
and Orson Pratt's faith-founded, but rational treatment of LDS theology,
dictated the extensive attention their pronouncements received in this
work.

******

I owe a debt of gratitude to a number of men—active, retired, or
deceased—of the faculty of Religious Instruction at Brigham Young
University for the intellectual and spiritual impact they have had on my
life. In ways, both direct and indirect, they are a part of all that I may have
accomplished.

I am most appreciative of the time and effort Lyndon W. Cook, the
publisher, has expended in making valuable literary and technical
suggestions and in endeavoring to assure the overall quality of this work.

My thanks to Connie Jensen, my present secretary, who cheerfully
typed and retyped the final draft, and also to Barney Madsen who worked
on the original manuscript.

As always, I am indebted to my wife, Bonnie Lou, for her undeviating
faith and support throughout this sometimes frustrating enterprise.

Finally, a big hug to my daughter, Tracy Ann Tallent, who accompanied me when I lectured on this subject some years ago and thereafter
encouraged its expansion into book form.

PART ONE

God and His Creations

CHAPTER ONE

The Two Universes

There are places where the night sky appears to be one vast canopy of lights—motionless, yet moving, remote, yet at our fingertips. The emotional impression is that those far-flung worlds are virtually countless in number. However, reason reminds us that on the clearest and darkest of nights the unaided human eye can only perceive the incoming light rays of some seven thousand heavenly bodies. Still, the emotional impression is much closer to the ultimate truth than the visual fact: there are not only millions, but billions and *trillions* of worlds to be found within the interlocking eternities of endless space.

The Times of Motion

Although the stars comprising a given galaxy appear to the astronomer to be in aimless, random motion, they are, nevertheless, under the ultimate control of an overruling Providence. Invisible hands direct this stellar traffic down the trackless highways of galactic space. These bodies, with their planetary systems, constitute wheels within wheels of time and motion.

The earth orbits the sun at 66,500 miles per hour while the sun and its system is circling the core of our galaxy, the Milky Way, at approximately 600,000 miles per hour—making one complete revolution in 200 million years. The Milky Way is, in turn, believed to be orbiting a supercluster of 2,500 nearby galaxies at something over one million miles per hour while simultaneously moving outward through space at an estimated speed of over 300,000 miles per hour. All is in motion; yet all is controlled by the unerring hand of the Almighty.

> And again, verily I say unto you, he hath given a law unto all things, by which they move in their times and their seasons;
> And their courses are fixed, even the courses of the heavens and the earth, which comprehend the earth and all the planets.
> And they give light to each other in their times and in their seasons, in their minutes, in their hours, in their days, in their weeks, in their months, in their years—all these are one year with God, but not with man.[1]

While the actual population of the heavens is, and will remain, numberless to mortal man, astronomers have discovered that it is far greater than was formerly supposed.[2] Astrophysicists using increasingly powerful and sophisticated instruments (such as the radio telescope) have discovered or postulated such exotic things as quasars, pulsars, black holes, and anti-matter. Consequently, we now know that the universe is not only far larger but also much more complex than was formerly supposed.

Man stands like some tiny creature upon this pebble of time and looks outward into eternity. He is mistakenly thought to be only a microscopic part of the riddle of existence, the solution to which appears as remote and as elusive as the outer limits of the universe itself. But does the universe have limits? Although probing ever deeper into the distant reaches of space, astronomers find no end to it or its galactic inhabitants. Its horizon, like that of the earth, seems to move with the mover leaving us to wonder if it is not a shoreless continent of incomprehensible proportions and indeterminate form.

How long a time was required to bring it, with all of its diversity, to its present state of organization? How old is it? What is its lifespan? Will it live

----

[1]D&C 88:42-44. Orson Pratt defined "one year with God" as being "celestial time." (D&C, 1890 ed.) Facsimile two, figure one in the *Book of Abraham* supports Pratt's view.

[2]The telescope was not invented until 1608. It has only been in the last century that astronomers have learned that the actual number of stars far exceeds the few thousand formerly thought to exist—being estimated at 10^{28} or ten octillion.

forever or is it self-doomed to oblivion? What is the sum and substance of its laws, forces, elements, and structures? How do they relate to one another? In brief, what is the nature of its anatomy and physiology?

And how did it all come to be? Is it the handwork of God or the chance result of incredibly fortuitous interaction between matter and energy? How the universe was formed *is* critically germaine to why it was formed. If it is a self-begotten accident, a child of chance, then there is no purpose to it; it just is. For there cannot be purpose without a purposer. Consequently, the "why" of things cannot be considered apart from the "how" of things.

Unless a creative mind, a supreme being, a God—call it what we will—is the primal cause behind all law and all creation, they cannot be purposeful in any ultimate sense. And if the whole of creation is purposeless, its parts are purposeless. Thus, if the universe is devoid of lasting meaning, then man is equally meaningless and his life is written on the wind.

Three Cosmogonies

In this regard, science provides us with scant comfort. Currently, there are three major theories of cosmogony. The most widely accepted of them predicts the eventual destruction of the universe and, therefore, the victory of death over life.

The "Steady-State" hypothesis posits a relatively stable but expanding universe, *without beginning or end*, in which the hydrogen (the chief component in nuclear fusion) needed to perpetuate the system is being continually produced out of nothing.

This *ex nihilo* hydrogen is used to form new stars which replace those that die, and also to fill in the elementary voids left by the galaxies as they continue to move outward and away from their common center and from each other. The "Steady-State" is generally considered the least tenable of the three cosmogonies.[3]

Almost all contemporary astrophysicists hold to a second theory—the

---

[3]The Steady-State theory violates the accepted principle of conservation of matter and energy (that matter and energy can neither be created nor destroyed)—a view held by Joseph Smith: "The pure principles of element are principles which can never be destroyed; they may be organized and re-organized but not destroyed. They had no beginning and can have no end." (HC, 6:308, 309. See also *ibid.*, 5:393.)

"Big-Bang."[4] Many billions of years ago virtually all matter was concentrated into a single mass of incomprehensible density with internal temperatures in the trillions of degrees—the ultimate supernova.[5] When this mass—"the cosmic egg"—became critical, it exploded, hurling its contents into space, thereby simultaneously increasing its dimensions while reducing its density.

However, as the universe continues to expand, the galaxies, in moving ever farther apart, will cause inter-galactic space to become ever emptier. This will cause the irreplaceable hydrogen within the galaxies to be used up. The galaxies, with their star systems, will fade and die and the universe will be no more.

Since the universe appears to be expanding at a steadily *decreasing* speed (due to the braking effect of the gravitational pull of the galaxies upon one another), most astrophysicists believe that it will eventually slow to a stop, reverse direction, and then crash in upon itself in a disintegrating implosion.

The third theory, known as the "Oscillating Universe," is something of a synthesis of the Steady-State and Big-Bang cosmogonies. It suggests that the universe is passing through repeated cycles of contraction and expansion. Upon reaching its ultimate point of expansion, gravitational force will bring the already slowing universe to a halt; it will then reverse itself and contract once more into a single mass. When this mass reaches a critical density and temperature, a new "big-bang" will occur and a new hydrogen universe will be born.[6]

Which, if any, of the current cosmogonies will prove correct? Can hydrogen be created out of nothing as is required by the "Steady-State"? Did the universe explode into being only to suffer eternal extinction as suggested by the "Big Bang"? Or is it a self-perpetuating system, endlessly

---

[4]A term coined by a Russian-American physicist, George Gamow.

[5]A supernova is a star of very great mass that suddenly releases all of its energy in one vast nuclear explosion, causing its virtual disintegration as its gaseous contents are hurled far into space. At the time of explosion, a supernova may equal or exceed the brilliance of the entire galaxy in which it is located. In 1054 a supernova was visible in daylight for 23 days.

[6]This scenario depends upon the presence of an adequate gravitational force to stop and reverse its motion. If such a force is lacking, the dead universe is expected to continue its outward voyage forever—the ultimate "Flying Dutchman."

dying and reincarnating itself as maintained by advocates of the Oscillating theory?

The Cosmogony of Scripture

What is the truth? Were billions of years involved in the evolution of the universe as we observe it today? Did *everything* begin this way? Did the entire universe with its myriad galaxies and star systems have a common moment of conception, a relatively common length of gestation, and, therefore, a relatively common birthday?[7] And if God was back of it all, did he reveal himself in one magnificent burst of capricious creativity?

Scripture's answer to all of these questions would seem to be "no." The Almighty did not begin and end his involvement in either natural or human affairs once and for all. He is not a deistic god.

His work and his glory is to bring to pass the immortality and eternal life of man. (See Moses 1:39.) That is an *endless* work, therefore the organization of new worlds in accomplishing that work is equally unending. This is why his course is one eternal round. (See D&C 3:2; 35:1.)

Worlds come and worlds go, and at least some of them do so *individually*. God is more than a mass producer. Moses learned that fact from the Creator himself.

And the Lord God spake unto Moses, saying: The heavens, they are many, and they cannot be numbered unto man; but they are numbered unto me, for they are mine.

And as *one* earth shall pass away, and the heavens thereof even so shall *another* come, and there is *no end to my works*, neither to my words.[8]

---

[7]It should be understood that astrophysicists do not claim that all stars were created simultaneously. While they believe that the galaxies were formed as a result of the primal "big-bang," new stars are and will continue to be formed for billions of years to come. Hence, astronomers speak of both first and second generation stars—meaning those formed as a result of the original "big-bang" and those (such as our sun) formed later from the debris of supernova.

[8]Moses 1:37, 38. (Italics added. Hereafter all italics will be by the writer except when otherwise indicated.) Joseph Fielding Smith stated that an earth such as ours passes away, not to death, but to higher estates of life and glory. (See *Doctrines of Salvation*, 1:72, 73.)

Enoch also understood the ongoing nature of God's creations. He testified that "were it possible that man could number the particles of the earth, yea, millions of earths like this, it would not be a beginning to the number of thy creations; and *thy curtains are stretched out still.*" (Moses 7:30.)

Abraham learned, literally from the hand of the Lord, that the organization of new worlds is an endless process reaching into the mists of eternal time:

> And he said unto me: My son, my son (and his hand was stretched out), behold I will show you all these. And he put his hand upon mine eyes, and I saw those things which his hands had made, which were many; and they multiplied before mine eyes, and I could not see the end thereof. (Abraham 3:12.)

Although God may follow the creative process theorized by astrophysicists where some planets, stars, and galaxies are concerned, he is not bound by the physical laws of the known universe. Just as all men are not mortal—some being spirits, some translated, and some resurrected—so, too, some spheres are formed of spirit matter, some of gross matter, and some of a combination of the two. Thus, worlds may be organized under different principles, of different materials, at different times, and for different purposes.

It is very likely that most, if not all, of the observable stars and galaxies are temporal in nature; they have been formed purely "for signs and for seasons." The "eternal worlds" are as undetectable as are those higher orders of humankind which dwell beyond the veil of mortality. Those earths or "lands" shown Moses were specifically designed to be immortal and were probably organized in sequence in this eternity.[9]

The universe *in toto* is not a monolithic miracle, blown into existence at a given moment; it is a living organism, the cellular structure of which is in a constant state of flux. And earth is no mere by-product of the gaseous remains of some long gone supernova. It is a purposeful and independent act of God—a celestial enterprise destined to fill the measure of its creation both in time and eternity. (See D&C 88:19, 20, 25.)

Present estimates of the age of the universe vary from thirteen to

---

[9]See Moses 3:29. In speaking of the creation of this world, Joseph Smith said: "The grand councilors sat at the head in yonder heavens and contemplated the creation of the *worlds* which were created at the time." (HC, 6:307.)

twenty billion years and that of our solar system from four and one half to five billion years. What is the likelihood that these figures are even approximately correct?

If God is engaged in an ongoing, never-ending program of organization, the question of the age of the universe as such is meaningless. We might as well ask how long it took to build Rome or London since these cities have long histories of growth and development spanning centuries of building up, tearing down, and general expansion.

Even assuming (as astrophysicists do) that the overall life-span of the universe can be measured in the trillions of years, in which stars will continue to be born and die, the allotted time is still too brief to meet the demands of revealed truth. Scripture argues for an *infinite* life-span where certain worlds are concerned.

However, the theories advanced by modern astronomy are supported by a considerable amount of impressive technical data which cannot be gainsayed. And it all seems to point to one conclusion: the universe is slowly but surely dying. Certainly the theological implications of this dour prognosis are most profound. Mankind can have no enduring reason for being if it is trapped in a terminal and, therefore, in an ultimately meaningless state of existence. But God is not a character in any play written by scientists. He has spoken of worlds that go on forever.

Where does the truth lie? There is but one answer: wholly with God and partially with man. Each bears witness to reality as each experiences it; this accounts for the apparent discrepency between their testimonies.

Divine science is infinite in experience and, therefore, infinite in knowledge. It comprehends the end as well as the beginning. Doing so, it can testify to the transcending power of life over death—an eternal truth human science has not experienced and, therefore, cannot know.

Because the fall permeates man's environment and delimits his field of experience, his science is equally circumscribed. It is the science of a kingdom of change and decay; everything in it bears the hallmark of mortality. In this kingdom, men and worlds share a common fate.

Thus, astrophysicists believe that stars are produced from great clouds of loose hydrogen atoms which evolve first into protostars[10] and then into true stars which pass through a basic life cycle of birth, maturity, old age, and death. Their longevity depends upon their size and structure and is thought to vary from as little as one million years to more than a trillion years. But regardless of lifespan, every star, along with every galaxy, is doomed to come to an end.

---

[10]Clusters of trillions of atoms.

The degree to which this generally accepted scenario will prove accurate remains to be seen. While there is no reason to dispute the reported observations of current stellar activity, the long-range conclusions extrapolated from those observations are another matter.

But whatever the fate of the observable universe as such, astrophysicists cannot be certain that there are not divinely-appointed exceptions to its governing laws. Here we come to the crossroads of knowledge; it is precisely at this point that we must turn from faith in man to faith in God. It is here that the science of earth should humbly yield to the science of Heaven.

Eternal Worlds

The Creator has informed us that the natural order is but the dim reflection of a higher order which is immeasurably superior to it in character and perfection. Beyond this visible universe of finite time and death lies an invisible one—one that is spiritual, and, hence immortal.[11]

This unseen universe is the place of the Father's many enduring mansions—the realms of immortal glory. Revelation speaks of them as *"the eternal worlds,"* (D&C 132:55, 63) the greatest of which are the promised lands of "the begotten sons and daughters unto God." (D&C 76:24.) They include those Zions which God has taken to his "own bosom from all eternity to all eternity." (Moses 7:31.)

Whereas the mortal stars in our fallen system are characterized by relative instability and change, the *eternal* stars are realms of perpetual tranquility and unspeakable beauty. They are the everlasting homes of resurrected life. Abraham saw some of them by means of the Urim and Thummim:

----

[11]Paul declared Christ to be the Creator of all things "visible and invisible." (Colossians 1:16.) Worlds are immortal when they are spiritual rather than temporal in character. (See D&C 88:27.) Like a resurrected body, their original spirit organization has become "inseparably connected" or fused to its temporal counterpart. (See D&C 93:33; Alma 11:45.) This fusion of spirit with element produces a unified spiritual body, the nature of which is far different from that of those worlds of gross materiality perceived by men. Consequently, we cannot see them for spirit "can only be discerned by purer eyes" than mortals possess. (See D&C 131:7, 8.)

And I saw the stars, that they were very great, and that one of them was nearest unto the throne of God; and there were many great ones which were near unto it;

And the Lord said unto me: These are the governing ones; and the name of the great one is Kolob, because it is near unto me, for I am the Lord thy God: I have set this one *to govern* all those which belong to the *same order* as that upon which thou standest.[12]

Note that the temporal order is governed by the spiritual order, the lesser by the greater. The controlling and sustaining energy which flows through the visible universe has its fountainhead in the realms of the Gods. The beginning-land of all eternal things lies far beyond man's searching eyes.

Paul's words to the Corinthians might well be paraphrased by a humble astronomer: "I see through a telescope darkly." Yet scientists do not labor in vain; the universe they search is a magnificent part of the Almighty's dominions—an unlimited reservoir of raw materials from which he continues to fashion new worlds. Some of these are destined for habitation in the realms of everlasting light and life. (See Revelation 21:23-25.)

A veil of darkness, of limited capacity to know, hides those realms from us. (See D&C 82:5; 84:49; 112:23.) Still, a few worthy men have been privileged to have that veil partially lifted. Joseph Smith and Sidney Rigdon testified: "By the power of the Spirit our eyes were opened and our understandings were enlightened, so as to see and understand the things of God." (D&C 76:12. See 110:1.) They were then shown those eternal worlds which no man-devised instruments can ever discover or probe. In summing up their experience they wrote:

But great and marvelous are the works of the Lord, and the mysteries of his kingdom which he showed unto us, which

---

[12]Abraham 3:2, 3. One evidence of the transcendent nature of these prefected "governing" realms is the incredible length of Kolob's period of rotation—one thousand earth years. No known star begins to equal it. (See Abraham 3:4.) In explaining the significance of selected symbols in facsimile number two of the Book of Abraham, Joseph Smith spoke of certain worlds as "holding the key of power also, pertaining to other planets." See, in particular, his explanations of figures two and five.

surpass all understanding in glory, and in might, and in dominion . . . .

Neither is man capable to make them known, for they are only to be seen and understood by the power of the Holy Spirit, which God bestows on those who love him, and purify themselves before him. (D&C 76:114-117.)

Science is no more capable of proving or disproving the existence of immortal worlds than it is of proving or disproving the existence of immortal men. But if we have faith in the existence of one, can we doubt the existence of the other?

Earth is shrouded in darkness, in a firmament of gross physical matter.[13] It is cut off from that divine atmosphere which envelops the eternal kingdoms. Indeed, the whole physical universe apparently lies behind a curtain of unperfected element. In due time, that curtain will be lifted. The righteous will then behold what natural eyes have never beheld: glorious immortal beings and glorious immortal worlds—an order of endless duration, the science of which is as exalted above the science of this universe as the Gods are exalted above men.

---

[13]In Mormon thought, matter is divided into two basic classes: gross matter (called element) which fills the observable universe, and refined matter (spirit). (See D&C 93:33-35.) The nature of spirit matter precludes its detection by mortals who are composed of gross matter. Joseph Smith said, "There is no such thing as immaterial matter. All spirit is matter, but it more fine or pure, and can only be discerned by purer eyes; we cannot see it; but when our bodies are purified we shall see that it is all matter." (D&C 131:7, 8.)

CHAPTER TWO

God and Natural Law

The working assumption of modern science is that reality is circumscribed by those things which can be physically perceived. Thus, for all practical purposes, whatever is not discernable through the senses comes within the pale of philosophy or religion. Obviously, this includes all things spiritual or supernatural.[1] Most scientists, therefore, go about the business of explaining the universe as though God were either nonexistent or irrelevant.[2] They honor the art, but ignore the Artist. Such is their myopia. It is argued that this non-theistic approach is necessary if science is to remain objective and if it is to present a consistent explanation of reality. How could science be science if it allowed for the possibility of miraculous intervention in the natural order?

Some theists, not wanting to rule God out entirely, maintain that man's ways are also God's ways; that he is not only bound by law, but by the same laws—natural and moral—to which men are subject. Thus, for them, Deity is a Cosmic Scientist who, in the process of discovering the

---

[1]Because Mormonism views reality as being on a continuum, the term "supernatural" is seldom used in theological discussion.

[2]This generalization pertains to the dominant philosophy of science. There are a number of respected, competent scientists who do not limit either their faith or their discipline to a purely mechanistic approach.

self-existent laws of nature, and by obedience to them, produced the universe—the ultimate technological achievement.

This view is appealing because it provides us with a sense of continuity where law is concerned, but it requires God to abdicate in favor of his own handiwork. He did not simply discover law, he *created* it! Joseph Smith taught that God had the power "to institute laws whereby the rest of the spirits could have a privilege to advance like himself." (HC, 6:312.) Of the natural order, the Prophet said: "God has made certain decrees which are fixed and immovable; for instance,—God set the sun, the moon, and the stars in the heavens, and *gave them their laws*, conditions, and bounds, which they cannot pass, *except by His commandments*." (HC, 4:554.) Orson Pratt also recognized that God is the formulator of law:

> The Latter-day Saints say, that the Lord of Hosts who has given us laws, adapted to our condition as free agents, has also given laws to these material worlds, by which they act and by which they are preserved for a great, and wise and good purpose, to sustain unnumbered myriads of animated beings, who are by numerous other laws adapted to these worlds, and enjoy life therein . . . .*God is the great Author of all law*, and is just as able to counteract a law, as he is to continue a law. (JD, 21:237, 238. See also 18:317; 21:321.)

John Taylor asked: "Who has implanted certain principles in matter and in all creation? God has done it." (JD, 25:215.) God can create, revoke, and overrule law as he chooses. He is omnipotent where nature is concerned. Limiting God's agency cannot be defended scripturally. But, as Joseph Smith noted: "It is the constitutional disposition of mankind to set up stakes and set bounds to the works and ways of the Almighty." (HC, 5:529.) And he warned: "I say to all those who are disposed to set up stakes for the Almighty, you will come short of the glory of God." (HC, 5:554.)

Despite this, some are unwilling to give the Almighty even a subordinate role in Creation. Naturalists maintain that the "great first cause" was not God, but self-existent natural law.[3] Law simply *is*. And it is sovereign. Its mechanistic operations produced the universe. Witless circumstance created all things by nuclear force, gravitation, and electromagnetism. Thus, proponents of a godless cosmogony maintain that a universe which

---

[3]The philosophy that the universe evolved as a totally self-generated, self-directed, and self-sustaining system is called naturalism.

challenges the best scientific minds to unravel its mysteries, understand its workings, and apply its principles is, itself, nothing more than the product of blind law.

Evolution and Natural Law

This working article of faith among thorough-going naturalists explains the pervasiveness of the evolutionary doctrine among cosmologists, geologists, paleontologists, biologists, and other scientists. While men should not be faulted for advancing any hypothesis they choose in their search for truth, some can be justifiably criticized for practicing sleight of hand and transforming questionable theory into unquestionable fact.

Such unscientific science has led to the widespread practice of arbitrarily dismissing every theory but the evolutionary theory for the origin of the universe, the earth, life, man, and human culture. For too many intellectuals, evolution is the key which unlocks the door to all beginnings.

Why do these men insist upon exalting theory to the heights of incontrovertible fact? Whatever their motives, one thing is indisputable: not a single aspect of the companion theories of cosmic, organic, and cultural evolution is dependent upon any mind, any power, any cause or any god other than natural law itself. Evolution is a self-generating process.

The naturalistic approach to the question of origins is defended as being objective, but the dogmatic stand of some of its practitioners suggests that their "objectivity" is actually a euphemism for pride. No human enterprise can justify the absence of humility—the recognition of God's works and ways and man's fundamental dependence upon him. (See D&C 59:21.) A proud science is no more excusable than a proud man. Orson Pratt observed:

> Now, the Lord has powers beyond those with which we are acquainted. He has almighty powers. He has only intrusted us his children of mortality with a knowledge of some of the more gross principles and laws of this fallen creation, and when we, through hard study, search out the relation of one law to another, we think we are learned men; but I think when we learn in that great university the sciences of which the Lord our God is the great Teacher, we shall learn more rapidly and comprehend more easily the things of his kingdom, than we now do the things of time. (JD, 19:294.)

While the theistic science of the middle ages can be rightly criticized for its prejudices, some of its present offspring are guilty of an even greater sin: by enthroning law they have dethroned the Law-giver. The wedding of science to natural law is a marriage of convenience, not of necessity. Scientific research does not require the abandonment of faith in God's sovereignty over law. That faith, so emphasized in Christianity, was simply surrendered for the lesser faith of naturalism.

The history of science is usually taught in a manner to make religion—"the church"—an arch-villain in the piece. The persecution of Galileo and others is recounted in a manner to suggest that all religion is an enemy to open inquiry. Consequently, the notion is almost universal that in so far as the physical order is concerned, religion has nothing to say and no right to say it. The tyranny of blind faith has been supplanted by the tyranny of blind reason.

Modern evolutionary theory is a dark child of the unholy alliance between science and natural law. It is the construct of creation imposed by human reason in the absence of an overruling intelligence. In other words, evolution is the only process man can conceive of for creation without a Creator.

This is precisely why evolution, in all of its aspects, involves incredibly long periods of time. It is illogically assumed that anything can happen if there is sufficient time. The failure to demonstrate so naive a notion does not deter evolutionists from repeating it like a litany.

However, the truth is that there are aspects of creation that are truly miraculous. They involve laws which transcend the understanding of man—laws which were and are uniquely employed by the Almighty in his own creative labors. But those who insist upon explaining everything on strictly naturalistic principles deny the miraculous and, perforce, the Miracle Worker.

Uniformitarianism

Naturalism gave birth to the now widely held theory of uniformitarianism.[4] In its absolute form, this postulate does not allow for the miraculous intervention of God in the cosmic order of things.

Uniformitarianism is the working hypothesis of those scientists con-

---

[4]Uniformitarianism was first espoused by Charles Lyell (1797-1875) in *Principles of Geology*. It is the *a priori* assumption that basic physical processes have remained unchanged, or uniform, throughout time. Thus, all past and present phenomena in the astronomic, geologic, and biologic orders were caused by the self-same process.

cerned with all that happened prior to man's advent on earth. Such research poses a dilemma: "If man cannot know anything he has not experienced, how can he determine the facts relative to the origin of the universe, the earth, life, man, etc.?" The answer provided by uniformitarianism is that the constancy of nature's processes can be assumed—the past can be experienced by observing the present. That is, the unknown can be extrapolated from the known.

This view of reality was prophesied by the apostle Peter who wrote that in the last days men would say: "All things continue *as they were* from the beginning of creation." (2 Peter 3:4.) Uniformitarianism is a reasonable, justifiable, and, indeed, necessary postulate of science. However, it is neither demonstrable nor verifiable. Therefore, it should not be considered more than a working hypothesis. When it is affirmed dogmatically, its proponents cease to function as authentic scientists.

Uniformitarianism is not unlike a detective's *ex post facto* investigation of a murder for which there were no eye witnesses. He studies the scene of the crime, notes the available evidence, and then *theorizes* as to the guilty party. But innocent men have been hanged and many false notions have been advanced only to be abandoned in the light of new facts. While human limitations render this procedure necessary for a theoretical understanding of the past, still it is a risky business at best, calling for the greatest reticence in arriving at even tentative conclusions.

Opposing the doctrine of uniformitarianism is catastrophism, the belief that cataclysmic changes have and will occur from time to time in the course of God's overruling providence. Catastrophism is supported scripturally in connection with the accounts of the creation, the fall, the flood, the death and second coming of Christ, the millennium, the end of the earth, and other important events both past and future. Such catastrophic events serve to disprove the theory of uniformitarianism with its implicit repudiation of divine intervention in human and natural affairs.

The Testimony of Scripture

For those who are "ever learning, and never able to come to a knowledge of the truth," all is nature, all is chance, all is purposelessness. However, central to all that God has made known is one eternal truth—a truth sensed by the simplest savage and the merest child: creation testifies to a Creator. Life is purposeful. We are not the hapless victims of chance. Joseph Smith observed:

> But if this life is all, then why this constant toiling, why this
> continual warfare, and why this unceasing trouble? But this life

is not all; the voice of *reason*, the language of *inspiration*, and the Spirit of the living God, our Creator, teaches us, as we hold the record of truth in our hands, that this is not the case, that this is not so; for, the heavens declare the glory of God, and the firmament showeth His handiwork; and a moment's reflection is sufficient to teach every man of common intelligence, that all these are not the mere productions of *chance*, nor could they be supported by any power less than an Almighty hand. (HC, 2:14. Italics in the original.)

Scripture repudiates the philosophy of naturalism. It sustains the cosmological argument for God[5] by affirming that all things are dependent upon him for their organized existence:

And if ye shall say there is no law, ye shall also say there is no sin. If ye shall say there is no sin, ye shall also say there is no righteousness. And if there be no righteousness there be no happiness. And if there be no righteousness nor happiness there be no punishment nor misery. And if these things are not there is no God. And *if there is no God* we are not, neither the earth; for *there could have been no creation of things*, neither to act nor to be acted upon; wherefore, all things must have vanished away. (2 Nephi 2:13.)

The apostle Paul declared Jesus Christ to be the foundation of all organized things: "For by him were all things created, that are in heaven, and that are in earth, *visible and invisible*, whether they be thrones, or dominions, or principalities, or powers: all things were created by him, and for him. And he is before all things, and by him all things consist." (Colossians 1:16, 17.) The apostle John testified: "All things were made by him; and without him was not anything made that was made." (John 1:3.) Scripture is replete with such testimonies so that no one need doubt that the universe is a product of God's genius through the Lord Jesus Christ.

The teleological argument[6] is supported in scripture in such passages

---

[5]The essence of the cosmological argument is that every effect has a prior cause and that the ultimate and non-contingent first cause of all things is God.

[6]The teleological argument is that all things give evidence of purpose or design aimed at a meaningful destiny. Hence, if there is design there must be a Designer.

as the following: "Wherefore, it [the earth] must needs have been created for a thing of naught; wherefore there would have been no *purpose* in the end to its creation. Wherefore, this thing must needs destroy the wisdom of God and his eternal *purposes*, and also the power, and the mercy, and the justice of God." (2 Nephi 2:12.)

All eternity is organized into various kingdoms or systems of law with their appropriate bounds and conditions.[7] Nothing is left to chance, whether man, animals, vegetation, planets, stars, solar systems, or galaxies—all are governed by that matchless God who rules from the "bosom of eternity." (D&C 88:13.)

> He comprehendeth all things, and all things are before him, and all things are round about him; and he is above all things, and in all things, and is through all things, and is round about all things; and all things are by him, and of him, even God, forever and ever. And again, verily I say unto you, he hath given a law unto all things, by which they move in their times and their seasons; And their courses are fixed, even the courses of the heavens and the earth, which comprehend the earth and all the planets. (D&C 88:41-43.)

> The Lord declared that "any man who has seen any or the least of these hath seen God moving in his majesty and power." (D&C 88:47.) This is why the Psalmist wrote, "The heavens declare [bear witness of] the glory of God; and the firmament sheweth his handiwork." (Psalm 91:1.) Everything in the universe witnesses of God's existence, nature, and genius. To deny him one must deny reality itself; reality is a synonym for God.

The Lord told Adam:

> And behold, all things have their likeness, and all things are created and made *to bear record of me*, both things which are temporal, and things which are spiritual; things which are in the heavens above, and things which are on the earth, and things which are in the earth, and things which are under the

---

[7]See D&C 88:36-39. If the universe were not a complex network of interrelated systems of law, it could not properly be referred to as a cosmos, and science as we know it would be an impossibility.

earth, both above and beneath: all things bear record of me. (Moses 6:63. See 2 Nephi 11:4; Helaman 8:24.)

The avowed atheist, Korihor, tried to deny the undeniable God. He wanted a sign before he would believe. But Alma rebuked him:

Thou hast had signs enough; will ye tempt your God? Will ye say, Show unto me a sign, when ye have the testimony of all these thy brethren, and also all the holy prophets? The scriptures are laid before thee, yea, and all things denote there is a God; yea, even the earth, and all things that are upon the face of it, yea, and its motion, yea, and also all the planets which move in their regular form do witness that there is a Supreme Creator. (Alma 30:44.)

Indeed, the world has had signs enough. God is witnessed on every hand; all creation testifies of its Creator! We are literally immersed in a sea of testimony that he lives and that he rules over all things, both animate and inanimate. The works of God are purposeful works. The undeniable design affirms the Designer.

CHAPTER THREE

The Creative Power of God

*Behold, great and marvelous are the works of the Lord. How unsearch-
able are the depths of the mysteries of him; and it is impossible that man
should find out all his ways. And no man knoweth of his ways save it be
revealed unto him; wherefore, brethren, despise not the revelations of
God. (Jacob 4:8.)*

While God has the freedom to roam from one end of eternity to the
other (comprehending every dimension of time), man is bound to the
present, to the whatness of things as they *now* exist. This is why the vast
majority of physical scientists necessarily concern themselves with the
practical rather than the theoretical aspects of their various disciplines.
They seek to understand the present mechanics of the universe, and their
discoveries of some of its governing principles have led to the impressive
technological achievements which bless and curse us today. Consequently,
the more speculative question of how the cosmic mechanism came into
being has been left to a comparatively few scientists, the astrophysicists.

Similarly, almost all of those who have treated the earth's beginnings
from a scriptural standpoint have concentrated on the physical process
while virtually ignoring the ultimate spiritual means by which that process
came about. Stressing divine ends while ignoring divine means leaves us
with a less complete and, therefore, a less valid understanding of creation
than is necessary. For the Creator has revealed some information as to
why and how he created this planet. That knowledge, although limited, is

21

too precious to be ignored. We can better appreciate the transcending powers by which God accomplishes his purposes by contrasting them with those mundane means available to man.

How Man Controls Nature

While the scientific progress of man cannot, and should not, be gainsayed, still, when the methods used to achieve that progress are compared with those of God, we must confess that human science is quite primitive. Man rules primarily by coercion; force is the chief principle he employs in achieving conformity to his will. This has become even more the case with the natural order as modern technology has enabled man to modify his physical environment with ever-increasing success. Machines and explosives are used to gouge and reshape the earth, to level its hills, crumble its mountains, alter the course of its rivers, and bury the land under ribbons and splotches of asphalt and concrete.

Man moves the earth. It does not move itself in response to man's will. Nor does it willingly respond to man's higher intelligence, it is coerced by it. This fact explains, in part, why the earth has turned and will yet turn against man and why it does not yield of its strength to him.

With the passage of time, man's uses of nature have become increasingly unnatural and, therefore, at variance with the *eternal natural* order of things. Having sown the wind of gluttonous, rapacious disregard for the earth and her ecological integrity, mankind now faces the prophecied onslaught of latter-day judgments, of nature in rebellion against her despoilers.

But man is so acclimated to his fallen state (and to the unnatural use of force which his fallen state necessitates), that he thoughtlessly assumes that there can be no other. It is generally believed that both man and nature can only be controlled by superior strength—that might not only makes for right, but for rule. This fallacious attitude has not only led to most human suffering but also to a misunderstanding of how God works in nature.

The Divine Mind

Whereas man tends to view nature as an antagonist to be conquered and subdued, the God of nature is its chief protagonist. He works in harmony with nature. He does not coerce it. Instead, he *wills* its cooperation. Thus the Lord exercises dominion over all lesser gradations of intelligence by virtue of the perfection of intelligence which is his glory.[1]

Joseph Smith equated mind with intelligence when he said: "The mind or the intelligence which man possesses is co-equal [in existence] with God himself. (HC, 6:310.) Therefore, it is not inappropriate to say that God's rule is the rule of intelligence, of mind. This is his glory. Consequently, the expression "mind over matter" has merit, for, ultimately, mind does control matter.[2]

The overruling power of the divine mind stems, at least in part, from the fact that all matter possesses intelligence or spirit. The eternities are filled with an infinitude of matter, stamped in greater or lesser degree with that omnipresent hallmark of divinity called the Spirit of the Lord.[3] To the degree that this Spirit is present in any particle of matter, it may be said that mind or intelligence is also present. Brigham Young taught:

> There is an eternity of matter, and it is all acted upon and filled with a portion of divinity . . .[it] is capacitated to receive intelligence . . .[it] can be organized and brought forth into intelligence, and to possess more intelligence, and to continue to increase in that intelligence.[4]

---

[1]See D&C 93:36. Joseph Smith taught that "God himself, finding he was in the midst of spirits and glory, because he was more intelligent, saw proper to institute laws whereby the rest could have a privilege to advance like himself." (HC, 6:312.)

[2]In Mormon theology all existing realities possess materiality; mind, spirit, and intelligence should be thought of as higher expressions of matter rather than immaterial essences. (See D&C 131:7.) Joseph Smith spoke of element or chaotic matter as that "in which dwells all the glory." (HC, 6:308.)

[3]The Spirit of the Lord is variously referred to as the light of Christ, the light of truth, the Spirit of God, the Holy Spirit, and so on.

[4]JD, 7:2, 3. See also *ibid.*, p. 285. Sixteen years later President Young added: "As far as we are concerned we suggest the idea that there is an eternity of life, an eternity of organization, and an eternity of intelligence from the highest to the lowest grade, every creature in its order from the Gods to the animalcule." (General Conference, October 8, 1875.)

He further said that life is present in every variety of matter, of whatever form, throughout "all the eternities." (JD, 3:277.)

The obedience of God's lesser creations to his will results from their being infused with his Spirit to the point that they become, as it were, extensions of it.[5] For the Spirit of the Lord permeates all of the creations of God and is "the power thereof by which they were made." (D&C 88:9.) Further, this Spirit "proceeds forth from the presence of God to fill the immensity of space." (D&C 88:12.) It is "the light which is in all things, which giveth life to all things, which is *the law by which all things are governed*, even the power of God who sitteth upon his throne, who is in the bosom of eternity, who is in the midst of all things." (D&C 88:13.)

Since the Spirit of the Lord is "the law by which all things are governed," it follows that the absence of the Spirit would result in chaos. There could be no universe—no order—were it not for the unifying influence of the Spirit. Orson Pratt said:

> All these universal laws that appear so prominently before us from day to day are nothing more than the operations of that all-wise Spirit which we are told is 'round about and in all things,' and which acts according to certain laws prescribed by the Almighty...Take away this Spirit, and you would immediately see some things going up, others down; some moving horizontally; one portion of the earth would divide from the other; one part would be flying here and another there. (JD, 2:340.)

Because the Spirit of the Lord permeates all things, God may be said to be omnipresent in all things: "He comprehendeth all things, and all things are before him, and all things are round about him; and he is above all things, and in all things, and is through all things, and is round about all things; and all things are by him, and of him, even God, forever and ever."[6]

---

[5]This doctrine should not be confused with animism, the belief that *immaterial* souls or spirits constitute the animating principle in all things. The Spirit of the Lord is material, cohesive and all-pervading.

[6]D&C 88:41. For an excellent discourse based upon these and related verses in D&C 88, see B.H. Roberts, "The Nearness of God," discourse delivered in the Salt Lake City Tabernacle, 15 March 1914.

Commenting on God's omnipresence, Brigham Young said that "there is no portion of space where he is not. There is no element in existence that does not contain him; no matter whether it be in its primitive, or in an organized state, he is through it and round about it. God fills immensity."[7]

The Most High possesses holy omnipotence. He acts with perfect faith, in harmony with all things organized and unorganized. All lesser gradations of intelligence respond to his will, not by coercion, but by affinity. Those who, by their faith, realize a like exaltation will rule as he rules. To them is the promise: "The Holy Ghost shall be thy constant companion, and thy scepter an unchanging scepter of righteousness and truth; and thy dominion shall be an everlasting dominion, and without compulsory means it shall flow unto thee forever and ever."[8]

Divine Faith

While it may appear erroneous to associate the principle of faith with a deity who is, to all intents, both omniscient and omnipotent, faith is essential to any being exercising any degree of agency. This includes God himself. Faith is as intrinsic with him as any other principle of intelligence (light and truth) flowing forth from the fountainhead of glory. And where there is glory, there is spirit, even the Spirit of the Lord. The greater the manifestation of the Spirit, the greater the faith and the greater the works produced thereby. Jesus, "being full of the Holy Ghost" (for he was endowed with "all power, both in heaven and on earth") was enabled by his own perfect faith to perform his miraculous works.[9]

Thus God lives by faith as it self-exists in perfection within his own being; it is an inevitable concommitant of the knowledge and power he has

---

[7]Discourse of February 12, 1854, Church Archives. Brigham Young is not referring to the limited individual spirit in God which is an inseparable part of his resurrected personage, but to the omnipresent Spirit of the Lord referred to in D&C 88:12, 13, 41.

[8]D&C 121:46. See 1 Nephi 9:6; 2 Nephi 9:20; Alma 26:35; Mosiah 3:5; 4:9; D&C 38:1, 2 and Moses 1:6.

[9]See Luke 4:1; D&C 93:17. God's faith is said to be non-contingent, meaning that is not dependent upon anyone or anything other than himself. It is perfect confidence, based upon perfect knowledge, that he can do anything he chooses to do. See Abraham 3:17; D&C 3:1-3.)

acquired in the course of his own progression. It is the dynamic source of his works.

While it is often thought that faith and knowledge are mutually exclusive, in actuality, they are coexistent principles continually interacting upon one another.[10] Consequently, one's faith is basically proportionate to the knowledge—valid or not—which produced it and which is, in turn, produced by it. (See Romans 10:14.) Our limited knowledge gives us the faith to do *some* things: God's limitless knowledge gives him the faith to do *all* things.

Thus, knowledge produces faith and faith produces greater knowledge which then becomes the basis for a greater faith, and so on and on to higher and higher levels of knowledge and faith. God stands at the apex of this process; his knowledge and faith are perfect and they co-exist in him with all other divine attributes as *indivisible* principles. Indeed, without faith ("the moving cause of *all* action") God would not be God.[11]

Paul declared that "through faith we understand that the worlds were framed *by the word of God*, so that things which are seen were not made of things which do appear." (Hebrews 11:3.) In commenting on this passage, a lecture prepared under Joseph Smith's direction defined faith as that inherent principle of power by which God organizes all things. "Take this principle or attribute—for it is an attribute—from the Deity, and he would cease to exist." (Lectures on Faith, No. 1, par. 16.)

The principle of faith is whole and holy (being unalloyed with any imperfection) in God. Consequently, when he exercises his faith and releases the infinite power of his mind, all nature obeys. Faith—as it exists in God—is the *alpha* and the *omega* of all things. Hence, we read that "the whole visible creation, as it now exists, is the effect of faith. It was faith by which it was framed, and it is by the power of faith that it continues in its

---

[10]This does not contradict Alma's statement: "Faith is not to have a perfect knowledge of things." (Alma 32:21.) While knowledge (via experience) of a given thing eliminates the need for faith in *that* thing, it does not eliminate the need for faith pertaining to things which have not yet been experienced. Jesus was obliged to draw upon his own faith each time he performed a new miracle. Thus we can have a perfect knowledge of that which has been done and at the same time exercise faith in that which is yet to be done (See Alma 32:34-36.)

[11]See *Lectures on Faith*, No. 1, par. 12. These lectures were given at the "School of the Elders in Kirtland, Ohio, in the winter of 1834-35. They appeared in all editions of the *Doctrine & Covenants* before 1921.

organized form, and by which the planets move round their orbits and sparkle forth their glory. So, then, faith is truly the first principle in the science of THEOLOGY." (*Lectures on Faith*, No. 7, par. 5.)

The purest faith and, therefore, the greatest knowledge is that which originates with the Spirit of the Lord. This is eternal faith; it alone can produce those works which will endure beyond mortal time. Such is God's faith and, therefore, such are God's works. Only as man partakes of his Spirit and manifests such faith, will his works be infused with immortality.

The Divine Word

The purest manifestation of faith is the spoken word. And the spoken word of God, being the word of faith, is more than verbal communication; it is both an energizer and a transmitter of power. Thus, in explaining what it means to work by faith, the seventh Lecture on Faith states:

> We answer—we understand that when a man works by faith he works by *mental exertion* instead of physical force. It is by *words*, instead of exerting his physical powers, with which every being works when he works by faith. God said, 'Let there be light, and there was light.' Joshua spake, and the great lights which God had created stood still . . . *Faith, then, works by words; and with these its mightiest works have been, and will be, performed.* (*Lectures on Faith*, No.7, par. 3.)

We have but little conception of the beauty and the power of man's primeval language. Far from being a savage tongue consisting of animal-like grunts and growls, the language of Earth's first inhabitants possessed a clarity and comprehensiveness of expression far beyond that of any contemporary mode of speech. It was for Adam and Eve and their righteous children altogether "pure and undefiled." (See Moses 6:5, 6, 46.)

For, unlike modern tongues, it was uncorrupted by the presence of any foreign words or derivations; the curse of Babel was yet to occur. Nor was it defiled by any profanities, obscenities or similar expressions of uncleanness. The Adamic tongue was meat and drink to the human spirit—nourishing, sustaining, and strengthening the whole soul. (See Deuteronomy 8:3; Amos 8:11; Matthew 4:4.) However, with the passage of time, this food of the spirit, like much food of the body, became ever more corrupt, denatured, and shorn of its vitality and power.

Today, language is frequently used to obscure rather than to communicate ideas and emotions. It is employed as an offensive weapon against the truth, as a propaganda missile calculated to guilefully mislead and, thereby, subvert others—as Satan subverted Eve—to the deceiver's will. On every turn we find glaring examples of this abuse of the divine principle of communication.

The unadulterated word of God is letter and spirit in union—a living soul. When spoken, it can be so "powerful and great" that it cannot be expressed in written form. (Ether 12:25.) And when written under the inspiration of the Almighty, it can be so charged with his Spirit that—as was the case with the revelations of the brother of Jared—they cause "the overpowering of man to read them."[12]

An assembled multitude of Nephites and Lamanites heard even more sublime language as it fell from the lips of the purest of men, the resurrected Son of God:

> The eye hath never seen, neither hath the ear heard, before, so great and marvelous things as we saw and heard Jesus speak unto the Father
>
> And no tongue can speak, neither can there be written by any man, neither can the hearts of men conceive so great and marvelous things as we both saw and heard Jesus speak. (3 Nephi 17:16, 17.)

How fitting that such exalting words should flow forth from the soul of the most exalted man!

The pre-mortal Christ told the brother of Jared: "And at my command the heavens are opened and are shut; and at my word the earth shall shake; and at my command the inhabitants thereof shall pass away, even so as by fire." (Ether 4:9.) The Only Begotten was God incarnate, the living embodiment of the mind, the faith, and the word of the Father— "the Word" which was "made flesh." (John 1:1, 14. See D&C 93:4-11.) He is the instrument by which the Father translates his will into tangible action and accomplishment: the "word of my power," (Moses 1:32, 35; 2:5.) which is "the power of my Spirit." (D&C 29:29, 30.) "Word" and

-----

[12]Ether 12:24. The presence of the Spirit of the Lord in the writing of scripture is the critical ingredient which distinguishes true from false revelation. This is why William McLellan, who had criticized the revelations of Joseph Smith, could not successfully meet the Lord's challenge to produce one of his own equal to the most inferior of those in the *Book of Commandments*. (See D&C 67:4-9 and HC, 1:224-226.)

"Spirit" are, therefore, virtual synonyms.[13] The Father's words and works are endless, (see Moses 1:4, 38.) and they are all fulfilled in and through the Son who said: "I am the same which spake, and the world was made, and all things came by me." (D&C 38:3; 1 Nephi 17:46; Mormon 9:17.)

The very particles of the earth are in harmony with, and therefore, subject to his will. He speaks and the earth obeys:

> Yea, by the power of his voice doth the whole earth shake...Yea, and if he say unto the earth—Move—it is moved...Yea, if he say unto the earth—Thou shalt go back that it lengthen out the day for many hours—it is done.[14]

Earth's obedience to divine will helps to explain why the Lord said that "the earth abideth the law of a celestial kingdom." (D&C 88:25.)

Commenting on this fact, Orson Pratt said that "This would seem to indicate that there is something connected with the earth itself, wherein it has an agency; and that because of the exercise of its agency, and keeping the law, it should be crowned with celestial glory. The materials out of which our earth is formed, are also governed by law. Not only the earth as an organized world, but the very materials themselves, are governed by laws." (JD, 21:233, 234.)

The Rebel

The term "obey" is not one a scientist would use in connection with his manipulations of matter and energy. However, it is used in scripture to express the relationship between God and his creations. But man is a rebel where God is concerned. Although human life is the highest order of intelligence to be found anywhere, mankind has the most difficulty har-

---

[13]Since the power of God's Spirit is as one with Christ—being personified in and through him—there is no contradiction in identifying the "word" with both Christ and the Spirit of God. (See D&C 84:45; 93:16, 17.)

[14]Helaman 12:7-17. Nature is not only obedient to the Creator's will, it also manifests empathy toward him—being involved with him. For while God is *not* nature, He is in nature. By his Spirit he is "in all things, and is through all things." (See D&C 88:41; JD, 21:233, 234.)

monizing its will with that of the Supreme Intelligence.[15] (Perhaps the very superiority of man's mind combined with the complexity of his nature is at the root of the problem.)

Endowed with a high degree of moral agency, man is free either to obey or disobey his Creator as he chooses. An all-wise Father wills life-giving principles for his children but, like many mortal parents, he must sadly acknowledge, "Men do not always do my will." (D&C 103:31.) Hence, scripture declares men to be foolish, vain, proud, devilish, boastful, and rebellious toward God: "For they do set at naught his counsels, and they will not that he should be their guide." (Helamen 12:6.) Men pit their agency against the agency of God with ineviatable pain and sorrow.

Such is not the case with those lesser orders of life and intelligence which lack agency in its higher and more extensive forms. They are essentially creatures of instinct, other-directed rather than self-directed.[16] Being so, they are responsive to the divine will and they are secure in the divine order of things.[17] Thus, all nature is obedient to nature's God.

But man is a child, not a creature, of that God. As such he is above and apart from nature; his race comprises the lords of creation. He is free as nature can never be. If man would be free (as Christ is free), he must emulate nature's example and humble himself before nature's God. Only in this way can he enter into union with the Father and become a co-ruler of his works.

Those who choose to disregard nature's example will be out of harmony with the eternal order of things and, therefore, unfit for absolute rule in that order. They forfeit the power and the glory of sonship and divine dominion.

Men of Power

But for some of God's truly holy sons, a portion of that power and dominion is vouchsafed them in mortality. Their faith in him has released

---

[15]Brigham Young said: "Man is the only object you can find upon the face of the earth that will not abide the law by which he is made." (JD, 9:140. See also p. 246.)

[16]The animal kingdom is characterized by gradations of intelligence which allow for greater or lesser degrees of instinctual behavior. (See D&C 77:3; Revelation 4:6 and HC, 5:343, 344.)

[17]As such, the animals fill the measure of their creation and will enjoy eternal felicity in the kingdom of God. (See D&C 77:3.)

his power in their behalf. Scripture is replete with instances of miracles being wrought by their spoken word.

Enoch, that "slow of speech" patriarch, was promised, "all thy words will I justify; and the mountains shall flee before you, and the rivers shall turn from their course." (Moses 6:34.) This divine promise was fulfilled to the letter, "so powerful was the *word* of Enoch, and so great was the power of the *language* which God had given him." (Moses 7:13. See also JST Genesis 14:30, 31.)

Moses drew down the power of God in the ten plagues and the dividing of the Red Sea, but he was later chastised for disobedience. When the Israelites clamored for water, Jehovah told Moses: "*Speak ye* unto the rock before their eyes; and it shall give forth his water." (Numbers 20:8.) But instead of using the *pure word* of faith, Moses struck (coerced) the rock. As a merciful penalty for his disobedience, Moses was denied the privilege of bringing Israel into the promised land.

The mighty Joshua commanded: "Sun, stand thou still upon Gibeon; and thou, Moon, in the valley of Ajalon." And the sun and the moon obeyed the word of Joshua so that "there was no day like that before it or after it, that the Lord hearkened unto the voice of a man: for the Lord fought for Israel."[18]

Nephi told his unbelieving brothers: "If he should command me that I should say unto this [the Arabian Sea], be thou earth, it should be earth; and if I should say it, it would be done." (1 Nephi 17:50.) Little wonder Nephi wrote that he was not "mighty in writing like unto speaking." (2 Nephi 33:1.)

Men often ignore the inspired word. Nature does not. Jacob, Nephi's younger brother, wrote that their faith was so great "that we truly can *command* in the name of Jesus and the very trees obey us, or the mountains, or the waves of the sea." (Jacob 4:6.) Jacob further tells us that God created the earth and man "*by the power of his word.*" He then asks the question: "Wherefore, if God being able to speak and the world was, and to speak and man was created, O then, why not able to command the earth, or the workmanship of his hands upon the face of it, according to his will and pleasure." (Jacob 4:9.)

---

[18]Joshua 10:12-14. Whether the sun and moon literally stood still or, as Mormon explains, the rotation of the earth was slowed or even reversed, the event defies all of the known laws of physics. Its historicity is implicitly affirmed in Helaman 12:14, 15. The birth of Christ produced a similar miracle when a night without darkness passed in America. (See Helaman 14:3, 4; 3 Nephi 1:15, 19.)

The foregoing examples are sufficient to demonstrate the reality of the power of the spoken word when that word is in harmony with, and a manifestation of, the mind of the Almighty. Consequently, impressive as man's accomplishments appear to be, he is quite ignorant of those higher principles of faith by which an intelligent God and his sons rule through the spoken word. The works of the most brilliant men are primitive when contrasted with those of the Creator. Perhaps this is why God told Isaiah: "For as the heavens are higher than the earth, so are my ways higher than your ways, and my thoughts higher than your thoughts." (Isaiah 55:9.)

PART TWO

The Earth

CHAPTER FOUR

Earth's Purposes

God is purposeful; he does nothing thoughtlessly or capriciously anymore than he leaves the operations of his kingdom, with its many mansions, to blind chance. Moses (who viewed some of the Creator's works through the infinite eyes of his Spirit) "beheld many lands; and each land was called earth, and there were inhabitants on the face thereof."[1] Upon seeing these other populated worlds, Moses asked why they had been created. The Lord responded: "For mine own purpose have I made these things." (Moses 1:31. See JD, 15:8.) The Lord explained that these worlds were prepared for the Father's spirit offspr-

---

[1] Moses 1:29. This, and related passages of scripture, led Orson Pratt and other commentators to conclude that all of the planets were inhabited, being in various stages of progression. (See JD, 19:287, 291-293.) Current astronomical information does not support such a notion insofar as this solar system is concerned. The Lord did not show Moses *all* of his creations. Instead he showed him "many lands" that, like Earth, were inhabited. In all likelihood, there are myriad stars and planets that are not inhabited by any form of organized life. Although Orson Pratt believed that all of the galactic systems were organized for "a greater and more glorious object," the Creator only told Moses that they were "lights in the firmament of the heaven to divide the day from the night: and let them be for signs, and for seasons, and for days, and years." (Genesis 1:14.)

ing who would thereby obtain physical immortality and eternal life or some state of happiness relative thereto. "And as one earth shall pass away, and the heavens thereof even so shall another come, and there is no end to my works, neither to my words. For behold, this is my work and my glory—to bring to pass the immortality and eternal life of man." (Moses 1:38, 39.) Joseph Smith wrote of the Only Begotten: "By him, and through him, and of him, the worlds are and were created, and the inhabitants thereof are begotten sons and daughters unto God." (D&C 76:24.)

God's work is man-centered; it pertains to the patriarchal order of the Holy Priesthood—everlasting in its duration and limitless in its growth. Rather than being only a minor accident in a universe of chance happenings, man is revealed to be the central reason creation exists and will endlessly expand!

Orson Pratt summed up this incredible truth when he said that innumerable inhabited worlds exist in various stages of progression "and there still remains no end, as it were, to the materials which will yet be organized into worlds, for the materials are infinite in quantity; they cannot be exhausted." (JD, 19:291. See also 14:240.)

Brigham Young affirmed this inexhaustible supply of unorganized matter when he said: "There is an eternity of matter, and it is all acted upon and filled with a portion of divinity. Matter is to exist; it cannot be annihilated. Eternity is without bounds and is filled with matter; and there is no such place as empty space." (JD, 7:2.)

Unless there is an infinite amount of matter and space, the divine labor of bringing to pass the immortality and eternal life of man must eventually come to an end. Were this to occur, God and his works, however great, would prove to be finite. Further, the immutable promise to those who gain exaltation and "a continuation of the seeds [posterity] *forever and ever*" would be broken. But this will never happen. The very nature of God assures the infinite organization of men, and of worlds to accommodate them. This planet is but one link in a genealogical chain of inhabited spheres reaching back far beyond Kolob and extending on into endless space.

A Home Away From Home

Earth was fashioned from an infinite reservoir of unorganized matter as a suitable home away from home for the spirit family of the divine Patriarch. Nephi taught: "Behold, the Lord hath created the earth that it should be inhabited; and he hath created his children that they should possess it." (1 Nephi 17:36) Those spirits who proved worthy were promised that they would inherit the earth forever.

But even those who did not obtain such an inheritance were to benefit immeasurably from coming to Earth. Doing so would mean the acquisition of a new dimension of the divine nature which would bring them greater self-realization and a far more rewarding life than could otherwise be known. In other words, heaven would be magnified and become more heavenly because it had been surrendered for a brief sojourn on Earth. This brings us to the second purpose for its creation.

A Tabernacle For The Spirit

It was foreordained that Earth should be unique among the planets in this solar system. It alone has the delicately-balanced environment suitable for life as we know it. Moreover, it alone possesses all of the essential elements necessary for the creation of physical bodies capable of a glorious quickening. Thus, Earth was to provide the raw materials for the formation of the third essential component of man's eternal being—the component which would transform his unembodied spirit into a living soul.[2]

Temporal (physical) man was "formed from the dust of the ground"—the good earth. (See Moses 3:7; Genesis 2:7.) God told Adam that "in the sweat of thy face shalt thou eat bread, till thou return unto the ground; for out of it wast thou taken: for dust thou art, and unto dust shalt thou return." (Genesis 3:19; Moses 4:25.) We are all "of the earth, earthy." (See 1 Corinthians 15:47; John 3:31; Job 34:15; Psalm 103:14 and 104:29.)

Earth is the mother of mothers in that all living organisms are comprised of elements taken from her body. All life—whether man, the mighty denizens of land and sea, a blade of grass or a microscopic organism—is an extension of Mother Earth. God established the earth as a living soul, a life-producing planet, not as a mere mass of inert matter.

Orson Pratt asked the rhetorical question, "What! is the earth alive too?" He responded, "If it were not, how could the words of our text [Isaiah 51:6] be fulfilled, where it speaks of the earth's dying? How can that die that has no life?" (JD, 1:281.) In a similar vein, Heber C. Kimball argued: "The earth cannot produce living things if it was dead...The earth is alive. If it was not, it could not produce." (JD, 6:36.)

Mother Earth was commanded to multiply and to increase the myriad

---

[2]Primal intelligence and the organized spirit constitute the first two components of a resurrected being. (See D&C 88:15; 93:29, 33-35; and HC, 6:311-313.)

life forms she has produced. (See JD, 9:336, 337.) Thus the principle of biogenesis also applies to her. Because she lives, we live. And she will continue to provide the raw material from which the temporal organisms of man and the "generations of the heavens and the earth" are fashioned until the end of time. For not until the last spirit has been embodied will the earth "answer the end of its creation."[3]

Even as the physical earth is a reflection of its spiritual image, so is man's physical body patterned after the form of his spirit.[4] The things of time, however darkly, mirror the things of eternity. Joseph F. Smith taught that the "things upon the earth, so far as they have not been perverted by wickedness, are typical of things in heaven. Heaven was the prototype of this beautiful creation when it came from the hand of the Creator, and was pronounced "good."[5]

True evolution had its beginnings in the primeval, spirit state of living things, and it is from that state that all things unfold in accordance with their God-determined nature and destiny. (See Ether 3:15, 16; Moses 3:4-9.) This is how they "fill the measure of their creation"—the measure God determined when they were organized as spirit entities.

The Father is a resurrected being of spirit and element. Therefore, he is a microcosm of all reality, all materiality. There is no principle of life existing anywhere in the eternities that is not represented in him. Having subdued and sanctified all materiality, his joy is absolute and his dominion limitless. His spirit children aspired to become like him. But they understood that such a sublime life was possible only when the spirit was clothed upon with a physical tabernacle.

> For man is spirit. The elements [gross matter] are eternal, and spirit [pure matter] and element, inseparably connected, receive a fulness of joy; And when separated, man cannot receive a fulness of joy. (D&C 93:33.)

Thus, the spirits of men came to earth in order to acquire *element* so

---

[3]See D&C 49:16, 17 and Rodney Turner, *Woman and the Priesthood* (Salt Lake City: Deseret Book Co., 1972), pp. 201, 202.

[4]This does not mean that the physical body is an exact duplicate of the spirit. The spirit was brought forth in perfection by holy parents. Such is not the case in this fallen world where many factors can lead to physical malformation and improper development.

[5]Joseph F. Smith, JD, 23:175. See also JD, 8:43; 15:305; 18:243.

that it might become an integral part of their beings forever. All this, in pursuit of happiness—the "object and design of our existence." (HC, 5:134.) As we learn to subject element, the flesh, to the will of our spirits, and our spirits to the will of the Father, we will find joy.

A Proving Ground

Although the earth was patterned after a heavenly realm, it was foreordained that it should fall and become a telestial planet of the lowest order—the setting for man's last and bitterest oppositions. No longer would the Father's children know the love, the security, and the guidance of a holy home. Earthlife would make them strangers and pilgrims in an alien world of pain, sorrow, strife, and frustration—a world over-shadowed by the dark presence of their former adversary in the war in heaven.

Satan awaited man's coming to this outpost of eternity with grim determination; souls not won in the presence of God would be conquered in his absence. (See Moses 4:1-4; D&C 29:36-40; 76:25-29.) And so a third purpose for Earth was to provide some of the Father's children with an opportunity for further trial and development under new and demanding conditons.

The manner in which God's commandments were kept would determine the eternal destinies of these spiritis: "And they who keep their first estate shall be added upon; and they who keep not their first estate shall not have glory in the same kingdom with those who keep their first estate; and they who keep their second estate shall have glory added upon their heads for ever and ever." (Abraham 3:25, 26.)

Would absence make the hearts of the children grow fonder? Or would it be a case of "out of sight, out of mind"? Would they keep God's commandments on earth as they had done in heaven? Would they be as successful in rejecting the overtures and blandishments of Lucifer in a new world as they had been in the old one? Would they continue to grow from grace to grace in light and truth, in their quest for salvation? Could they learn to rule gross matter and not be ruled by it? Would they, in acquiring a tabernacle of element, be able to master that organism and, with divine help, sanctify it so that it could dwell forever with holy beings?[6]

The answers to these questions would be highly variable. The manner in which each spirit child had already used the gift of agency made for

---

[6]Joseph Smith said: "We came to this earth that we might have a body and present it pure before God in the celestial kingdom." (TPJS, p. 181.)

great variety in the overall composition of the heavenly host. The family had already become quite diverse in so far as individual capacity, obedience, progress, and achievement were concerned: the premortal achievements of men and women would affect their opportunities and performances in mortality. The competence and diligence with which the children of God obeyed his laws in their first estate have profoundly affected their opportunities for spiritual growth and development in their second estate. Spiritual scholarships were given to the Father's most meritorious sons and daughters—the noble and great ones—whom he determined to make his "rulers" on earth in both time and eternity.[7] Hence, the doctrine that principles of intelligence acquired in mortality will magnify the individual in eternity was also applicable to man's premortal estate. (See D&C 130:18, 19.)

God's great servants from Adam to the present day were foreordained in the councils of heaven. Speaking of his own prophetic calling, Joseph Smith declared: "Every man who has a calling to minister to the inhabitants of the world was ordained to that very purpose in the Grand Council of heaven before this world was. I suppose that I was ordained to this very office in that Grand Council." (HC, 6:364.)

If those who were foreordained to be the elect of God keep their second estate with the same diligence manifested in their first estate, they will have proven themselves in "all things whatsoever the Lord their God shall command them." (Abraham 3:25.)

In a vision of the redemption of the dead, President Joseph F. Smith saw Joseph Smith and a number of other leaders of the Church in the spirit world and wrote: "I observed that they were also among the noble and great ones who were chosen in the beginning to be rulers in the Church of God. Even before they were born, they, with many others, received their first lessons in the world of spirits and were prepared to come forth in the due time of the Lord to labor in his vineyard for the salvation of the souls of men." (D&C 138:55, 56.) This vision took place October 31, 1918 and was canonized by the LDS Church in 1976.

While certain spirits were judged "noble and great," others proved relatively inferior in overall character. The gross infidelity toward God of some men in this world may very likely be the mortal fruits of their

---

[7]In observing that Moses was to stand as God to the Israelites, Joseph Smith said: "I believe those Gods that God reveals as Gods to be sons of God, and all can cry, 'Abba, Father!' Sons of God who exalt themselves to be Gods, *even from before the foundation of the world*, and are the only Gods I have a reverence for." (HC, 6:478.)

rebelliousness in the pre-earth life. To a greater or lesser degree, this causative principle probably applies to all men.

Lucifer is the prime example of one whose conduct in heaven determined his fate on earth. He failed to "keep" his first covenants with the Father. His rebellion was total; his judgment was final. Lucifer and his followers are denied the blessing of physical incarnation. Consequently, they will not obtain a "glory" in any earthly "kingdom."[8]

Others, while not joining Lucifer's rebellion, failed to be as obedient in keeping (or magnifying) their first estate as did their nobler brothers and sisters. These less qualified spirits "shall not have glory in the same kingdom with those who keep their first estate."[9] The manner in which individuals progressed in the pre-mortal life became a key factor in determining their possibilities on earth.[10] Mortality—in terms of its op-

---

[8]Joseph Smith said, "The great principle of happiness consists in having a body. The devil has no body, and herein is his punishment." (TPJS, p. 181. See also Abraham 3:28; Moses 4:1-3 and Jude 6.)

[9]Note that Abraham 3:26 does not say that those who fail to keep the first estate are denied glory; it says that they do not have glory *in the same kingdom* with those who keep their first estate. J. Reuben Clark commented on this passage: "I am not undertaking to declare doctrine or Gospel, but as I read that, and as I understand it, it means that after we, so to speak, have been taken out, those who have kept their first estates, and we are not the only ones, there remains the great over-plus. They do not have the same heritage, the same kingdom, the same glory, that we shall have, and they have and can fall into the terrestrial, the telestial, and then the Doctrine and Covenants tells us there is a kingdom without any glory. (D&C 88:24.) My point is that we were not equal at the beginning as intelligences; we were not equal in the Grand Council; we were not equal after the Grand Council." (CR, Oct. 6, 1956, pp. 83, 84.)

[10]The fact that all men are born equal in innocence before God (D&C 93:38) does not mean that all men are born equal in spiritual and intellectual attainments. If they were, the foreordination of noble and great spirits would be negated and become meaningless. Parley P. Pratt observed that "although some eternal intelligences may be superior to others, and although some are more noble, and consquently are elected to fill certain useful and necessary offices for the good of others, yet the greater and the less may both be innocent, and both be justified, and be useful, each in their own capacity; if each magnify their own calling, and act in their own capacity, it is all right." (JD, 1:258.)

portunities for spiritual growth and development—is largely the harvest of seeds sown in that former life. And just as yesterday's sowing dictated today's harvest, so will today's works dictate the character of mankind's tomorrows.

The foregoing view of mortality as a period of trial and testing must be qualified. As has been stated, many spirits enter this world under conditons which do not allow for any genuine opportunity to obey such revealed commandments as are found in the law of Moses or the gospel of Jesus Christ. Joseph Smith described these peoples as "heathens."[11] Being without divine law (administered through the Priesthood), they will be judged in accordance with the moral and spiritual understanding they possess.[12]

Destiny Of Little Children

In addition to the above classes, literally billions of the Father's children have died in infancy or early childhood and, consequently, will never be "tried and tested" in so far as an earthly probation is concerned.[13] They accomplished the primary purpose of mortality—the acquisition of a physical tabernacle. This is the one universal objective of every earthbound spirit; all else is variable and relative.

In describing a vision given him January 21, 1836, Joseph Smith declared that "all children who die before they arrive at the years of

----

[11]In his poetic paraphrase of *Doctrine and Covenants*, section 76, Joseph Smith described these candidates for the terrestrial kingdom as follows: "Behold, these are they that have died without law; The heathen of ages that never had hope." (See *Times and Seasons*, 4 (February 1, 1843): 82-85.)

[12]See Romans 2:12; 2 Nephi 9:25-27; 29:11; Alma 29:8. It is for this reason that those who "died without law" (D&C 76:72) are declared to be heirs of the terrestrial kingdom. As a group, they apparently failed to qualify for celestial glory. In connection with the Savior's advent we read: "And then shall the heathen nations be redeemed, and they that knew no law shall have part in the first resurrection; and it shall be *tolerable* for them." (D&C 45:54.)

[13]Another class of spirits that will be spared the trials of this telestial world and the temptations of Satan are those who are priviledged to be born during the Millennium and who are resurrected prior to the "Little season" when Satan is loosed. (See D&C 45:30-32, 58; 101:28-31.)

accountability, are *saved* in the celestial kingdom of heaven." (D&C 137:10.) Thus, these spirits are spared the necessity of a mortal probation.

This doctrine has been interpreted by some as an unqualified assurance that literally every deceased child will attain celestial glory. Others have suggested that it applies only to the offspring of the saints or to those "born under the covenant." The Prophet's statement appears to be an addendum to the basic revelation in that it follows the declaration that "all men" will be judged in terms of their works and the desires of their hearts. The salvation of little children (who are adult spirits) is surely in harmony with this principle. If so, then it would seem that all of those children who die, who would have accepted the gospel had they lived, are the ones Joseph Smith beheld "in the celestial kingdom of heaven." However, this is a moot point which must await further revelation.

The Prophet subsequently suggested that the very temperment of some of the Father's children was such as to make mortality an unnecessarily harsh ordeal for them. Consequently, "the Lord takes many away, even in infancy, that they may escape the envy of man, and the sorrows and evils of this present world; they were too pure, too lovely, to live on earth; therefore, if rightly considered, instead of mourning we have reason to rejoice as they are delivered from evil, and we shall soon have them again." (HC, 4:553. See also Moroni 8:10.)

Nor will these brief visitors to earth be subjected to the temptations of Satan or the trials and vicissitudes associated with our fallen world at any future time. Joseph Fielding Smith maintained:

Satan cannot tempt little children in this life, nor in the spirit world, nor after their resurrection.[14]

They are "alive in Christ, even from the foundation of the world." (Moroni 8:12.) They are pure and spotless before God by virtue of the atonement. (See Mosiah 3:16.) There is no barrier of sin between them and their eternal Father; they return to his presence. Brigham Young declared that "they swarm in the Courts of Heaven; there are myriads and myriads of them there already, and more are going continually." (JD, 14:230. See also 23:126.)

Joseph Smith comforted bereaved parents in saying, "A question may be asked—'Will mothers have their children in eternity?' Yes! Yes!

---

[14]*Doctrines of Salvation*, 2:57. Italics in original.

Mothers, you shall have your children; for they shall have eternal life, for their debt is paid." (HC, 6:316.) While not defining the term "eternal life," Joseph Smith seemed, in this instance, to equate it with the phrase "saved in the celestial kingdom." (D&C 137:10.) Although the atonement *saves* little children in that heaven, of itself, it does not *exalt* them there.[15] Consequently eternal life and exaltation may not always have the same connotations. For example, in the *Book of Mormon* eternal life is contrasted with eternal death and means salvation in the kingdom of God as opposed to damnation in the kingdom of the devil. (See Alma 4:4; 1 Nephi 14:7; 2 Nephi 2:28, 29; 10:25.)

While deceased young children have been declared heirs of the celestial kingdom, the question of their exaltation therein is yet to be resolved by any revelation from the Lord. Brigham Young remarked that such children "are to receive an exaltation" but then went on to qualify the statement by adding: "Should it be that they are not capable of dwelling as fathers and mothers—of becoming enthroned in glory, might, majesty, and power—they may enjoy to a fulness, and who can enjoy more?"[16] This reflects his view that a "fulness" is determined by one's capacity and that men are equal when their respective capacities are "filled to overflowing." (See JD, 4:268, 269; 7:7.)

Wilford Woodruff was uncertain of the precise state of deceased young children after the resurrection:

With regard to the future state of those who die in infancy I do not feel authorized to say much. There has been a great deal of theory, and many views have been expressed on this subject, but there are many things connected with it which the Lord has probably never revealed to any of the Prophets or

---

[15]William Clayton's journal entry for 18 May 1843 records the following: "I asked the Prest. [Joseph Smith] wether children who die in infancy will grow. He answered 'No, we shall receive them precisely in the same state as they died ie no larger. They will have as much intelligence as we shall but shall always remain separate and single.'" Andrew F. Ehat and Lyndon W. Cook, *The Words of Joseph Smith: The Contemporary Accounts of the Nauvoo Discourses of the Prophet Joseph* [Provo: Religious Studies Center, 1980], p. 136, n. 22.)

[16]Discourse of Brigham Young, October, 24, 1860, Church Archives. Spelling corrected.

patriarchs who ever appeared on the earth. There are some things which have not been revealed to man, but are held in the bosom of God our Father, and it may be that the condition after death of those who die in infancy is among the things which God has never revealed; but it is sufficient for me to know that our children are saved . . .With regard to the growth, glory, or exaltation of children in the life to come, God has not revealed anything on that subject to me, either about your children, mine or anybody else's, any further than we know they are saved. (JD, 18:32, 34. See also 10:367.)

Joseph F. Smith said that deceased children "will inherit their glory and their exaltation, and they will not be deprived of the blessings that belong to them . . .All that could have been obtained and enjoyed by them if they had been permitted to live in the flesh will be provided for them hereafter. They will lose nothing by being taken away from us in this way." (*Gospel Doctrine*, p. 453.)

Historically, terms such as "eternal life," "exaltation," "salvation," and "saved" have been used quite loosely. For this reason, it is most unwise to impose a more precise definition on any of them than is explicitly warranted in a given text.

The doctrine that all children who die before the age of accountability are saved in the celestial kingdom has been objected to on the grounds that the accident of premature death is hardly a just reason for saving anyone. Why should those who are subjected to the trials of mortality risk all for salvation when little children, who presumably risk nothing, are guaranteed salvation? The question implies that the Lord acted arbitrarily in sparing certain spirits the ordeals of mortality. But he is no respecter of persons. Nor is he capricious; salvation in his presence is not a matter of chance. Like every other blessing, it is based upon obedience to irrevocable law. He responds to all in accordance with the manner in which they exercise their moral agency.[17]

Indeed, without such agency we could not choose to "keep" or lose

---

[17]See D&C 29:36 and 1 Nephi 17:35. Blessings granted are blessings merited. Gospel covenants bring special privileges to those who honor them. For example, Joseph Smith taught that "when a seal is put upon the father and mother, it secures their posterity, so that they cannot be lost, but will be saved by virtue of the covenant of their father and mother." (HC, 5:530.)

the blessings of the first estate. We have been working out our salvation from the very beginning of our association with God. For as Elder Melvin J. Ballard declared: "Long before we were born into this earth we were tested and tried in our pre-existence."[18]

Only in the premortal world was the Father's *entire* spirit family obliged to face the opposition represented by Lucifer and thus be proven as to their spiritual integrity. And so it seems that, for some, a decisive judgment was made in the first estate, but, for others, it will follow their works in the second.[19] It is fruitless to conjecture as to the relative worthiness of any given spirit. And it is incorrect to say that only the good die young. The work of God required that many of his noblest sons and daughters be foreordained, to live to maturity, to parent their unborn brothers and sisters, and to fulfill many other missions related to the salvation of man.

The basic question—"Are little children heirs of the celestial kingdom because they die, or do they die because they are heirs of the celestial kingdom?"—brings us back to the issue of God's culpability in their deaths. Does he cause the deaths of a favored class of adult spirits before they attain the age of accountability in the flesh? Assuredly not! A moment's reflection on the historic practices of foeticide and infanticide, together with the many other immoral circumstances under which children die, should make it obvious that God has no part in these crimes against innocence.

However, being omniscient, the Lord foreknows all things. But he does not foreordain, much less predestine, all things. As Jesus noted: "Woe unto the world because of offences! for it must needs be that offences come; but woe to that man by whom the offence cometh!" (Matt. 18:7.) The Lord foresees the offences which will befall little children. This seership enables him to place each spirit in that mortal condition which will insure it those blessings and opportunities to which it is entitled.

That the course of our mortal lives was foreknown not only to the Lord, but, to some extent, to ourselves was the conviction of President Joseph F. Smith who believed that the Savior "possessed a foreknowledge of all the vicissitudes through which he would have to pass in the mortal

---

[18]*Sermons and Missionary Services of Melvin J. Ballard,* comp. by Bryant S. Hinckley (Salt Lake City: Deseret Book Co., 1949), pp. 247-48. The entire host of heaven was begotten before this earth was organized.

[19]The second estate includes man's post-mortal sojourn in the spirit world.

tabernacle . . .If Christ knew beforehand, so did we. But in coming here, we forgot all, that our agency might be free indeed, to choose good or evil, that we might merit the reward of our own choice and conduct."[20]

The Lord knows the end from the beginning. He knows how men will exercise their agency, what the consequences will be, and how their actions will affect others. He beheld the tapestry of human history long before the warp and woof of the individual lives comprising that tapestry were drawn from the skein of time.

All that he does is done with but one grand objective in view: the eternal welfare and happiness of each of his sons and daughters. When we stand before him in the final judgment, all will acknowledge that "he counseleth in wisdom, and in justice, and in great mercy, over all his works." (Jacob 4:10.)

The Worthy Dead

There is another class of spirits whose situation lies somewhere between that of little children who die and those who accept the gospel in mortality and thereby become heirs of the celestial kingdom. This third group of celestial candidates consists of those who would have received the gospel in the flesh had the opportunity been afforded them. It is this class of spirits for whom the doctrine of salvation for the dead is designed. The Lord informed Joseph Smith:

> All who have died without a knowledge of this gospel, who would have received it if they had been permitted to tarry, shall be heirs of the celestial kingdom of God; also all that shall die henceforth without a knowledge of it, who would have received it with all their hearts, shall be heirs of that kingdom; for I, the Lord, will judge all men according to their works, according to the desire of their hearts. (D&C 137:7-9. See also D&C 128:5.)

In this sense, the earth is not only a proving ground for the living but for the dead as well. Man's preparatory or probationary period begins with birth and ends with resurrection. (See Alma 12:24; 42:4-13.) The afterlife (a continuation of the second estate), is, therefore, a segment of

---

[20]Joseph F. Smith, *Gospel Doctrine*, 7th ed., pp. 13, 14. His statement was in reply to a letter on the general subject from Elder Orson F. Whitney.

that period in which the message of salvation is proclaimed to those spirits held captive behind the gates of hell in the prison-house of death.[21] The judgement is based upon the deeds done in the body. Therefore, as pertaining to one's final destiny, no losses can be incurred after death. The dead will, by repenting, qualify for their merited salvation.[22] They cannot sin so as to jeopardize it. The level of divine law obeyed in the premortal and the mortal estates determines the level of divine law (and, therefore, divine blessings) which can be attained after the resurrection. (See D&C 88:20-39.)

A World of New Experiences

Another valuable purpose for earthlife is related to, but goes beyond, the matter of mortality being a time of trial and testing for the children of God. Life on the newly-formed planet required that man's spirit be veiled in flesh. An "iron curtain" of unsanctified element would bar his view of and association with heavenly things.[23] This fall (or subjugation of the spirit) was necessary if man was to have those unique experiences that mortality alone could provide. As Orson Pratt noted: "We learn by our experience many lessons we never could have learned except we were tabernacled in the flesh." (JD, 14:242. See also 19:288; 21:198.)

There was no other way by which the spirit offspring of the Father could become like him. They must undergo such experiences as would

---

[21]See D&C 76:73; 88:99; 128:22; Isaiah 24:22; 42:7; 61:1; Matthew 5:25, 26; 18:34, 35; John 5:25; 1 Peter 3:18; 4:6; *Gospel Doctrine*, pp. 472-476.

[22]The teaching of Amulek (Alma 34:30-35) that there can be no spiritual labor performed after death applies to those who have ample opportunity to repent in mortality but procrastinate doing so. Such persons cannot perform a post-death labor which will qualify them for salvation in the celestial kingdom, but they can and must repent of all of their sins if they are to qualify for even a lesser salvation.

[23]Brigham Young spoke of man's physical veil: "We are now clothed upon with mortal flesh which veils the vision of the eternal spirit, that we cannot perceive what is going on in those eternal elements that have passed through a routine of changes until they have secured to themselves an eternal organization both in body and in spirit, and [in] the tabernacle, and out of it." (Discourse of February 12, 1854, Church Archives.)

give them the peculiar knowledge of good and evil he possessed. For as Brigham Young said: "The only key to open the door of knowledge is experience." (Discourse, October 1, 1854, Church Archives.)

Our divine Parent is able to comprehend the trials and sufferings of his children because he has had similar experiences at an earlier stage of his own life. Brigham Young maintained that it would be foolish to petition a God "who never had any experience in the adverse fortunes of mortal life." The Lord can respond compassionately to our pleas for support in times of tribulation because he "never operates . . .beyond his own capacity . . .If he has received his exaltation without being hungry, cold, and naked; without passing through sickness, pestilence and distress, by the same rule we may expect to be exalted to the same crown, to the same glory and exaltation."[24]

The Savior had to drain the bitter cup his Father gave him because there was no other way for him to fulfill the plan of salvation. The bitter-sweet cup of mortality is likewise necessary for those who aspire to become joint-heirs with Jesus Christ in all that the Father possesses. Joseph Smith declared that "men have to suffer that they may come upon Mount Zion and be exalted above the heavens." (HC, 5:556.)

Even those whose mansions will be located in lesser heavens will have benefited immeasurably from the mortal experience. Because of their brief sojourn on earth, they will be blessed with unfailing happiness—for "man is that he might have joy." The contrast between their second and their final estate will be overwhelming. They will appreciate the wisdom and the goodness of divine law as never before. They will realize just how heavenly *any* heaven is in comparison with life in a fallen world.[25]

It is only by tasting the bitter that we can prize the sweet. It was not until man was thrown into an alien condition of struggle and privation that he could rightly judge the advantages of his former estate. Mortality provides God's family with those essential experiences which produce the

---

[24]Discourse, October 1, 1854, Church Archives. Orson Pratt made this same point. (See JD, 19:289.) Jesus' own life reflects this view. Alma taught: "And he will take upon him death, that he may loose the bands of death which bind his people; and he will take upon him their infirmities, that his bowels may be filled with mercy, according to the flesh, that he may know according to the flesh how to succor his people according to their infirmities." (Alma 7:12. See also Hebrews 2:18; 4:15.)

[25]Even the glory of the telestial heaven, the least of the kingdoms, is described as surpassing all understanding. (See D&C 76:89.)

sincere gratitude men must feel if they are to fully appreciate the blessings of immortal glory.

Few prophets have understood this principle better than Wilford Woodruff who remarked:

> Whoever goes back into the presence of God our eternal Father . . .will also learn that he has placed us here that we may pass through a state of probation and experience, the same as he himself did in his day of mortality . . .these things are necessary in order to enable us to comprehend good and evil, and to be prepared for glory and blessings when we receive them. As the Apostle argues very strongly in the Book of Mormon—'If we never taste the bitter how will we know how to comprehend the sweet? If we never partake of pain how can we prize ease? And if we never pass through afflication, how can we comprehend glory, exaltation and eternal blessings? (JD, 18:32, 33.)

The happiness of the spirits in the premortal estate will be multiplied exceedingly when they are added upon via the resurrection with those tabernacles of flesh and bone the earth provided. Thus, all but the unrepentant sons of perdition will partake of that measure of the "more abundant life" commensurate with their spiritual attainments in their first and second estates. Earth will have filled the measure of its creation in providing those essentials which make it possible for the children of God to demonstrate their ability to "do all things whatsoever the Lord their God shall command them."

These are but a few of the purposes for which Earth was organized; others will be treated in subsequent chapters. But the whole truth as to the *why* of Earth's organization will not be known until the Lord comes in glory and reveals "the purpose and the end thereof."

CHAPTER FIVE

Earth's Beginnings

The Lord's course is "one eternal round"—a divine creative cycle in which all things are organized first spiritually and then temporally. In the resurrection, the spiritual and the temporal are commingled, becoming one, perfected, immortal creation. This process fulfills the Lord's decree that "the first shall be last, and that the last shall be first." (See D&C 29:30-32 and JD, 18:243.)

The earth was brought forth in harmony with this principle of duality. Initially it was organized as a spiritual sphere (or heaven) which, in time, became the pattern for its second organization as a physical planet.[1]

Parley P. Pratt wrote that "the earth and other planets of a like sphere, have their inward or spiritual spheres, as well as their outward or temporal. The one is peopled by temporal tabernacles, and the other by

---

[1]See D&C 93:35; 101:25; 131:7. In an official statement on "The Origin of Man" the First Presidency wrote: "The creation was two-fold— firstly spiritual, secondly temporal. This truth, also, Moses plainly taught—much more plainly that it has come down to us in the imperfect translations of the Bible that are now in use. Therein the fact of a spiritual creation, antedating the temporal creation, is strongly implied, but the proof of it is not so clear and conclusive as in other records held by the Latter-day Saints to be of equal authority with the Jewish scriptures." (*The Improvement Era*, 13 [November, 1909], p. 76.)

spirits. A vail [sic] is drawn between the one sphere and the other, whereby all objects in the spiritual sphere are rendered invisible to those in the temporal." (Parley P. Pratt, *(Key to Theology*, p. 125.) 9th ed. (Salt Lake City. Deseret Book Co., 1943).

The Spirit World

Although the creation of the spirit world remains a divine mystery, that which has been revealed (in scripture and through modern prophets) concerning the earth and man provides a basis for a partial understanding of its nature and purpose.[2] There are symbiotic ties uniting all creation into one harmonious whole; life is bound to life in ever widening circles which extend to the fartherest reaches of eternity. Thus, in compelling ways, Earth and man share a common origin, law and destiny, so much so that the one becomes somewhat analogous of the other.[3] The following parallels between the two may, therefore, be tentatively inferred.

As man is a dual being of spirit and flesh, so is the earth a dual creation; it was organized first in spirit and then in element. And even as the human spirit is the very "core" of man, so may we think of the spirit world as the "foundation" of the earth. (See Job 38:4; Zechariah 12:1; D&C 45:1; 128:18 and 132:63.)

The spirit world, like the human spirit, was fashioned of highly refined spirit matter; it is by nature an immortal sphere. Being so, it is invisible to us mortals because such matter "is more fine or pure, and can only be discerned by purer eyes." (D&C 131:7. See also JD, 3:368.)

The spirit body of Christ was the prototype of the human spirit and, in turn, of its physical tabernacle. (See Ether 3:15, 16; D&C 77:2.) So, too, was heaven the model followed by the Gods in fashioning the spirit world and, in turn, this planet. Brigham Young observed: "All things were created first spiritual, and then temporal. Everything in the spirit world was presented as we see it now, and this temporal earth was presented there." (JD, 18:243.) Joseph F. Smith agreed: "Things upon the earth, so far as they have not been perverted by wickedness, are typical of things in heaven. Heaven was the prototype of this beautiful creation when it came

---

[2]The terms earth and world are often used interchangeably. However, at times "earth" refers to the planet, while "world" denotes mankind—especially the wicked. (See JS-M 4, 31, 55, and D&C 45:22.)

[3]God bears witness of his creations and his creations testify of him. (See D&C 88:47; Moses 6:63.)

from the hand of the Creator, and was pronounced 'good'." (JD, 23:175.) But neither the earth or man have remained "good." Both have fallen; the former because of the latter. Still, their original patterns are unchanged; only their reproductions have become flawed. (See JD, 14:231.)

Even as the human spirit was begotten of divine parents who endowed it with a portion of their own holiness and perfection of mind and body, so was the spirit world brought forth in the presence of the Gods of the "eternal worlds" as a deathless realm of transcendent grandeur—a sphere of order and serenity where, under glorious skies, life thrived and beauty abounded in fruits that never decayed and flowers that never faded. Heber C. Kimball recounted a description of the spirit world given him by Jedediah M. Grant during his last illness in which Grant spoke of the perfect order which existed among the righteous dead who were organized "in perfect harmony" as families. Grant went on to describe the magnificent structures in the spirit world, adding that the least of these were superior to Solomon's temple. The gardens, too, transcended any to be found on earth with some plants having "fifty to a hundred different colored flowers growing upon one stalk." (JD, 4:135, 136.) Joseph Smith is reported to have described the spirit world as being so desireable that men would forfeit mortality to be there.[4]

It is a popular, but erroneous, assumption that the righteous "go to heaven" as soon as they die. Some Latter-day Saints have believed and taught this because of the statement of Alma: "Behold, it has been made known unto me by an angel, that the spirits of all men, as soon as they are departed from this mortal body, yea, the spirits of all men, whether they be good or evil, are taken home to that God who gave them life."[5] However, the "home" to which the dead go is not the celestial world, but

---

[4]Under the date of August 19, 1877, Charles L. Walker recorded the following: "He [Wilford Woodruff] referred to a saying of Joseph Smith, which he heard him utter (like this) That if the People knew what was behind the vail, they would try by every means to commit suicide that they might get there, but the Lord in his wisdom had implanted the fear of death in every person that they might cling to life and thus accomplish the designs of their Creator." (*Diary of Charles Lowell Walker*, 2 vols., A. Karl and Katharine Miles Larson, eds., [Logan: Utah State Univerity Press, 1980], 1:465-66. See also JD, 14:231; 17:442 and 26:192, 193.)

[5]Alma 40:11. See also Ecclesiastes 12:7. Orson Pratt believed that the dead return to God's literal presence after which some are then cast out. (See JD, 2:238.)

the spirit earth. Joseph Smith declared that "the righteous and the wicked all go to the same world of spirits until the resurrection."[6] Brigham Young explained that the dead "do not pass out of the organization of the earth on which we live." (JD, 3:368.)

Thus, when men "shuffle off this mortal coil," they return to God in the sense that they return to that spiritual condition in which they were first begotten. As with all things which the Lord has created, the spirit of man "remaineth in the sphere" in which God created it. (Moses 3:9.) As the human spirit dwells in and about its temporal body, so is the spirit world in close proximity to its physical counterpart. In a discourse given in 1856, President Young taught that the spirit world "is incorporated within this celestial system.[7] Can you see it with your natural eyes? No . . .Is the spirit world here? It is not beyond the sun, but is on this earth that was organized for the people that have lived and that do and will live upon it." (JD, 3:368, 372. See also JD, 3:69, 95 and 11:26.)

Brigham Young said further that if the Lord would permit it, "you could see the spirits that have departed from this world, as plainly as you now see bodies with your natural eyes." (JD, 3:368.) Joseph Smith taught that the glorified spirits of the just "are not far from us, and know and understand our thoughts, feelings and motions, and are often pained therewith." (HC, 6:52.)

Creation Of The Physical-Spiritual Earth

The authorized accounts of the creation of the earth were written by Abraham and Moses between three and four thousand years ago.[8] Abraham's information was based initially on ancient records and, subsequently, on his own seer powers. By means of the Urim and Thummim and by face to face instruction from the Lord himself, Abraham watched

---

[6]HC, 5:425. The parable of Lazarus and the Rich Man (Luke 16:19-31) confirms the Prophet's statement. (See JD, 3:94-96 and 11:126.)

[7]The earth is a "celestial system." Brigham Young said that "the earth is very good in and of itself, and has abided a celestial law." (JD, 2:302, 303. See also D&C 88:25.)

[8]Abraham lived about B.C. 2000, Moses about B.C. 1300.

the creative process unfold.[9] Moses also conversed with Jehovah face to face and received like instruction from him;[10] indeed, the Lord actually dictated the account which bears Moses' name.[11] Thus, by vision and by direct, verbal revelation two witnesses were raised up to testify of the divine truth concerning Earth's beginnings.

It is noteworthy that both Abraham and Moses received their independent revelations of the creation prior to their respective encounters with the ruling powers of Egypt. Being God's own witnesses of truths long shrouded in myth and fantasy, they stood unawed before the learning and sophistries of the ancient world. It is to their untarnished testimonies— together with those of later prophets—that we now turn for revealed knowledge of Earth's beginnings.[12]

----

[9]Abraham's initial knowledge of creation was obtained from the records of the prediluvian patriarchs: "Therefore a knowledge of the beginning of the creation, and also of the planets, and of the stars, as they were made known unto the fathers, have I kept even unto this day." (Abraham 1:31. See also Abraham 3:1, 11, 15, 22.)

[10]See Moses 1:40, 41. In an official pronouncement on the origin of man, Joseph F. Smith and his counselors in the First Presidency wrote: "The omnipotent Creator, the maker of heaven and earth—had shown unto Moses everything pertaining to this planet, including the facts relating to man's origin, and the authoritative pronouncement of that mighty prophet and seer to the house of Israel, and through Israel to the whole world, is couched in the simplest clause: 'God created man in his own image.'" (*The Improvement Era*, 13 [November, 1909]:76.)

[11]The second and third chapters of the writings of Moses (as found in the *Pearl of Great Price*) are an expanded, but otherwise parallel, version of Genesis 1-2. In most instances, the former will be cited.

[12]In the General Conference of the Church, October 8, 1875, Brigham Young declared: "We admit the history that Moses gives of the creation or organization of this earth, as stated in his writings, to be correct." Joseph F. Smith said: "The Bible account, being the most rational and indeed *only historical one* of the creation and the dealings of God with men, we are constrained to accept it, in the main, as truth." (JD 15:326.)

A Spiritual Account?

Many Bible scholars believe that Genesis 1 and 2 contain disparate versions of creation erroneously combined into a single narrative. Some LDS scriptorians have concluded that these chapters comprise two different creation narratives—the first spiritual, the second temporal. This dual accounts theory is thought to resolve certain apparent inconsistencies stemming from the fact that the organization of vegetation, animals, and man during the third, fifth and sixth days of creation, respectively, is followed by another account in near reverse order—man, vegetation and animals—on the seventh day of creation.[13]

Orson Pratt resolved this apparent contradiction by suggesting that all forms of life were created as spirit entities on the fifth and sixth days of the same creation week in which the physical earth was formed:

> We learn, therefore, when speaking of this spiritual creation, that not only all the children of men, of all generations, and of all ages, were created spiritually in heaven, but that fish and fowls, and beast, and all animated things, having life, were first made spiritual in heaven, on the fifth and sixth days, before bodies of flesh were prepared for them on the earth. (JD, 21:200. See also 15:243; 16:318.)

But there are several objections to Elder Pratt's view. The first is that it requires Moses' account to become a somewhat confusing admixture of the two creations: the physical on the first four days, and the spiritual on the fifth and sixth days. It also ignores the question of vegetation on the third day. Was it spiritual or physical at that time?

Perhaps a more important objection to this theory is that man would not have been begotten in spirit until *after* the physical earth was organized, Abraham, however, is explicit in declaring that all mankind existed as "spirits" or "souls" *before* the Gods went down to form the earth. (See Abraham 3:22-4:1.) Perhaps Elder Pratt intended to limit his comments to non-human life forms.[14]

----

[13]Genesis 1 and 2 is paralleled verse for verse in Moses 2 and 3 and, to a lesser extent, by Abraham 4 and 5.

[14]In the same address, Pratt said that "the beasts, etc., were formed on the sixth day or period." (JD, 21:201.)

Joseph Fielding Smith maintained that there is no extant account of the spiritual organization of the earth or its inhabitants:

> Now I repeat, the account in Genesis one and two, is the account of the physical creation of the earth and all upon it, but the creation was not subject to mortal law until after the fall. It was, therefore, a spiritual creation and so remained until the fall when it became temporal, or mortal.[15]

Consistent with the Lord's principle of "line upon line," it appears that the Lord has revealed what is essentially one, sequential, intergrated chronicle of the physical creation. The evidence suggests that the narratives of both Abraham and Moses pertain to events *after* the organization of the spirit earth and all spirit forms of life were a *fait accompli*.

Abraham's vision of creation began with a prologue in which the great patriarch was shown a portion of the cosmos as it existed in eternity—a descending order of spheres from immortal Kolob (the greatest of the everlasting stars shown him) on down to our temporal moon, sun, and earth. Their relative positions in the cosmic hierarchy were based upon their "times of reckoning" which, in turn, were declared to be analogous to the relative order of the "intelligences" over which God presided. (See Abraham 3:2-19.)

Abraham then beheld the pre-mortal estate and its inhabitants—"the intelligences that were organized *before* the world was."[16] These spirits or souls were to be "added upon" with physical tabernacles (Abraham 3:26.) Abraham then heard one "like unto God" tell his companions:

> We will go down, for there is space there, and we will take of these materials, and we will make an earth whereon these may dwell; and we will prove them *herewith*, to see if they will do

---

[15]Smith, *Doctrines of Salvation*, 1:75, 76. (Italics in original.)

[16]Abraham 3:22. Since Abraham saw that the spirits of men were already in existence before the creative week began, Orson Pratt's view that man was spiritually organized on the sixth day of that week seems untenable. (See JD 21:200.)

all things whatsoever the Lord their God shall command them.[17]

That these "spirits" had already been proven in terms of the "first estate" is shown by the fact that "among all these there were many of the noble and great ones." Since their worthiness as spirits had been established, it only remained for them to demonstrate like virtue on a physical-temporal earth. Abraham's account of the creation of that "proving" earth then follows.

Whereas Abraham figuratively stood among the Gods of the pre-mortal world when witnessing the creation, Moses' vantage point was the physical earth as it existed in his day. He described three visions given him by way of prologue to his creation account. In the first vision, Moses was shown "the world upon which he was created" together with "all the children of men which *are*, and which *were* created."[18] The second vision was a magnification of the first. He again "beheld the earth, yea, even *all* of it, and there was not a particle of it which he did not behold, discerning it by the spirit of God." In like manner, he discerned *each* of its "numberless inhabitants." (Moses 1:27, 28.)

Having totally comprehended this earth, Moses was given a third vision in which he was shown many other lands which were also called "earth," for they, too, were inhabited. (Moses 1:29-32.) This awesome knowledge prompted him to ask the Lord why and by what means they had been made. Moses was told that they existed to bring to pass God's work and glory—the immortality and eternal life of man—and that they had been created by the Only Begotten Son. (Moses 1:30-33 and 39.)

Lest Moses desire to know more concerning these other earths, the Lord cautioned: "But only an account of *this* earth, and the inhabitants thereof, give I unto you." Moses responded: "Be merciful unto thy servant, O God, and tell me concerning this earth and the inhabitants thereof, and also the heavens, and then thy servant will be content."[19] The

---

[17]Abraham 3:24, 25. That the entire human race existed as spirits before the physical earth was formed is also supported by Moses 3:4, 5 and D&C 49:16, 17. See also D&C 38:1 and JD, 21:290.

[18]Moses 1:8. Moses may have seen the spirit earth as well as the physical earth.

[19]Moses 1:35, 36. Moses must have been unaware at that time of the existence of Abraham's creation narrative. Otherwise he would have known how and why this earth was organized. It is fortunate that a second account was provided since Abraham and Moses constitute two witnesses to the same vital truth.

Lord then dictated his own account of the creation of the physical earth—
the "earth upon which thou standest."[20]

> And now, Moses, my son, I will speak unto thee concerning *this
> earth upon which thou standest*; and thou shalt write the things
> which I shall speak.
> And in a day when the children of men shall esteem my words
> as naught and take many of them from *the book which thou shalt
> write*, behold, I will raise up another like unto thee; and they
> shall be had again among the children of men—among as
> many as shall believe.[21]

At no point in the subsequent narrative does the Lord ever suggest
that he is speaking of a spiritual creation. Indeed, if such were the case, his
parenthetical explanation in Moses 3:5 (which, significantly, parallels
Abraham 5:5) that *all* life was organized spiritually before any life existed
"naturally" on this planet becomes a confusing redundancy.[22] Then too,
both writers described the primal earth as being immersed in water ("the
deep") from which the "dry land" did not emerge until the third day.
Water consists of gross element not to be found in a purely spiritual realm.
(Vicarious baptism for the dead is an earthly ordinance which is made
necessary, in part, by this very fact.) (See D&C 128:12-14.) Also, Abraham
and Moses began their accounts with the formation of the earth with its
sea, land, and atmosphere. If they were alluding to the earth's spiritual
creation—and nowhere in their texts do they even infer this—then no

---

[20]Moses 1:40. See also Moses 2:1. Apparently the Lord dictated the
same creation narrative to Joseph Smith. (See Moses 1:42.) The fact that
God, not Moses or some unknown scribe, is the author of the biblical
account of the creation has been lost from the Genesis account. In the
Book of Moses the first person "I, God," is used in contrast to the third
person "God said," in Genesis.

[21]Moses 1:40 and 41. This revelation marked the beginning of the
books of Moses.

[22]Note that these verses refer only to the spirit origin of the various
life forms, not to the earth per se. Joseph Fielding Smith said, "The
statements in Moses 3:5 and Genesis 2:5 are *interpolations* thrown into the
account of the physical creation, explaining that all things were first
created in the spirit existence in heaven before they were placed on this
earth." (*Doctrines of Salvation*, 1:76. Italic in original.)

scriptural account of Earth's physical formation exists. No further reference to the origin of the earth *per se* is forthcoming from either writer.

Finally, if, as Orson Pratt suggested, the physical earth was fashioned on the seventh day, then, contrary to both accounts, the "heaven and the earth" were not completed by the end of the sixth period and, therefore, the seventh was not earth's first sabbath on which God "rested from all his work which he had made."

The Gods of Creation

Prior to organizing the earth, the three members of the Godhead covenanted with each others as to their respective roles and responsibilities in the enterprise. Joseph Smith said that this covenant was everlasting and that it "relates to their dispensation of things to men on the earth; these personages, according to Abraham's record, are called God the first, the Creator; God the second, the Redeemer; and God the third, the witness or Testator."[23]

That "God the first" is called the Creator does not contradict the doctrine that Christ is also a creator. The Father accomplishes his works by and through the Son. (Moses 1:33. See also Colossians 1:16.) Then too, the "fulness of the Father" is the fulness of Godhood. (See Colossians 1:19; 2:9 and D&C 93:12-16.) The powers exercised by those subordinate to the Father are possessed in their totality by him. Hence, in his attributes, powers, and glory he is a composite of all the Gods. In this sense he is the Creator, the Redeemer, and the Testator at one and the same time. The Father shares his powers and attributes with others so that their callings are extensions of his authority. The Most High God possesses all the gifts and powers of those who serve under him even though he may not always exercise them. Thus, Jesus Christ, in exercising the creative

---

[23]TPJS, p. 190. The Prophet also said: "Any person that has seen the heavens opened knows that there are three personages in the heavens who hold the keys of power, and one presides over all." (TPJS, p. 312. See also p. 370.) While there is but one true God, a plurality of deities share that title. (See D&C 20:28; Alma 11:26-44; John 17:20-23; 1 Corinthians 8:5, 6 and Colossians 2:9.)

power of the Father became the Creator, "the Father of the heavens and of the earth, and all things that in them are."[24]

In harmony with the Prophet's statement, Brigham Young referred to the three personages who were subsequently involved in the actual labor of creation:

> It is true that the earth was organized by three distinct characters, namely, Eloheim, Yahovah, and Michael, these three forming a quorum, as in all heavenly bodies, and in organizing element, perfectly represented in the Deity, as Father, Son, and Holy Ghost.[25]

Thus, while the Genesis prologue—"in the beginning God created the heaven and the earth"—is correct, the term, God, should be viewed as a collective noun. The record of Abraham is explicit in stating that a plurality of Gods organized the heaven and the earth. [26] In a vision of surpassing wonder, the great patriarch was taken back through time to a point in eternity prior to "the beginning" and shown the very council in which the decision was made to organize this planet. While he did not specifically identify the Gods of Creation, he wrote of one who stood among the noble and the great ones who was "like unto God," who led those who were with him in organizing the earth. (Abraham 3:23, 24.)

It appears that he who was like unto God is the second ranking

---

[24]Ether 4:7. See also Mosiah 15:1-4; Talmage, *Articles of Faith*, appendix two, pp. 466, 467 and *Jesus the Christ*, p. 33. Speaking of those who become the sons of God, John Taylor said, "They, through the atonement might be exalted, by obedience to the law of the Gospel; *to the Godhead.*" *Mediation & Atonement*, p. 133.

[25]JD, 1:52. Michael the archangel was given the name, Adam, upon coming to earth. (See D&C 27:11; 107:54; 128:21.) There is no scriptural account of the actual naming of Adam.

[26]See Abraham 4 and 5. A plurality of Gods is also indicated in Genesis 1:26: "And God said, Let *us* make man in *our* image." (See Moses 2:26 which indicated that the Father was speaking to his Only Begotten.) See also John 1:14, 18 and 1 John 4:9.

member of the Godhead, the Lord Jesus Christ. This is supported by the direct word of God to Moses that "I am the Beginning and the End, the Almighty God; by mine Only Begotten I created these things; yea, in the beginning I created the heaven, and the earth upon which thou standest."[27] Christ's appointment was made in a "grand council" convened for the purpose of planning the earth's organization. Joseph Smith stated:

> The head God called together the Gods and sat in grand council to bring forth the world. The grand councilors sat at the head in yonder heavens and contemplated the creation of the worlds which were created at the time . . .In the beginning, the head of the Gods called a council of the Gods; and they came together and concocted a plan to create the world and people it. (HC, 6:307, 308. See also HC, 6:475, 476.)

This decision was subsequently made known to the hosts of heaven who "shouted for joy" when the foundations of this planet were laid.[28] Joseph Smith may have been alluding to this same occasion when he said: "At the first organization in heaven we were all present, and saw the Savior chosen and appointed and the plan of salvation made, and we sanctioned it." (TPJS, 181. See also p. 365.) According to the Prophet, this, or a similar council was held "in Kolob."[29]

Matter Unorganized

The Creator said to his companions: "We will go down, for there is space there, and we will take of these materials, and we will make an earth

---

[27]Moses 2:1. That the Only Begotten was the chief organizer of the earth is so well attested in both ancient and modern scripture as to make extended discussion unnecessary. (See Moses 1:32, 33; D&C 38:13; 76:23, 24; John 1:1-14 and Colossians 1:16.)

[28]See Job 38:4-7. Commenting on this passage Orson Pratt asked: "Do you relize that you and I were there? Can you bring it to your minds that you and I were among the happy number that shouted for joy when this creation was made?" (JD, 1:55.)

[29]See Joseph Smith's poem, "A Vision" (a paraphrasing of D&C 76), *Times and Seasons*, Nauvoo, Illinois, 4 (February 1843), pp. 82-85. Kolob is an immortal sphere having governance over "the same order" of worlds of which this earth is a part. (See Abraham 3:3.)

whereon these may dwell." (Abraham 3:24.) The materials which the Gods then organized were not created in the traditional *ex nihilo* sense of the word. From nothing comes nothing. The word *create* was translated from the Hebrew word *baurau*. Joseph Smith taught that *baurau* does "not mean to create our of nothing; it means to organize; the same as a man would organize materials and build a ship."[30] The Prophet further taught that "God had materials to organize the world out of chaos—chaotic matter, which is element, and in which dwells all the glory. The pure principles of element are principles which can never be destroyed; they may be organized and reorganized, but not destroyed. They had no beginning and can have no end." (HC, 6:308, 309.)

Since element is uncreated and uncreatable, it can be said that the earth—and everything else—is ageless insofar as its materiality is concerned. And since matter can be organized and reorganized, it is conceivable that at least some of the earth's "materials" were drawn from earlier creations.

Joseph Smith taught that this earth was "organized or formed out of other planets which were broken up and remodeled and made into the one on which we live."[31] Orson Pratt, characteristically, carried this idea to the point of hyperbole when he wrote: "How many thousands of millions of times the elements of our globe have been organized and disorganized; or how many millions of shapes or forms the elements have been thrown into in their successive organization and disorganizations . . .is unknown to us mortals."[32]

Heber C. Kimball advanced a provocative thought—which he realized some would call "foolish philosophy"—when he asked the rhetorical question: "Where did the earth come from? From its parent earths." (JD, 6:36.) While this unadorned concept appears altogether naive, it may yet prove correct. Living things beget living things after their own kind. This principle not only assures a continuity of life from generation to

---

[30]HC, 6:308. The Prophet also taught that the earth existed in "an elementary state, from eternity." (HC, 3:387. See also TPJS, 181; JD, 12:238 and 19:286; 24:61 and 26:27.)

[31]Andrew F. Ehat and Lyndon W. Cook, *The Words of Joseph Smith: The Contemporary Accounts of the Nauvoo Discourses of The Prophet Joseph* (Provo, Religious Studies Center, 1980), p. 60.

[32]Orson Pratt, *The Seer*, pp. 248, 249. See JD, 16:316; 18:293, 294; 20:274 and 21:322.

generation, but from world to world as well. If such be the case, it is not too far-fetched for Elder Kimball to suggest that earths are products of other earths. Every living earth may, in God's own way, be organized from a "seed" or nucleus—"from its parent earths." If so, then all of the Creator's works are literally linked to one another in an unbroken chain reaching from one eternity to another!

Was the debris of entire planets used in forming this small earth? And what was the consistency of that debris? Was it fine, gaseous particles or comparatively rough conglomerate? Responding to this question, Orson Pratt wrote:

> We are not to suppose that these elements, before they were collected, were formed into solid masses of rocks and other hard substances: and that these came rushing together—rocks being piled on rocks, breaking, crashing, and rending into millions of fragments. But no doubt through the operation of antecedent forces, there had been a complete disorganization or dissolution of the bodies, composed of these elements in that prior state or existence anterior to the foundation of the present globe: this being the case, the elements being separate, and apart, and widely diffused, were in a condition to come together in a state of particles, instead of aggregate masses.[33]

But whatever the primal state of the earth's "clay," it was miraculously fashioned upon the wheel of the divine Potter.

"God spake, chaos heard, and worlds came into order by reason of the faith there was in HIM." (Lectures on Faith, No. 1, par. 22.) Orson Pratt sought to explain how this miracle occurred in terms of his knowledge of Newtonian physics.[34]

---

[33]*The Seer*, p. 249. See also JD, 13:248 and 21:32. B. H. Roberts believed that this planet had been created, inhabited, and destroyed in an earlier age and that its "fragments" were then reorganized into the present earth, after which man and other forms of life were "brought from some other world to our own." (*Man's Relationship to Deity*, pp. 279-282.)

[34]Orson Pratt lectured extensively on the subject of astronomy at the Deseret University (now the University of Utah). His lectures were compiled and published by Nels B. Lundwall under the title *Wonders of the Universe*, in 1937.

Jehovah spake—the elements came rushing together, not by their own power, but under the action of the self-moving forces of His Spirit . . .every particle moving toward the great common center with a resultant force, varying inversely as the square of its distance from every other particle.—They [modern philosophers] would have called it the law of gravitation: while those better acquainted with the origin of the force would have called it the law by which the Spirit of God moves together the particles of matter. (*The Seer*, p. 249.)

"And the Gods watched those things which they had ordered until they obeyed." (Abraham 4:18.) Matter unorganized, infused with the Spirit of the Lord—"the law by which all things are governed"—responded and a new world was born. And all without the sound of hammer or chisel! The Creator pronounced it "very good."

Place of Creation

Astronomers theorize that about 8.5 billion years after the beginning of the universe (or 4.5 billion years ago), our sun and its satellites[35] were formed by the condensation of gaseous materials indigenous to our galaxy, the Milky Way. [36] *Where* the earth was formed may profoundly affect *how* it was formed. A different location for the primal creation would virtually negate the condensation theory of formation in so far as the earth is concerned.[37] While scripture is silent on the matter, modern

---

[35]The planets may have been formed before the sun; the sequence is uncertain.

[36]This is called the Condensation Theory. It was preceded by the theory that the planets were formed as a result of a collision between our sun and another star. Condensation is thought to be the typical way all stars are formed from galactic materials.

[37]There are very real objections to the condensation theory of the formation of our solar system which prompt astronomers to emphasize that it is only a working hypothesis.

66   *The Footstool of God*

prophets have taught that the earth was not organized in this solar system.[38]

Joseph Smith prophesied: "This earth will be rolled *back* into the presence of God, and crowned with celestial glory." (TPJS, p. 181.) Obviously, the earth could not be "rolled back" into the presence of God unless it had once been in his presence. That such had been the case was the teaching of Brigham Young who taught that the earth "will go back into the presence of God, where it was first framed." (JD, 9:317. See also 7:163; 8:8.) He further remarked: "When the earth was framed and brought into existence and man was placed upon it, it was near the throne of our Father in Heaven." (JD, 17:143.) This implies that the earth was organized in the vicinity of Kolob, the heavenly body Abraham saw "nearest unto the throne of God." (Abraham 3:2, 3.) Such was Elder John Taylor's understanding in writing that the earth "was first organized, near the planet Kolob."[39]

There is a universal principle of affinity which applies to all things; like does attract like, in time, and in eternity. (See D&C 88:40.) Spirits mingle with spirits, mortals with mortals, and resurrected beings with other resurrected beings. Any extensive or prolonged commingling of one class with another is not to be found. Indeed, the plan of salvation envisions eternal degrees of glory where men and women of similar natures are homogeneously grouped together. This principle is equally applicable to all heavenly systems.

The order of the universe observed and described by our astrophysicists is essentially different from that order to which the earth belonged in its primeval childhood. Being a spiritual organization, one endowed with immortality, the earth was governed by and moved in harmony with other worlds of like nature. One senses the rightness and the appropriateness of

---

[38]That the earth was organized independent of the sun and the other planets is suggesed by the creation accounts of both Moses and Abraham. They state that the earth was provided with light on the *first* "day" or "time," and that the sun did not become its light source until the *fourth* "day" or "time." (See Genesis 1:2-13; Moses 2:2-13 and Abraham 4:2-13.) The earth must have been rotating on its axis from its formation since night and day resulted from the presence of its *initial* light source on the first day.

[39]John Taylor, "Origin and Destiny of Woman," *The Mormon* [New York] (August 29, 1857), as quoted in N. B. Lundwall, *The Vision*, p. 146.

the inspired teachings of the first three presidents of the Church. Both man and the planet on which he now dwells were brought forth as deathless creations in the presence of God. Both have fallen and become wanderers in a corner of an alien kingdom.[40]

The "Week" of Creation

How much time was involved in the earth's total organization? Genesis literalists maintain that all was accomplished in six, twenty-four hour periods. But Moses' account does not provide us with any yardstick by which to measure the length of his creative "days." Even assuming that they were of equal length, there is nothing in the text to suggest their duration. Hence, Brigham Young's comment:

It is said in this book (the Bible) that God made the earth in six days. This is a mere term, but it matters not whether it took six days, six months, six years, or six thousand years. The creation occupied certain periods of time. We are not authorized to say what the duration of these days was, whether Moses penned these words as we have them, or whether the translators of the Bible have given their words their intended meaning.[41]

However, the yardstick that Moses failed to provide may be found in the writings of Abraham. His account of creation is but a subdivision of an all-encompassing revelation given him through the Urim and Thummim before he went into Egypt. (See Abraham 3.) These instruments functioned in part as a divine telescope through which Abraham saw stars of awesome magnitude which the Lord denominated "the governing ones." Among the stars which he saw was Kolob, the star nearest the

---

[40]The word planet is taken from the Greek *planetes* meaning wanderer.

[41]JD, 18:231. George Q. Cannon cited Joseph Smith as teaching that the six days of creation were six periods of the Lord's time. Cannon believed that these periods were compatible with the views of geologists. (See JD, 14:61.) In 1871, Orson Pratt said the length of creation was unknown (JD, 14:234, 235.) In 1873 he cited Abraham's account as evidence that it was six thousand years. (JD, 16:317.)

throne of God, meaning, "nearest to the celestial, or the residence of God."[42]

The Lord further informed Abraham that Kolob belonged to the highest order or system of worlds, having the same "seasons" and the same measurement of time as that of the celestial dwelling place of God himself:[43] "one revolution was a day unto the Lord, after his manner of reckoning, it being one thousand years according to the time appointed" for the earth upon which Abraham stood.[44] But while Abraham equates one of the Lord's days with a thousand earth years, does he use the term "day" in the same manner when treating the Creation?[45] It seems that he does. Note that he consistently employs the terms "day" and "night" as

------

[42]See the explanations of figures 1 and 2 of facsimile number two in the *Book of Abraham* which parallel the information provided in Abraham 3:2-4.

[43]God is not immaterial, therefore he is not beyond time. Like him, time is eternal, but its measurement is relative. He measures time according to the rotation of his celestial world even as we measure time according to the rotation of our earth on its axis. The length of a "day" is determined by the star or planet upon which one lives. For example, a "day" on the sun is twenty-seven times longer than a "day" on earth. Joseph Smith taught: "In answer to the question—Is not the reckoning of God's time, angel's time, prophet's time, and man's time, according to the planet on which they reside? I answer, Yes." (D&C 130:4, 5.)

[44]Abraham 3:4. Compare Psalm 90:4 and 2 Peter 3:8. The Lord's reckoning of time is, indeed, awesome. Astronomers know of no star that is so massive as to require a thousand earth years to complete one rotation on its axis. Little wonder that Kolob is "First in government [and] the last pertaining to the measurement of time." (See figure 1, facsimile 2, *Book of Abraham*.) The Lord has revealed that the sum of all the systems of time governing all heavenly bodies equals one celestial year: "And they give light to each other in their times and in their seasons, in their minutes, in their hours, in their days, in their weeks, in their months, in their years—all these are one year with God, but not with man." (D&C 88:44.)

[45]John Taylor equated the word "time" in Abraham's account with "epochs" and "ages" and distinguished between them and the term "day" as used by Moses. He felt that Abraham's record "agrees precisely with many geological facts that have puzzled so many of this generation." (JD 25:215.)

referring to the presence or absence of light, *not* to any given period of time. (See Abraham 4:5, 8, 13, 19, 23, and 31.) Thus, a day and a night equal a *time*. Six evenings and mornings (days)—six times—are covered in Abraham 4.

Then too, unlike Moses (who describes each creative day only in terms of the earth's diurnal cycles—"the evening and the morning"), Abraham describes them in terms of both *days* and *times*. First he tells us that "from evening until morning" was Earth's period of darkness and that "from morning until evening" was its period of light. He then states that each round of darkness and light equals one "day" or one "time." Thus, it appears that he employs the two terms so as to distinguish between the character of a "day" on Earth and a "time" on Kolob; for while they were of equal duration, they were dissimilar in nature. Whereas a "day" on Earth was characterized by alternating periods of darkness and light, a "time" on Kolob, the realm of the Gods, *knew no darkness* "from evening until morning" or "from morning until evening."

In all likelihood, the Gods produced night and day—alternating darkness and light—on the empty and desolate planet by causing it to rotate on its axis in the presence of its primeval light source. One complete cycle of darkness and light constituted a "day" or a "time." But were earth's pre-fall days equal to those of Kolob? Did both worlds reckon time the same way? If they did, then Abraham has told us that creation was between six and seven thousand years in length.[46] There is evidence that such was the case.

It is in the context of the Lord's reckoning of time that Abraham presents his account. His treatment of the various phases of the work, in terms of first, second, third, etc., times, implies celestial times—one thousand year days. This is evidenced by his consistent and singular usage of the word "time" throughout his account. Nowhere does he attempt to redefine the term or to disassociate it from God. Indeed, he continues to refer to "time" in the same way even after concluding his account of the creation. In writing of subsequent events, Abraham tells us that Adam was warned that he would die "in the *time*" in which he ate

---

[46]To this figure some LDS scriptorians add the six thousand years since the fall, making the overall age of the earth about thirteen thousand years. (See Hyrum L. Andrus, *God, Man and the Universe*, pp. 315, 316, 329, and Melvin A. and M. Garfield Cook, *Science and Mormonism*, chapter VIII.)

the forbidden fruit.[47] Abraham then explains that a new measurement of time has not been introduced on the earth that would give the word "time" a different connotation: "Now I, Abraham, saw that it was after the Lord's time, which was after the time of Kolob; for as yet the Gods had not appointed unto Adam his reckoning."[48]

Abraham's meaning is clear: Adam was on God's time or Kolob's time during his sojourn in Eden. In all likelihood, the Gods appointed Adam his new reckoning of time when he, and the earth, fell from immortality to mortality. That is, eternal time ended and mortal time began when Adam fell from the presence of God. Besides, how could it have been otherwise? According to Joseph Smith, time is relative, being measured in terms of the world on which one dwells. Because the Garden of Eden was on the earth, and because Garden of Eden time was also the Lord's time, it logically follows that Earth time before the fall was equal to the Lord's time. There is no basis for assuming that Adam was on one time system while the planet on which he lived was on another.

Joseph Smith's poetic paraphrase of "The Vision" (D&C 76), suggests that the "council in Kolob" and the "grand council" (HC, 6:307) which was convened to plan the earth are one and the same. If this is correct, it would be altogether reasonable for the Gods to schedule their labors in terms of their *own* time frame. The seven times or days of creation would, therefore, equal seven days on Kolob, or seven thousand years on this fallen planet.

It has been argued that the creation "days" may have varied in length and/or that they may have been interspersed with pauses of indeterminate duration. Also, Earth's organization may have begun

---

[47]Adam was 930 years old when he passed away. This was seventy years before the "day" on which he transgressed ended. (See Genesis 5:5; Moses 6:12; JD, 16:317 and 26:200.) The original manuscript of Joseph Smith's translation of Genesis indicates that Adam was almost 1,000 years old at his death.

[48]Abraham 5:13. "When this earth was created, it was not according to our present time, but it was created according to Kolob's *time*, for the Lord has said it was created on celestial time which is Kolob's time. Then he revealed to Abraham that *Adam was subject to Kolob's time* before his transgression." (Joseph Fielding Smith, *Doctrines of Salvation*, 1:79. Italics in original.)

long before the "first time" and simply been completed in connection with the introduction of light.[49] Consequently, the earth itself could be older, perhaps much older, than thirteen thousand years.

These objections cannot be disregarded, but the weight of scriptural evidence is against them. As before stated, each of the six days comprising the creation week were computed in terms of the measurement of time employed by the Gods on Kolob. These times are apparently fixed and precise. It would seem, therefore, that the only way the days enumerated by Abraham and Moses would have varied in length (since they are defined in terms of alternating darkness and light) would have been for the rate of rotation of the earth to have been altered from one creative day to another. But there is neither evidence nor justification for such tampering with the clocks of Earth and Kolob. Indeed, to have done so would have rendered meaningless the words of Abraham and Moses on this point. Likewise, there is no indication of any creation pauses by the Gods until the seventh time *when they rested* from all their labors. The spiritual significance of that rest would be diminished by any pre-sabbath sabbaths.

Why would the Gods interrupt a project which they had counseled to complete "on the seventh time"? Certainly fatigue or lack of blueprints or materials or workers would not have prompted any delays. Other than Abraham's testimony, the most compelling reason for believing that all was accomplished within a pre-determined period of time is found in modern revelation. The seven one thousand year days of creation are paralleled by the seven one thousand year days of the earth's temporal existence.[50] Thus, the initial career of the earth from its birth to its death is only a matter of about two celestial weeks!

---

[49]This possibility was expressed by Charles W. Penrose who felt that geology had "demonstrated the fallacy of the idea that the earth is such a young planet in the universe." He added: "How many ages upon ages passed from the time called 'in the beginning,' to that when God called forth the light out of the midst of the darkness, cannot be gleaned from any revelation or scripture ancient or modern, that is now known to man." (*The Improvement Era* [May, 1909], p. 507.) Other LDS leaders have also tended to support the accepted position of geologists. Prominent among them was James E. Talmage, "The Earth and Man" and John A. Widtsoe, *Joseph Smith, As a Scientist*, chapter VII.

[50]Joseph smith wrote: "The world has had a fair trial for six thousand years; the Lord will try the seventh thousand Himself." (HC, 5:64.)

As previously noted, the Lord moves in cycles. His work is one eternal round (D&C 3:2; 35:1), a repetitive sequence wherein the first is as the last and the last is as the first. (See D&C 29:30.) This principle applies with equal validity to both men and worlds: they are first spiritual, then temporal, then spiritual again. (See D&C 29:31, 32.)

The spiritual and the temporal stages of the earth's existence are inextricably associated with the pre-mortal and post-mortal missions of Jesus Christ. Indeed, his activities on Earth's first sabbath are parallel with, and prophetic of, his activities on Earth's second (millennial) sabbath. Both are the Lord's day; both are a thousand years in length. The profound relationship between the first and the second sabbath is set forth in a modern revelation which states that "as God made the world in six days, and on the seventh day he finished his work, and sanctified it, and also formed man out of the dust of the earth, *even so*, in the beginning of the seventh thousand years will the Lord sanctify the earth, and complete the salvation of man." (D&C 77:12. See also JD, 15:262, 263 and 16:325.)

A question not considered in the previous discussion of earth's total age is: Did the Gods need six thousand years to create the earth? If not, why did they extend their labors over that length of time?[51] One possible reason is that they wished to teach mankind a vital principle—that mortals possess two natures, each of which must be recognized and respected. To do this there must be a proper balance between the temporal and the spiritual, between physical activity and spiritual *rest*, between daily bread and the bread of life. (See Matthew 4:4; 6:11; Luke 11:3 and John 6:35 and 47-41.) This, they did, first by example and then by precept. (See Exodus 20:8-11 and D&C 59:10.) Having finished all of their works, they rested on the seventh day and "the Lord blessed the sabbath day, and hallowed it."

The fact that the seven "days" of the creation "week" will be followed by another seven thousand year period pertaining to the earth's "temporal existence" (D&C 77:6) suggests that the pivotal events pertaining to this earth were foreordained with a kind of prophetic symmetry. It is as though the destiny of man and this earth had been plotted as a divine chiasmus, the central point being the atonement and resurrection of Jesus Christ in the meridian of time. Therefore, the

---

[51]The labors of each creative day were accomplished *within*, not throughout that day. (See JD, 15:263, 264.)

THE EARTH'S DUAL WEEKS[a]

Years	1000	2000	3000	4000	5000	6000	7000

CREATION (left) — FALL (right)

Earth's Physical—Spiritual Organization and Preparation

7000: Coming of Adam — God With Man

Days	1	2	3	4	5	6

First Sabbath

Years	1000	2000	3000	4000	5000	6000	7000

FALL (left) — END OF EARTH (right)

Earth's Temporal Existence

7000: Coming of Christ — God With Man

Days	1	2	3	4	5	6

Second Sabbath

[a]The chart is only representative of the general pattern of events from the Creation to the Millennium. Neither the actual number of years since the fall nor the precise time of the Lord's coming is known.

major prophetic milestones—from the foundation of the world to the first coming of Christ—are to be passed again, but in an inverse, modified order. All this, from first to last and from last to first, within a time frame of two celestial weeks, or approximately fourteen thousand years.[52]

The Earth's Age

The suggestion that this planet is only thousands of years old is considered ludicrous by contemporary geologists who calculate its age to be about 4.6 billion years. While scripture fails to support geologists on this point, a letter written by William W. Phelps (a close associate of Joseph Smith) to William Smith states that "eternity . . .has been going on this system (not this world) almost *two thousand five hundred and fifty five millions of years*."[53] Phelps indicated that this information was gleaned—apparently by Joseph Smith—from the, as yet, unpublished portions of the writings of Abraham and Joseph.[54] To say that eternity has been "going on" for some two and a half billion years in the "system" of which the earth is a part is most revealing. Eternity is often defined as the endless continuum of existence which lies on either side of mortality.[55] But eternity is also defined as a single epoch or cycle of creation, redemption, and perfection—one "round" of God's work and

---

[52] It is appropriate that all things should be *centered* in Christ since he is "the first and the last." (D&C 100:4. See also Revelation 2:8.)

[53] *Times and Seasons*, 5 (January 1, 1854), p. 758. (Italics in the original.) The letter was dated Nauvoo, December 25, 1844. The "records" alluded to were separate rolls of papyri purchased for Joseph Smith in Kirtland, Ohio, in July 1835. (See HC, 2:235, 236.) John Taylor seems to have elaborated on the Phelps' letter in an editorial entitled "The Living God" which appeared in the *Times and Seasons* for February 15, 1845. Taylor later incorporated some of this editorial into his *Mediation and Atonement*.

[54] On several occasions, Joseph Smith made reference to the knowledge he had gained concerning God and his creations while translating the records of Joseph and Abraham. (See TPJS, 190; HC, 3:27; 5:63, 64 and 6:476.)

[55] To God the mortal state is but an imaginary point on the road of eternal time. (See D&C 29:31-34.)

glory. This earth and all others associated with it are bound together through their mutual Redeemer and by common bonds of Spirit and truth. (See D&C 88:49-61.) Thus, because of the spiritual darkness which now prevails on *this* earth, "all eternity is pained." (D&C 38:11, 12. See also Moses 7:36, 37, 40, 41 and 56.) When the Savior was crucified on *this* earth, the sons and daughters of God on other worlds also responded to that cosmic event. (See D&C 76:23, 24; 1 Nephi 19:12 and Moses 7:55 and 56.) Finally, sometimes eternity connotes the sum of all particular extensions of eternal time: "Thou hast taken Zion to thine own bosom, from all thy creations, from all eternity to all eternity."[56]

The primal earth had a dual nature, being both spiritual (or immortal) and physical (or corporeal) in composition. Joseph Smith stated that it was physically organized "out of chaos—chaotic matter, which is element, and in which dwells all the glory." (HC, 6:308.) This in-dwelling glory of the primal earth was the Spirit of the Lord which permeated it with quickening, sustaining power, thereby rendering it an immortal body.[57] It remained so until the fall.

Being immortal throughout its pre-fall state, the earth was, for all intents and purposes, ageless. This makes it impossible to determine its real age from the post-fall data with which science is obliged to work. The dating methods currently employed to measure the age of rocks, fossils, and various organic objects are virtually useless when applied to the total lifespan of the earth.[58] The dating problem is further compounded by the unprecedented cataclysmic changes which occurred in connection with the fall, the flood, and the atonement. Catastrophism, not uniformitarianism, has characterized earth's history from the beginning. Only God knows what has happened to Earth's time clock. According to Abraham, the Gods finished all of their labors by the Saturday evening of their celestial week—a period of 6,000 years. But while the enterprise was to be concluded within that time frame, the

---

[56]Moses 7:31. See also *Times and Seasons*, 6 (February 15, 1845), p. 809.

[57]See D&C 88:41 and Moses 1:5. The physical-spiritual character of the pre-fall earth has led to its being described as a terrestrial world of paradisaical glory.

[58]For a conservative LDS treatment of the dating problem see Melvin A. Cook and Melvin G. Cook, *Science and Mormonism*, Chapter IX, Deseret Book Co., Salt Lake City, 1973.

actual amount of time spent in carrying out each phase of it must have been minimal. (Mortals labor only a portion of each twenty-four hour day.)

As we have already noted, the Gods rule by the power inherent in their spoken word: "I am the same which spake, and the world was made, and all things came by me." (D&C 38:3. See also Jacob 4:9.) The Gods are miracle workers. Can finite man ever hope to understand their science? Moroni asked: "Who shall say that it was not a miracle that *by his word* the heaven and the earth should be?" (Mormon 9:17.)

The miracles of Jesus prove that God is bound neither by time nor by law as we mortals experience time and law.[59] For example, the natural processes involved in wine production require many months of planting, growing, harvesting, pressing, and fermentation. Yet Jesus, employing higher laws of organization instantaneously produced wine which was superior to the natural product. (See John 2:1-10.)

Science is also able to speed up the processes of nature—both creative and destructive—and quickly accomplish what would ordinally take many years. In a thousand ways, the earth is subdued, modified, transformed, and utilized to produce new products and conditions in a micro-fraction of the time any conceivable "natural" process might entail. So, too, the time required to bring the earth with all of its myriad life forms into existence would depend entirely upon the processes employed. Orson Pratt argued that the great events prophecied for the future need not take place through the slow, progressive methods ascribed to geology. (See JD, 18:318 and 19:284, 285.) Declaring God to be "the greatest chemist there is," Pratt said that God can "make a tree into rock in one night or one day . . .or he can let it lie until it pulverises [sic] and blows to the four winds, without petrifying, just as he pleases." (JD, 15:126, 127.)

While the prophecies pertaining to the future destiny of the earth, together with the historical account of God's dealings with man, do not provide scientific proof that the Lord did not move at a glacial pace in the beginning, they certainly do not support such a notion. Would the ways of that God who changes not be so different in the dim past from

---

[59]This may be one reason why God is excluded from any strictly scientific system. Such a system depends upon the consistent operations of natural law for its own validity and reliability. But miracles are, by definition, modifications of natural law which virtually strip the scientist of his science.

his ways in the historical present or the on-rushing future? Why would he suspend his omniscience and omnipotence to become a passive spectator in the universe throughout the eons of creation? If he did, then he is, indeed, longsuffering! And humble! For then it was not he, but natural law that created the heavens and the earth and all things therein.

But such is not the case, God fashioned this earth, and he did not even begin to do so until *after* the entire human race had been begotten as spirits in the pre-mortal world. (See D&C 49:17 and Moses 3:5.) Is it reasonable to assume that billions of spirits were kept waiting billions of years while those who were sent down to organize this planet cast their priesthood powers aside and deferred to the very forces that that priesthood was designed to control?

This is but one of countless worlds being continuously formed by the Gods to provide for the ever-expanding family of Man. They are not neophytes in the business of creation. Nor are they fools. Indeed, as Paul asked, "Hath not God made foolish the wisdom of this world?" (1 Corinthians 1:20.) Why do men insist upon defending the mirror image of the truth? The earth did not create man, Man created the earth. Earth is not where man first set his foot, but where he last set his foot. His origin is not down in the dust, but up among the stars. He is not the offspring of primates, but of Gods. His ever-receding origin is not to be found in East Africa, but on Kolob—and beyond.

Harmonizing Abraham and Moses

Some exegetes see Abraham's record as essentially the divine design of creation, the implementation of which was later described by Moses. This view is based in part on Abraham 5:5 which seems to indicate that all that had been treated in chapter four was but the "plan"—the agenda—of the Gods.[60] However, when the textual integrity of Abraham and Moses is not violated by the introduction of extraneous concepts or materials—when their records are allowed to speak for

---

[60]The term "plan" appears but once in Abraham's account (4:21) where it is apparent from the context that it is used in terms of an *on-going* enterprise, not a tentative scheme. Like architects overseeing the construction of a mighty edifice, the Gods observed that "their plan was good."

themselves—it becomes apparent that they are, in fact, two harmonious descriptions of the same magnificent event.[61]

Chapter four begins with the statement that the Gods "organized and formed the heavens and the earth." This is followed by Abraham's account of the origin of day and night, the atmosphere, the dry land, and its surrounding "great waters." All of these events are described in the past tense as completed actions. Phase one of the labors being completed, the Gods then *prepared* the sea, land, and atmosphere for their future denizens. These preparations are also described in the past tense.

As the sixth time drew to a close, a second council was held in which they reaffirmed their purposes (as expressed in the first creation council—3:24; 5:3) to populate the newly-formed planet with man and all other animated things. (Abraham 4:26-5:2.) All this is stated in terms of intent not completion: "We *will* bless them. We *will* cause them to be fruitful. We *will* give them every herb, etc." The sixth time ended with the Gods saying: "We *will do* everthing that we have said, and organize them; and behold, they *shall be* very obedient. And thus we *will finish* the heavens and the earth, and all the hosts of them."[62] Although the earth was made in six celestial days, it was not finished until it was filled with life in all of its varieties.[63] When the sixth day ended, Earth was a magnificent, but empty, house—without furnishings or occupants.

The second creation council concluded with the Gods reaffirming a decision they had made before beginning their labors: "On the *seventh* time we will *end* our work, which we have counseled; and we will *rest* on the seventh time from all our work which we have counseled."[64] The narrative resumes in Abraham 5:4: "And the Gods came down and

---

[61]After allowing for the different circumstances under which each was produced, their terminology, emphases, sequence of events, and overall composition prove strikingly similar.

[62]Abraham 4:31-5:1. Chapter divisions are quite arbitrary.

[63]Abraham 5:2. Verse 3 is not a restatement of verse 2. It is Abraham's parenthetical confirmation of the fact that the Gods did end their labors on the seventh time, just as they had originally planned.

[64]Orson Pratt stated: "On the seventh day the Bible says that God ended his work. He did not altogether end it on the sixth, but he ended it on the seventh." (JD, 15:243.)

formed these the generations of the heavens and of the earth, when they were formed in the day that the Gods formed the earth and the heavens."[65] Thus, the Gods came *down* to do that which they (at the close of the sixth time) had recommitted themselves to do: to organize—not the earth—but physical life in all of its varieties—"the *generations* of the heavens and of the earth."

That the final creation council took place after the physical planet was prepared and ready to receive the spirit "hosts" seems indisputable: "For the Gods had not caused it to rain upon the earth when they counseled to do them, and had not formed a man to till the ground." If the earth did not already exist, it would be ludicrous for Abraham to speak of rain failing to fall upon it! And that man—male and female—did not come to Earth until after the second council is shown by the fact that the formation of Adam's physical body from the dust of the ground *follows* the first mist-like rain. (See Abraham 5:7-9, 20; Moses 3:7-9, 19 and D&C 77:12.) Orson Pratt understood such to be the case:

> There was no flesh upon the earth until the morning of the seventh day. On that morning God made the first fleshly tabernacle and took man's spirit and put within it, and man became a living soul—the first flesh upon the earth—the first man also. Though it was the seventh day, no flesh but this one tabernacle was yet formed. No fish, fowl and beast was as yet permitted to have a body of flesh.[66]

A previously quoted revelation to the Prophet Joseph Smith affirms this fact in words that cannot be gainsayed: "God made the world in six

---

[65]Abraham 5:4 and Moses 3:4 employ the term "day" as a collective noun for the combined "days" or "times" of creation. These verses serve to explain that the life forms which were to be placed on earth were not created *after* the earth was formed but in conjunction with all that was done during the creative "day." The creative "day" thus included both the spiritual and the physical organization of the heavens and the earth and all the hosts thereof. Time and eternity were combined in one creative day. (See JD, 14:235.)

[66]JD, 21:200. See also JD, 15:243 and 16:317. Among others who have taught that man was placed on earth prior to any animals was John Taylor. (See JD, 18:327.)

days, and on the *seventh day* he *finished his work*, and sanctified it, and also *formed man* out of the dust of the earth."[67]

Abraham's account is far more than a plan of creation. True, he refers to two major councils held by the Gods—one, before their labors had begun, and another in connection with the sixth "time" of those labors-but this only expands our understanding of, and appreciation for, the total creative process as seen through the eyes of that ancient seer who beheld the work of those Gods from beginning to end. Those who regard Abraham's account as but the *design* (spiritual or otherwise) of creation tend to view Moses' narrative as the physical implementation of that design. Consequently, they argue that the earth was not only prepared for, but supplied with, biological life beginning with vegetation on the third day. This assumption is primarily based upon the use by Moses of the clauses "it was done as I spake" (2:5); "it was so, even as I spake" (2:6, 7, 11, 30); "it was done" (2:6); and "it was so" (2:9, 15, 24, 26). These expressions are thought to mean that a given act was carried out at the time it was willed. However, they can also be interpreted as meaning that all was done "in the manner God willed it to be done." Indeed, Abraham emphasizes this point: "It was so, even as they ordered" (4:7, 9, 11); "they were obeyed" (4:10, 12); they "watched those things which they had ordered until they obeyed" (4:18); "they would be obeyed" (4:21); "it was so, as they had said" (4:24); and "they would obey" (4:25). The unity of Abraham and Moses on this point is supported by the fact that both described the physical creation of man, vegetation, and animals in the context of all that transpired *after* the sixth day had ended and the seventh had begun.

In terms of the general tenor and sequence of creation, the inspired narratives of Abraham and Moses are altogether harmonious, being in almost perfect parallel. Each prophet-historian complements the other while at the same time describing Earth's beginnings from his own unique vantage point. Abraham, viewed creation from the standpoint of eternity. He looked *forward* in time to the yet-to-be-done work of the Gods. It is from his unique position that we are privileged to look, as it

---

[67]D&C 77:12. It is argued that the formation of man on the seventh day refers to his becoming mortal in consequence of the fall. But nowhere in scripture is man's fall spoken of as a formation. God *formed* Adam as an immortal being; Adam *became* mortal by his own act. Then too, Moses treats Adam's creation and subsequent fall in totally different portions of his record and in mutually exclusive contexts.

were, over the shoulders of the Gods as they both planned and executed the creative enterprises. Moses, on the other hand, viewed creation from the standpoint of this planet in its finished and fallen state. He figuratively looked *backward* in time as he was told of all that had happened to it from its inception to its fall. This explains why the Lord dictated the story of creation to him in the same sequence observed by Abraham, but without distinguishing between preparations for life and its placement on earth. As Moses could plainly see, all had been accomplished—"even as I spoke." Through the instrumentality of two of God's mightiest prophet-seers, we are privileged to learn of the creation from the perspective of God and man—of eternity and of time.

Summary of Creation

The creation involved two related, but distinct, regions in inner and outer space called heavens. The most proximate to the earth of these is the "firmament or expanse"—the realm of winged creatures and of that life-sustaining atmosphere which envelops the planet with diminishing density from the troposphere to the ionosphere.[68] Beyond this inner heaven lies the firmament of the heaven or the expanse of the heaven(s). It encompasses not only the sun and the moon, but the distant sidereal or starry heavens as well. (See Moses 2:14-17 and Abraham 4:14-17.)

As to the organization of the earth as such, all we are told is that it was formed in the beginning as an empty and desolate sphere whose lifeless, primordial sea stretched from horizon to horizon.[69] No winds blew across its darkened waters, no sound broke the awesome silence which enveloped it like a shroud and "darkness reigned upon the face of the deep, and the Spirit of the Gods was brooding upon the face of the

---

[68]See Moses 2:6-9, 20 and Abraham 4:6-9, 20. The word "firmament" (from the Latin *firmamentum*) is an unfortunate translation of the Hebrew *raqia* which suggests something extended or stretched out—an "expanse."

[69]Orson Pratt believed that the "submerged earth" may have existed "in the form of partial or imperfect organizations" for thousands or even millions of years before it emerged from the primordial sea on the third day of creation. (See JD, 18:316.)

waters."[70] Even as the unborn child is sustained by the oxygen and vital nutrients provided by its mother, so was the earth sustained by the Spirit of the Lord which brooded over it in the womb of creation.

Then, on the third day, the Gods spoke and the submerged land rose up out of the global sea.[71] The moment had come for the next phase of their labors to begin—the preparation of the heavens, the earth and the sea for life. Such life was possible because the darkness, which had initially enveloped the global sea, had vanished away on the very first

---

[70]Abraham 4:2, 6. The Hebrew term for "brood" does not mean to be despondent or anxious, but rather to overshadow or envelop. The Spirit of the Lord enveloped the earth so as to bring forth life much as a mother hen hatches her chicks with the warmth of her own body.

[71]Orson Pratt described the earth's natal day in more prosaic terms:

In the morning of our creation the gathering together of the particles was accomplished under such regular, harmonious and systematic laws, that there were no elevations of the land above the water. All the successive strata seemed to have arranged themselves *in a perfect spheroidal form*, conforming to the laws of gravity and rotation, as if they had been a fluid substance. So perfect was this arrangement, that *the land was completely enveloped in a flood of water*: no portion thereof was seen.

But soon the commandment came for the waters to be gathered together into one place, and for the dry or solid land to appear. This great event was unquestionably brought about under a system of fixed laws, no less definite than that of gravitation; but perhaps not so well comprehended by man. *The Spirit of God in association with the elements*, not only produces all the phenomena of gravitation, but also causes the elements to act upon each other, cohesively and chemically, when the particles are brought insensibly near to each other. (*The Seer*, p. 249. See also JD, 16:314.)

Sequence of Creation

Abraham	Moses (Genesis)	Time/Day	Creation Act
4:1, 2	2:1, 2	First	1. Heavens and earth organized . . . global "deep" covers earth
4:3-5	2:3-5	"	2. Light provided . . . Day and Night begin
4:6-8	2:6-8	Second	3. Atmospheric heavens formed between lower and upper "waters"
4:9, 10	2:9, 10	Third	4. Primal continent emerges from global sea
4:11-13	2:11-13	"	5. Land prepared for vegetation
4:14-19	2:14-29	Fourth	6. Sun, moon and stars organized to serve the earth
4:20-23	2:20-23	Fifth	7. Seas prepared for marine life and atmospheric heavens for fowl
4:24, 25	2:24, 25	Sixth	8. Earth prepared for land creatures
4:26-28	2:26-28	"	9. The Gods council to organize man, male and female
4:29, 30; 5:9	2:29, 30; 3:9	"	(All living things to be herbiverous)
5:6	3:6	Seventh	10. A mist waters the "dry land"
5:7, 8	3:7, 8	"	11. The first "flesh", man, is organized
5:6, 8-10	3:6, 8-14	"	12. Vegetation produced . . . a "garden" is planted
5:14-19*	3:18, 21-25*	"	13. First woman, Eve, is organized*
5:20, 21	3:19, 20	"	14. Animal kingdom organized in all its varieties

*As with man, woman's "organization" is symbolic. Whether woman was placed on earth before or after animal life is of little moment. However, both accounts are probably correct: woman was "formed" before the animals (as per Abraham), but not "brought" to man until after they had been named by Adam (as per Moses).

day of creation.[72] It had been replaced by spiritual light—the very glory of God.

Analysis of the foregoing chart indicates that the first three "times" were taken up with the formation of the planet with its global sea, the introduction of light (from a source other than the sun, moon, and stars), and the development of an atmosphere appropriate to the physical-spiritual character of the earth prior to its fall. Following this preliminary work, the Gods then *prepared* the risen earth (the dry land) and the waters for the various orders of life they were to subsequently sustain.[73]

The planet was probably devoid of even micro-organisms when first formed; it had to be prepared for planting, much as a farmer harrows

———————

[72]Moses 2:2 reads that God "caused" darkness to envelop the deep after the earth was formed. This led Orson Pratt to surmise that this was why earth's creation began in the *evening*. Perhaps the Lord produced the darkness by obscuring the light of the "self-luminous" matter composing the earth. Why God would choose to do such a thing is not explained. (See JD, 20:73, 74.) Beginning the day in the evening and ending it in the morning, or daylight hours, reflects the Hebraic background of the text. (The Jewish religious day is calculated from sundown to sundown.) Abraham and Moses consistently follow this formula. Then too, both Moses 2:3 and Abraham 4:3 simply refer to the presence of darkness at the time of earth's initial formation without suggesting any divine causation. On balance, it seems more likely that the earth was organized *in* darkness (a metaphor for chaos?) and thereafter brought into light, than that it was organized in light, hidden in darkness only to be restored to light again.

The lesser light of sun, moon, and stars is first mentioned on the fourth day of creation. The physical light of these bodies did not actually shine upon this earth until it had fallen. (See JD, 15:264; 16:314 and 18:316.) Brigham Young taught: "When the Lord said—'Let there be light,' there was light, for the earth was brought near the sun that it might reflect upon it so as to give us light by day, and the moon to give us light by night." (JD, 17:143.)

[73]It is interesting to note that the term "life" is first used by both Abraham and Moses in connection with marine life. This suggests that the higher definitions of life do not apply to vegetation. (See Abraham 4:20; Moses 2:20.)

and fertilizes his land before seeding or as an aquarium is readied for fish.[74] This preparatory work very likely included putting dormant seed of all kinds in the dry land which germinated on the seventh time when a mist rose up from the barren earth. (See Abraham 5:5-9; Moses 2:5-9.) Thus, they prepared the ground for vegetation, the waters for marine life, the heavens for fowl, and the earth for land creatures. In every instance, the Gods were either obeyed or saw that they *would be* obeyed.[75]

Having completed the physical organization and preparation of the earth the Lord explained to Moses: "I, the Lord God, had created all the children of men; and not yet a man to till the ground; for in heaven created I them." LDS doctrine affirms that the human race is comprised of the literal offspring of Deity, having been spiritually procreated by celestial parents. An official pronouncement to this effect was made by the First Presidency of the Church: "All men and women are in the similitude of the universal Father and Mother, and are literally the sons and daughters of Deity . . .Man as a spirit, was begotten and born of heavenly parents, and reared to maturity in the eternal mansions of the Father, prior to coming upon the earth in a temporal body to undergo an experience in mortality."[76]

The earth was made in six days; meaning that it was organized and prepared to receive physical life in all of its varieties within that time frame. All that remained to be done on that first sabbath morn was for the "generations of the heavens and of the earth"—the unembodied spirit hosts—to descend to the glorious planet and claim that life. And when there went up a "mist from the earth, and watered the whole face

---

[74]Brigham Young asked: "Shall I say that the seeds of vegetables were planted here by the Characters that framed and built this world—that the seeds of every plant composing the vegetable kingdom were brought from another world? This would be news to many of you." (JD, 7:285. See JD, 2:160 and 8:243.) Moses 3:8 may mean that the first seeds were planted on the seventh day.

[75]See Abraham 4:11, 12, 20-22, 24, 25 and Moses 2:11, 12, 20-22, 24, 25

[76]"The Origin of Man," First Presidency of the Church, (Joseph F. Smith, John R. Winder, Anthon H. Lund), *The Improvement Era*, 13 (November, 1909):78, 80.

of the ground," those dormant seeds which the Gods had long since placed in the dry land burst forth as grasses, plants, trees, and flowers to bless and sustain man and his animal dominions with "the good things which come of the earth." (Abraham 5:6 and Moses 3:6. See also D&C 59:17.)

Man becomes a living soul (an embodied spirit) at mortal birth. Animal kind, vegetation and the earth itself are similarly blessed. (See Moses 3:7, 9, 19; 7:48; D&C 29:30-32 and 88:15.) This planet became a living soul when the Gods, who had organized it first spiritually then physically brought its two "beings" together in their present temporary union.[77] At that moment the physical earth came uniquely alive.[78] For the spirit is the very breath of life. It sustains all mortal organisms and "giveth life." Death comes when that breath is permanently withdrawn. And as the body without the spirit is dead, so was this globe a dead planet (empty and desolate) in the absence of its spiritual counterpart.[79]

And so the earth came truly alive on the sabbath of the Gods. Michael, the archangel, having completed the initial phase of his foreordained assignment, condescended to become Adam—the "first flesh" and the "first man" to walk upon the new world.[80] While every

----

[77]Eventually the earth will die—"the end of the earth." Having passed away, it will then be prepared to come forth as an immortal world, a celestial kingdom.

[78]When created, the physical earth was *wholly* dependent upon the governing, sustaining power of the light of Christ—the Spirit of the Lord which "proceedeth forth from the presence of God to fill the immensity of space." (D&C 88:13. See also JD, 21:201.)

[79]In all likelihood, the earth is the only truly living planet in this solar system. The rest seem spiritless, devoid of even primitive organisms.

[80]The theory of organic evolution is virtually demolished by the revealed truth that man, not lesser species, was the first fleshy organism on the new-born earth. Theistic evolutionists to the contrary, at no point in either creation narrative is the word "flesh" equated with mortality. Moses is explicit: When the seventh day dawned, "there was not yet flesh upon the *earth*, neither in the *water*, neither in the *air*." Man was the first flesh upon the earth"—not *generic* man, but the man Adam, the first male who remained "alone" until the Gods provided him with a female helpmeet. It was this *immortal* woman, not his *immortal* animal companions, that the *immortal* Adam spoke of as "bone of my bones, and flesh of my flesh."

sabbath is made to bless man, the first was made to receive him! As Jesus, during his earthly ministery, made a suffering mortal "every whit whole" on the sabbath day, (John 7:23) so did the Creator, on an earlier sabbath, make man every whit *whole* when he breathed into him the breath of life and he became a living soul. And so through the veil of eternity came Adam, creation's lord, followed by his retinue of subjects—the generations of the heavens and the earth.[81]

When the Gods rested from all of their works, man partook of that rest as well.[82] His second estate began in an immortal garden, in paradise, in terrestrial glory—the glory which will envelop the earth when the Lord of the sabbath returns to sanctify it and to reendow it with the splendor it once knew.

---

[81]The various species were placed on the earth in a pre-ordained order even as each living soul will be resurrected in its appropriate order. (See D&C 77:3 and 1 Corinthians 15:22, 23.)

[82]It is intended that man should enter into the rest of God, even a fulness of God's glory, through the merits of Christ and obedience to his commandments. (See Jacob 1:7; D&C 19:9, 84:24 and 121:32.)

CHAPTER SIX

Fall of the Earth

In the beginning Earth was an immortal, physical sphere. Bathed in the light of celestial worlds, it partook of a paradisaical glory which it shared with man and all living things. How lovely was the new-born earth! There was nothing to hurt or to make afraid in all that holy mountain. (See Isaiah 11:9; 65:25.) Edenic conditions were world-wide. Life was the natural order; death was still a stranger. (See 2 Nephi 2:22; JD, 1:280-282 and 21:202, 323.)

> Every particle of air, of water, and of earth, was so organized as to be capable of diffusing life and immortality through all the varied species of animated existence—immortality reigned in every department of creation; hence it was pronounced very 'good.'[1]

All creation thrived under the benevolent reign of Adam, its God-anointed king. Like a father, he gave names to the denizens of the animal kingdom. And like faithful children, they accepted his kindly rule over them.[2] Neither was a threat to the other: earth was a garden, not a jungle. Life, not survival, was the issue, and it was free for all and secure for all.

---

[1]Orson Pratt, JD, 1:281. Elder Pratt explained the term "very good" in the context of those beings who were to inhabit the earth. (See *ibid.*, 328.)

[2]See Turner, *Woman and the Priesthood*, Chapter III.

Parley P. Pratt described that primeval paradise as a world where "everything that grew was just calculated for the food of man, beast, fowl, and creeping thing: and their food was all vegetable. Flesh and blood were never sacrificed, to glut their souls or gratify their appetites; the beasts of the earth were all in perfect harmony with each other; the lion ate straw like the ox, the wolf dwelt with the lamb . . .all was peace and harmony, and nothing to hurt nor disturb in all the holy mountains."[3]

The harmony between man and creature was paralled by the harmony between the earth and its vegetation. It was a weedless world. The many troublesome and harmful plants so common today—plants reflective of a fallen, telestial sphere—did not mar the land. Producing in her strength, earth affirmed the goodness of God and his pleasure in those things which strengthen the body, enliven the soul, please the eye, and gladden the heart.[4]

Nor was the immortal planet subject to the extreme climatic variations which characteize its present age. Instead of zones of frigid cold and torrid heat, a temperate to semi-tropical climate extended from pole to pole. Luxuriant forests, rich with all varieties of plants and animals, covered the land. Earth was at peace.

And so were the heavens. The mild, unified climate precluded any violent meterological activity such as hurricanes, tornadoes or severe electrical storms. There were only infant winds—light breezes.[5] It was a divine age; tranquility was the hallmark of every dimension of creation. Only with the passage of time did that splendid epoch give way to savage conditions. Our present harsh world is a product of devolution over a period of many centuries, a devolution marked by increasing violence and castrastophe as Eden faded from view.

The earth—like the sabbath—was made for man, not man for the earth. It exists because man exists. It is subject to a higher authority than impersonal natural law. Earth is the obedient servant of the Priesthood.

Adam was appointed God's surrogate. He received the keys of the Holy Priesthood—including "the keys of the universe"—before the earth

---

[3]Pratt, *A Voice of Warning*, p. 86.

[4]See D&C 59:18, 19; Pratt, *A Voice of Warning*, p. 86.

[5]The first reference to wind in the Bible is made in connection with the flood. (See Genesis 8:1.)

was organized.[6] As lord of creation Adam exercised universal dominion and stewardship. The destiny of the earth and every living thing upon it was bound up in him: Adam's fate would be the fate of all.

Fall of Man

According to both Abraham and Moses, Adam was alone in the Garden of Eden when the first commandment to man on this earth was given:

Of every tree of the garden thou mayest freely eat,
But of the tree of the knowledge of good and evil, thou shalt not eat of it, nevertheless, thou mayest choose for thyself, for it is given unto thee; but, remember that I forbid it, for in the day thou eatest thereof thou shalt surely die.[7]

In time, and according to the foreordained plan of salvation, earth's first and only immortal couple transgressed the commandment, thereby bringing upon themselves and their posterity the judgment of God—the natural consequences of violated law.[8]

The substance of their immortality was purged from their systems when they partook of the incompatible, blood-producing fruit.[9] Over a

---

[6]See Abraham 4:26-28; Moses 2:26-28. Joseph Smith said: "The Priesthood was first given to Adam; he obtained the First Presidency, and held the keys of it from generation to generation. He obtained it in the Creation, before the world was formed, as in Genesis 1:26, 27, 28. He had dominion given him over every living creature. He is Michael the Archangel, spoken of in the Scriptures." (HC, 3:385, 386.)

[7]Moses 3:16, 17. See also Abraham 5:13. Both accounts are silent as to when Eve learned of this commandment. She may have been taught it by her husband.

[8]Known as the "first judgment." (See 2 Nephi 9:6, 7 and Turner, *Woman and the Priesthood*, pp. 42, 43.)

[9]Joseph Fielding Smith declared: "Now when Adam was in the Garden of Eden, he was not subject to death. There was no blood in his body and he could have remained there forever. *This is true of all the other creations.*" (*Doctrines of Salvation*, 1:77, (italics in original.) See also Joseph Fielding Smith, *Man: His Origin and Destiny*, pp. 362-364.)

period of time their body chemistries were altered; they literally ate themselves into mortality.[10] A natural law had been broken; a natural consequence ensued.[11] However, the transgression of natural law does not, of itself, produce spiritual death;[12] only disobedience to the commandments of God can do that. Consequently, the Lord not only warned Adam against the lethal effects of the toxic fruit but also made it a point to forbid its use thereby making it a matter of moral law as well.[13] Had the Lord not made his counsel a matter of obedience, Adam would have become mortal and remained spiritually alive. The wages of his act were both natural and spiritual death because both natural and spiritual law had been transgressed.

The Garden of Eden

While the pre-fall earth was charged with glory far beyond that which it now enjoys, the Garden of Eden was especially blessed by the presence of the Father when he communed with Adam and Eve.[14] The Garden, therefore, symbolized the relationship all mankind once enjoyed with God and which will be had again by as many as qualify for it through the merits of the Savior. Its beauty and perfection also reflected the spiritual natures of its two human inhabitants. Virtue garnished their thought's unceasingly; heart and mind were innocent and uncorrupted:

---

[10]"When Adam and Eve had eaten of the forbidden fruit, their bodies became mortal from *its effects*, and therefore their offspring were mortal."—(Brigham Young, JD, 1:50, italics in original. See also JD, 1:282; 10:235; 16:388.)

[11]The fact that Adam could have purged mortality from his system and regained his lost immortality by partaking of the fruit of the tree of life indicates that natural law was involved in his fall. (See Alma 12:26; 42:3-5.)

[12]Spiritual death is alienation from God. It ranges from banishment from his literal presence to the total loss of the influence of his Spirit. Adam suffered the former; Satan will suffer the latter. (See Alma 42:7-9; D&C 29:36-42; 76:36, 37 and Revelation 20:9, 10.)

[13]Orson Pratt spoke to this point. See JD, 1:282.

[14]By the same token, the grove where Joseph Smith beheld the Father and the Son was rendered sacred and more glorious by their presence.

So near allied to beings o'er the sky,
Their minds were holy—every thought was high:
The stream of knowledge then was pure and broad,
For man held converse with th' Eternal God.[15]

Man's departure from the literal presence of the Lord is symbolized by Adam's expulsion from the Garden. He was removed from the Garden and, in time, the Garden was removed from the earth.[16] Its site now lies buried beneath the asphalt and concrete of a suburb of Kansas City where it is trodden by the feet of men and desecrated by the banal sprawl of shopping centers, service stations, theaters and all of the other refinements of twentieth-century civilization.[17]

The Garden of Eden was located in what is now Independence, Jackson County, Missouri—making America the oldest inhabited land on earth. This fact was revealed through Joseph Smith in connection with the designation of Independence as the site of the future city of Zion, the New Jerusalem. (See D&C 57:1-3.) Brigham Young remarked:

Now it is a pleasant thing to think of and to know where the Garden of Eden was. Did you ever think of it? I do not think many do, for in Jackson County was the Garden of Eden. Joseph has declared this, and I am as much bound to believe that as to believe that Joseph Smith was a prophet of God.[18]

---

[15]Eliza R. Snow, "Eden," *Poems, Regligious, Historical, and Political* (Liverpool: Printed by R. James, 1856.), p. 153.

[16]According to Brigham Young, it still exists in its spiritual state. See JD 14:231.

[17]Fortunately, the general area designated for the temple is used for religious purposes, being under the control of the Reorganized Church of Jesus Christ of Latter-day Saints, the Hedrikites and the LDS Church.

[18]*Journal History*, March 15, 1857, as quoted in John A. Widstoe, *Gospel Interpretations*, p. 254. See also JD, 8:67, 195, 211; *The Contributor*, 14:7-9. Heber C. Kimball taught the same: "and I will say more, the spot chosen for the garden of Eden was Jackson County, in the state of Missouri, where Independence now stands." (JD, 10:235, See ibid., 8:195.)

America is the choicest of all the lands of promise because it *is* the site of the Garden of Eden—the holiest spot on earth.[19] For this reason Zion, the New Jerusalem, cannot be built anywhere else—it must and will be located in Independence, Missouri, prior to the second coming of the Savior. (See D&C 97:19; 101:17-21. See also HC, 2:261, 262.) In the beginning, God walked and talked with his children in the Garden; he will do so again as part of the restitution of all things. After being driven from the Garden, the exiled pair settled some seventy miles north of Independence in what is now Daviess County, Missouri. In man's pristine language their new home was called Adam-ondi-Ahman—the land where Adam, the son of God, dwelt.[20]

Multiple Effects of the Fall

Although faithless men will not accept the revelations of God as a source of reliable information to understand the beginnings of this planet and its inhabitants, the fact remains that both Earth and man are far different from what they were when first organized. Earth is a fallen planet, man is a fallen race.

This truism is a key that would unlock the outer portals of much correct geologic and anthropologic knowledge if only men would use it.

----

[19]The Garden of Eden is the true and original hierocentric point—a holy center—where all things began. Certain world religions have borrowed the concept and designated such cities as Rome, Jerusalem, and Mecca as their most holy places.

[20]See D&C 116 and 78:15, 16, 20. John Taylor heard Joseph Smith identify Adam with the Daviess County site: "Indeed, it was stated by the Prophet Joseph Smith, in our hearing, while standing on an elevated piece of ground or plateau near Adam-ondi-Ahman (Daviess County, Missouri), where there were a number of rocks piled together, that the valley before us was the valley of Adam-ondi-Ahman; or in other words, the valley where God talked with Adam, and where he gathered his righteous posterity, as recorded in the above revelation [D&C 107:53-57], and that this pile of stones was an altar built by him when he offered up sacrifices, as we understand, on that occasion." (*The Gospel Kingdom,* p. 102.) A gathering of an even more momentous nature will take place in fulfillment of Daniel's prophecy (Daniel 7:9, 10) in connection with the preparations for the world coming of Christ. (See D&C 116; *Doctrines of Salvation,* 3:13, 14.)

But most will not. Uniformitarianism has become their ruling gospel: "All things continue as they were from the beginning of the creation." Thus they would limit the Almighty to one method of creation and one system of law. In doing so—to paraphrase Paul—they are ever learning about a fallen creation but never able to come to a knowledge of the truth of its primeval glory.

Similarities between Earth as it *is* and Earth as it *was* in the beginning are analogous to the similarities between the law of Moses and the law of Christ. (See D&C 88:21.) While they share some elements in common, they are so different in nature as to make any attempt at equating the one with the other an exercise in futility. They are related but different laws; they are related but different worlds.

For just as the carnal law of Moses supplanted the spiritual law of Christ (see D&C 84:18-27; JST Exodus 32:15-19; 34:12) so did telestial, physical law supplant the terrestrial physical law which governed the primal earth. And just as the carnal law of Moses cannot be superimposed on the spiritual law of Christ, neither can the telestial, physical laws—now observed on this planet—be validly superimosed, via a doctrine of un-iformitarianism, on the earth as it was in the beginning.

Fall From Primeval Time

No longer would earth's reckoning of time be like unto that of exalted worlds. The speed at which it rotated on its axis was apparently increased by a factor of 365,000! Its thousand year days were over, being foreshor-tened to a mere twenty-four hours. This acceleration of time, this speed-ing up of earth's heartbeat, was significant; it was a sign of its fall from immortality, it meant that its lifespan had become finite; its days were literally numbered.[21] Instead of living forever, its longevity was temporar-ily reduced to seven thousand years. (See D&C 77:6.) Thus, the earth fell from the time measurement of the highest to that of the lowest order of worlds. Indeed, even the moon is superior to it in this respect. (See Abraham 3:5.)

Fall From Primeval Light

No longer would Earth bask in the glorious spiritual light of Kolob. In being cast out of the presence of the Father, it, like man, became subject to

---

[21] It is intersting to note that, in general, the faster the heartbeat, the shorter the lifespan. For example, the heartbeat of some insects is so rapid that their lifespan is but a matter of hours.

and dependent upon the gross diminished light of the sun, moon, and stars.[22] Brigham Young stated: "When the Lord said—'Let there be light,' there was light, for the earth was brought near the sun that it might reflect upon it so as to give us light by day, and the moon to give us light by night."[23]

Fall From Primeval Place

> Thou, Earth wast once a glorious sphere
>   Of noble magnitude,
> And didst with majesty appear
>   Among the worlds of God.[24]

---

[22]The diminished glory of the earth stems in part from the fact that the sun itself is obliged to "borrow its light from Kolob through the medium" of still another "governing power."—(See the explanation of figure 5, Facsimilie 2, in the *Book of Abraham*.

[23]JD, 17:143. See also note 25. The sun and moon are mentioned in conection with the fourth creative day. These two bodies and possibly some stars, may have been formed at that time—making them younger than the earth. While some have thought our sun to be a celestial world (see *Doctrines of Salvation*, 1:88, 89), Orson Pratt believed otherwise. Describing the splendor of the future earth he added: "I will not say as the splendor of our sun, for it is not a celestial body. Although the light of the sun is very glorious, it will not begin to compare with that of this earth, when it becomes celestial and eternal and is lightened by the presence of God the Father. It is doubtful whether the children of mortality on other worlds, will ever behold the light of this earth, after it is made eternal, unless they happen to catch a glimpse of it by vision. God dwells in a world of light too glorious for mortal eyes to behold, unless aided by the Spirit of the living God." (JD, 19:290, 291. See also *ibid.*, 14:236, 237.)

[24]Eliza R. Snow, "Address To Earth." This poem was published in England in the *Millennial Star* 13 (Sept. 1, 1851): 272. The doctrinal acceptability of its contents was apparently recognized since it appeared in numerous editions of the LDS Hymnal between, at least 1856 and 1905. Eliza R. Snow was the sister of Lorenzo Snow, the fourth president of the LDS Church, the plural wife of Joseph Smith and, subsequently, of Brigham Young.

Brigham Young agreed with the foregoing sentiments: "When the earth was framed and brought into existence and man was placed upon it, it was near the throne of our Father in heaven . . .But when man fell, the earth fell into space, and took up its abode in this planetary system, and the sun became our light."[25]

Man is the key to the universe; his destiny dictates the destiny of all things. Therefore Adam's spiritual and temporal fall imposed a similar fate upon the heavens, the earth and all of their hosts. As he was driven from the Garden of Eden, from the presence of the Lord, so was the earth driven from God's presence and cast down to the outskirts of this galaxy.[26]

And when the earth fell, so did its heaven. Since the original firmament or atmosphere enveloping the planet was compatible with the bloodless, immortal natures of man and beast, it is likely that the "air" they breathed was more pure than the blood-transmitted oxygen which is the basis of mortal life. It may have been a life-sustaining element akin to, if not identical with, the Spirit of the Lord.[27] The placing of the earth in this solar system led to the necessary modification of its atmosphere so as to make it compatible with the oxygen-breathing requirements of the earth's

---

[25]JD, 17:143. Charles L. Walker recorded hearing Brigham Young state that "when this world was first made it was in a close proximity to God. When man sinned it was hurled millions of miles away from its first position and that was why it was called the Fall." (Charles Walker Journal, 13 July 1862, pp. 233, 234.) John Taylor also maintained that the earth "Had fled and fallen from where it was organized near the planet Kolob." (*The Mormon*, August 29, 1857.)

[26]President Young "gave it as his opinion that the Earth did not dwell in the sphere in which it did when it was created, but that it was banished from its more glorious state or orbit or revolution for man's sake." (Record of Acts of the Quorum of the Twelve Apostles," 1849 Record Book, p. 41, Church Archives.) (As quoted in Ehat and Cook, *The Words of Joseph Smith*, p. 84.) (See also p. 60, n. 12.)

[27]President Lorenzo Snow told the saints in St. George, Utah: "The whole earth is the Lord's. The time will come when it will be translated and be filled with the spirit and power of God. The atmosphere around it will be the spirit of the Almighty. We will breathe that Spirit instead of the atmosphere we now breathe." (*Millenial Star*, [August 24, 1899]: 546.)

then-mortal denizens.[28] In any event, both earth and man are cut off from the presence of the Lord by a very real veil of element. (Pratt, *A Voice of Warning*, p. 87.) The Savior's return will be attended by an unveiling of those glories which now lie hidden behind a curtain of gross materiality.

Fall From Immortality

The existence of plant and animal fossils which are thought to have originated in the so-called paleozoic era of geologic time[29] would appear to contradict the scriptural declaration that death was unknown on this earth until after the fall. (See Genesis 2:17; Moses 3:17; 6:48, 59; 2 Nephi 2:22 and JD, 16:358.) In an effort to reconcile scripture and paleontology, it has been suggested that plant and animal life antedated the coming of Adam by hundreds of millions of years in which the natural processes of birth and death (so vital to the theory of evolution) were taking place on the primitive earth. Then, as scripture affirms, God placed man in a special sector of the earth—the Garden of Eden—where the natural order of things was suspended during the pre-fall period. In other words, God created an oasis of immortal life in a global desert of death.

Such an Hegelian-like synthesis is appealing because it allows the scientific thesis of a mortal world to be joined to a scriptural anti-thesis of universal immortality. Unfortunately, the synthesis—as is usually the case where revelation and reason clash—is achieved at the expense of divine truth.[30]

The earth was organized in a totally different sphere than that in which it now finds itself. It was a physical and *spiritual* body—a soul. Having been created by God, it partook of his own excellence: "And I, God, saw *everything* that I had made, and behold, *all things* which I had made were *very good*"—meaning God-like: perfect and immortal.

----

[28]The indivisible character of the earth and its heaven is affirmed by the fact that "heaven *and* earth shall pass away," only to be followed by "new heavens *and* a new earth." See Matthew 24:35; D&C 29:23, 24; Ether 13:9.

[29]The paleozoic era extends from approximately 600 to 225 million years ago.

[30]The attempt to localize the scriptural activities of God so as to uphold the prevailing opinions of the sciences is also the technique employed in dealing with the universal flood and other problem areas. Convinced that science is correct, but not wanting to be labeled disbelievers, such apologists grant scripture a tithe of their faith.

One might as well argue that a mortal body possesses an immortal heart as to suggest that death reigned planet-wide except in a tiny paradise eastward in Eden. Joseph Smith explained that the book seen by John (Revelation 5:1) symbolized the things of God "concerning this earth during the seven thousand years of its continuance, or its *temporal existence*.'" (D&C 77:6.) This unqualified scripture admits of no other interpretation that that the *entire planet*, not the Garden alone fell into a temporal or mortal state less than seven thousand years ago.[31] Then too, the whole tenor of the creation accounts in scripture is to the effect that the Gods were dealing with the earth as an entity. Their labors pertained to all life, to "the generations of the heaven and the earth" as such, and not simply to a select group of immortals.

Adam's dominion was not limited to his stewardship over the animals found in the Garden, it was "over the fishes of the sea, and over the fowl of the air, and over the cattle, and over *all* the earth." (Moses 2:26. See also Abraham 4:26.) There could have been no universal fall if Adam had lacked universal dominion or if the major portion of the earth and its creatures were in a mortal condition long before Adam himself fell to that state.[32] On the issue of death, no honest synthesis of current scientific thought with the clear declarations of scripture is possible at this time. A choice must be made.

Fall Of Earth's Nature

The fall robbed the earth of its spiritual nature—the nature that rendered it immortal—so that, like Adam, it became spiritually diminished. It was no longer sustained by the enlivening power of the Spirit of God to the same high degree it had formerly enjoyed. It became a mortal world, a fallen, telestial kingdom ruled by a set of laws appropriate to its new condition. (See D&C 88:26-39.) As such, it was diminished in its life-sustaining powers. Spontaneity shifted from the production of fruits,

---

[31]In fact, there is no information on the fate of the Garden as such. It well may have been removed from the earth sometime after Adam's expulsion from it. (See Moses 5:2.)

[32]The fall of Adam was as universal as was the atonement of Christ; they were infinite acts of two immortal beings. (See 1 Corinthians 15:22.) Then too, if the earth did not undergo a universal fall, there would have been no need for a universal flood nor a universal baptism of fire and the Holy Ghost at the Lord's coming. The atonement and these three universal events are inextricably bound together.

flowers, and desirable vegetation to the growth of troublesome weeds and poisonous plants.[33]

In the beginning, earth's vegetation was wholly for nourishment and beauty: "Out of the ground made the Gods to grow every tree that is pleasant to the sight and good for food." (Abraham 5:9 and Moses 3:9.) Only one life-threatening thing—the tree of knowledge—was to be found anywhere. This paradisaical vegetation was modified and corrupted by the introduction of plant forms characteristic of the earth's present condition: "Thorns also, and thistles shall it bring forth to thee, and thou shalt eat the herb of the field."[34]

The introduction of alien telestial vegetation suggest another possibility: the introduction of alien animal life as well. While it is assumed that all creatures are descendents from pre-fall species, such may not be the case. Certain animals may have been as out of place on a paradisean earth as the thorns and thistles. For example, the dinosaur could well be a late-comer to this planet, arriving after the fall only to be destroyed in the flood. There are degrees of glory among animals as well as men. Since the different species are assigned to appropriate kingdoms after the resurrection, why not before as well?[35] In any event there has been a profound descending for the many "kindgoms" on this planet. Like Adam, they possess life, yet they experience death. Earth has become a heterogeneous realm of oppositions, variations, and contradictions.

The substitution of blood for spirit profoundly affected the dispositions of living things. As time passed, the trusting, harmless companions of man became fearful or threatening strangers. Creatures that had once lived side by side with their human keepers in mutual security and affection either fled at the sound of their approaching step or poised them-

---

[33] See Moses 4:24. Brigham Young taught: "The thistle, the thorn, the briar, and the obnoxious weed did *not* appear until after the earth was cursed." (JD, 1:50. Italic in original. See also Pratt, *A Voice of Warning*, p. 87.)

[34] Moses 4:24. The fruits of the Garden which had formerly sustained the immortal couple were no longer available to them. The tree of life had now become the "forbidden fruit."

[35] The "four beasts" of John's vision (Rev. 4:6-9) "represent the glory of the classes of beings in their destined order or sphere of creation, in the enjoyment of their eternal felicity." (D&C 77:3. See also HC, 5:343, 344.)

selves for attack. The lower order of vegetation, the "green herb," had been organized to sustain the higher kingdoms of man and animals:

> And to every beast of the earth, and to every fowl of the air, and to every thing that creepeth upon the earth, wherein there is life, I have given every green herb for meat: and it was so. (Genesis 1:30. See also JD, 16:358.)

Thus, like man, the entire animal kingdom had been herbiverous in the beginning. Neither purchased life at the price of another's death. The fall compromised this harmonious arrangement. The wily serpent which had willingly served as the instrument of Satan's attack on mankind, had, in doing so, become the "Judas goat" of all animal creation as well— peaceful munching and chewing gave way to clawing, ripping, and tearing. The bounds of the several kingdoms were breached; the divinely established order was disrupted. (See D&C 88:36-39.) Kingdom rose up against kingdom, species against species. The spoilers had arrived; man invaded and was invaded in turn. The Spirit of the Lord—of peace—no longer prevailed. World war had begun. (See Genesis 9:2-5.)

Subsequent Curses and Falls

Violation of the laws of God produces consequences which almost always affect the innocent as well as the guilty—the sins of the fathers are visited upon the children even as the sins of the children are often visited upon their fathers. (See Exodus 10:5; 34:7; Numbers 14:18 and Deuteronomy 5:9.) While a sin may be isolated, its bitter fruits seldom are; sooner or later, one way or another, others are obliged to partake of them. Earth was no exception. Mother Earth and her Redeemer are alike in that, while both were innocent, both were willing to be cursed for the sake of others. The curse of the fall was visited upon the earth because of Adam's transgression, even as the curse of the atonement was visited upon the Redeemer because of the sins of all mankind.[36]

But whereas the Redeemer descended below all things in one final, climactic sacrifice, the earth has been subjected to additional curses

---

[36]"Christ hath redeemed us from the curse of the law, being made a curse for us; for it is written: Cursed is everyone that hangeth on a tree." (Galatians 3:13. See Isaiah 53; Luke 22:42-44; Revelation 19:15; D&C 19:15-19; 133:50, 51.)

following her expulsion from the presence of God. Man's disobedience has swept him over one moral and spritual cataract after another. The fall of man has been followed by the falls of men. The earth has been cursed over and over again because of them. Parley P. Pratt wrote: "The great curses which have fallen upon the different portions, because of the wickedness of men, will account for the stagnant swamps, the sunken lakes, the dead seas, and great deserts." (Pratt, *A Voice of Warning*, p. 87.)

Cain

Earth was first defiled by Cain's murder of his brother, Abel. So heinous a crime had never before been committed among the children of Adam.[37] Murder! The blood of innocence had been wantonly shed in what is probably the most outrageous act of rebellion against God in human history.[38]

Mother Earth, the ultimate source of the physical body of him whose blood now seeped into her flesh, turned against Cain the husbandman whose livelihood she had made possible.

> And the Lord said: What hast thou done? The voice of thy brother's blood cries unto me from the ground.[39] And now thou shalt be cursed from the earth which hath opened her mouth to receive thy brother's blood from thy hand. When thou tillest the ground it shall not henceforth yield unto thee her strength. A fugitive and a vagabond shalt thou be in the earth. (Moses 5:35-37.)

---

[37]Satan, not Cain, authored the idea. (See Moses 5:29-31.)

[38]While the crucifixion of Jesus is the supreme example of the shedding of innocent blood, its perpertrators lacked Cain's knowledge of God. For this reason, Cain is Perdition while those who crucified Jesus are the subjects of salvation. (See Moses 5:18-25 and Acts 3:13-19.)

[39]The earth is defiled and justice is outraged when innocent blood is shed. That blood cries out for justice and if those who are responsible for administering justice ignore that voice, they become accessories to the crime. Although men betray justice, God does not: murdered innocence, and the earth that receives its blood, will be avenged. (See HC, 6:555; Alma 1:13; 2 Nephi 26:3; 3 Nephi 9:5-11 and Revelation 6:9-11.)

Cain was forced to wander the alienated earth that would no longer respond to his labors. He fled the land God had cursed against him and built a city named for his son, Enoch—the first city known to man.[40]

The Lord's judgment was altogether just. Cain, like his mentor, Satan, was a liar and a murderer from the beginning. (See John 8:44; D&C 93:25.) He was the original "Gadianton," being the founder of the organized kingdom of the devil among men. (See Moses 5:29-31, 43-55; Helaman 6:21-30 and Ether 8:14-26.) The murder of Abel unleashed a flood of conspiratorial evil upon the human family that has brought misery and death to millions of innocent souls caught in its wake. And the family of Cain provided the nucleus around which Satan marshalled his offensive against the kingdom of God. It is a tale of blood and horror. Cain's grandson, Irad, was murdered by his great grandson, Lamech, for violating his oath of secrecy as a member of Cain's society. (See Moses 5:49, 50.) Betrayed by his own wives, Lamech, like Cain, became an outcast. Still the forces of evil prospered; the kingdom of the devil spread its contagion throughout the earth:

> And thus the works of darkness began to prevail among all the sons of men. And *God cursed the earth with a sore curse*, and was angry with the wicked, with all the sons of men whom he had made; For they would not hearken unto his voice, nor believe on his Only Begotten Son, even him whom he declared should come in the meridian of time, who was prepared from before the foundation of the world. (Moses 5:55-57.)

The People of Canaan

The "sore curse" God imposed on the earth in Lamech's generation (probably in the third century after the fall) was followed by other instances of divine judgment. Enoch prophesied that the "people of Canaan" would launch a war of aggression against the weaker "people of Shum" and utterly destroy them. However, the Lord would turn the wine of victory to gall by cursing the conquered and occupied land:

---

[40]See Genesis 4:16, 17. This city is not to be confused with the City of Holiness founded by the patriarch Enoch some five centuries later. (See Moses 7:19.)

The land shall be barren and unfruitful, and none other people shall dwell there but the people of Canaan; for behold, the Lord shall *curse the land with much heat*, and the barrenness thereof shall go forth forever; and there was a blackness came upon all the children of Canaan, that they were despised among all people. (Moses 7:7, 8.)

Enoch

Enoch was instructed to carry the message of salvation to many lands with the Lord's warning: "Repent, lest I come out and smite them with a curse and they die." (Moses 7:10.) The faith of Enoch was such that the earth was responsive to his every command. With the spoken word alone he caused the earth to tremble, the mountains to flee, and the rivers to alter their courses. "All nations feared greatly, so powerful was the word of Enoch, and so great was the power of the language which God had given him." (Moses 7:13. See 6:31-34; JST Genesis 14:30-32 and Ether 12:24.)

This mighty patriarch, like many prophets who came after him, was also a military leader who led the people of God against their enemies, "and there went forth a curse upon all people that fought against God." (Moses 7:15.) And so judgment followed judgment in a mounting crescendo generation after generation.

Methuselah

Another "sore curse" was visited upon the earth in the days of Methuselah.[41] "And there came forth a great famine into the land, and the Lord cursed the earth with a sore curse, and many of the inhabitants thereof died." (Moses 8:4.) Whether this particular judgment triggered a general decline in the earth's fertility is unclear. However, such a decline did occur. In blessing his son, Noah, Lamech prophesied: "This son shall comfort us concerning our work and toil of our hands, because of the ground which the Lord hath cursed."[42] Saint as well as sinner eventually

----

[41]Methuselah remained behind when his father's City of Holiness was translated from the earth. (See Moses 7:68-8:2.) This curse came in the eighth century after the fall.

[42]Moses 8:9. This prophecy was made some 369 years after the birth of Methuselah in whose days the aforementioned famine occured.

suffered under the Lord's judgments, so that the earth, which was initially cursed against one man was finally cursed against them all.

Sodom

We would not know that a series of curses or judgments were visited upon the earth prior to the flood were it not for the revelations given to the Prophet Joseph Smith in the Book of Moses. Genesis mentions only the incident of Cain. However, Genesis does record the occasion after the flood when God cursed the notorious cities of Sodom and Gomorrah for their homosexual abominations. Abraham pled in vain for the preservation of Sodom when not even ten righteous persons could be found in the entire city. (See Genesis 18:20-33.) The degeneracy of the men of Sodom was such that they attempted to assault the two angels sent to save Lot and his family. (See Genesis 19:1-11.) When the sun arose the next morning, Lot and his two daughters (Lot's wife and sons-in-law had perished) were entering the village of Zoar.

> Then the Lord rained upon Sodom and upon Gomorrah brimstone and fire from the Lord out of heaven; And he overthrew those cities, and all the plain, and all the inhabitants of the cities, and that which grew upon the ground . . .And Abraham got up early in the morning to the place where he stood before the Lord: And he looked toward Sodom and Gomorrah, and toward all the land of the plain, and beheld, and, lo, the smoke of the country went up as the smoke of a furnace. (Genesis 19:24-28.)

Today, the fertile valley of Siddim, where once stood Sodom and Gomorrah, lies buried beneath the acrid waters of the Dead Sea. All around is barren desert, rocky desolation, and the silence of an empty land—mute, but profound testimony to the fact that the wages of sin is death.

Famine

The foregoing incidents combine to show one thing: nature turns against men when men turn against nature's God. The "natural" man, who is an enemy to God, is eventually cursed pertaining to the good things of the earth upon which he places so much stress and for which he commits so many crimes. Note that God's "curses" do not take the form of the exotic spells or the mysterious happenings found in fairy tales. Rather, they strike at man's physical life and his ability to sustain it. This is why God's curses usually involve natural calamities.

Famine-inducing drought is the natural disaster most frequently mentioned in scripture.[43] Indeed, the Lord has employed it to bring about the desired migration of men and nations. A prophesied famine befell the Chaldeans in the days of Abraham prompting his family's move to Haran in Mesopotamia. (See Abraham 1:29-2:1.) It was still raging when Abraham left Haran and journeyed to Canaan where it was also felt: "And there was a continuation of a famine in the land; and I, Abraham concluded to go down into Egypt, to sojourn there, for the famine became very grieveous." (Abraham 2:21.) A famine in the days of Isaac led him to consider migrating to Egypt until the Lord instructed him to remain in Canaan with the assurance that if he did so, the blessings of Abraham would become his blessings as well. (See Genesis 26:1-5.)

Had Isaac disobeyed the Lord, the story of Israel would most likely have been quite different; Israel might have been founded in Egypt rather than in the land of promise. This, the Lord did not intend and Israel was to be established in accordance with the covenants God had made with Abraham. So, at the right time, famine brought Jacob to Egypt as it had his grandfather, Abraham, more than a century earlier. The house of Israel followed Joseph into a strange land in search of survival—not merely, as they supposed, the survival of their lives, but more importantly their survival as an integral unit. For had Israel remained in Canaan, evidence suggests that they would have been either destroyed by their enemies or absorbed into the all-too-enticing culture surrounding them.[44] But as sojourners in Egypt, they were safe from the Canaanites and were permitted to live apart from the general society, thereby giving them time to gain strength and to establish their identity as a unique nation. The famine that made Joseph governor of Egypt and his family subject to his righteous stewardship was a blessing in disguise.

----

[43] Disease and pestilence are natural concomitants of famine and are, therefore, implied in this discussion.

[44] The killing of the Hivites by Levi and Simeon (Genesis 34) caused Jacob to fear: "I being few in number, they shall gather themselves together against me, and slay me; and I shall be destroyed, I and my house." (Genesis 34:30.) The danger of amalgamation is seen in Jacob's seeming acquiescence to the marriage of his daughter, Dinah, to Shechem and Judah's marriage to a Canaanite woman. (See Genesis 34:1-19; 38:1-3.)

Famine is a frequent motif in the story of ancient Israel. It accounts for Ruth (a Midianite) marrying an Israelite. (See Ruth 1:1-5.) It was inflicted on Israel for Saul's slaughter of the Gibeonites. (See 2 Samuel 21.) Elijah caused a famine when he sealed the heavens so that there was no rain for three and one half years. (See 1 Kings 17, 18 and Helaman 10:6.) Other references make it clear that God has cursed the earth with famine in the past and will do so in the future.[45]

A Testimony to Sin

It is apparent that at least some of the earth's bleak, inhospitable regions were once the dwelling places of very sinful men and women. Their defilement of themselves brought defilment to the lands they occupied. And as they moved from place to place, seizing the most desirable areas for themselves, they spread their moral contagion. This caused the curses of God to follow them, thereby intensifying the fall of the earth from her primeval glory.

Having brought desolation to their own habitations, the wicked abandoned them to the poor and the downtrodden. And it is the poor and the downtrodden we find ekeing out a bare existence today on cruel wastelands all over the earth. As has ever been the case, the wealthy and the powerful continue to appropriate the most productive, the most scenic, and the most valuable areas of city and country for themselves. The weak and the ignorant are allowed to remain on impoverished land only so long as the strong permit them to do so.[46]

Man's offenses against God compounded man's offenses against himself. For as more and more of the earth became less productive due to divine judgments, man turned with increasing fury and frequency against his fellow man in competition for earth's diminishing spoils.

It is noteworthy that history's first wars began immediately after the initial cursing of the earth in the days of wicked Lamech, apparently in the

---

[45]See 2 Kings 25; Isaiah 14:30; 51:19; Jeremiah 11; 14; 15; 16; 18; 21; 24; 27; 29; 32; 34; 38; 42; 44; 52; Ezekiel 5; 6; 7; 12; 14; 36; Matthew 24:7; Luke 21:11; Revelation 18:8; D&C 43:25; 86:7. Famine also figures prominently in the divine judgments cited in the Book of Mormon. See, for example, 2 Nephi 1:18; 6:15; 9:3; 12:4; 10:22, 23; Helaman 10:6; 11:4-15; 12:3.

[46]A case in point is the American Indian whose best lands were appropriated by the white race in many unconscionable actions.

third century after the fall. (See Moses 5:56; 6:15.) Man had finally come of age. Satan raged in the hearts of men and men raged in their hearts against their own blood. (See Moses 7:33.) James asked, "From whence come wars and fighting among you? come they not hence, even of your lusts that war in your members?" (James 4:1.) Would the wicked, in being cursed, remain on the least desirable portions of the earth if it were in their power to appropriate the uncursed lands of others? No. Is this not a prime cause of war? Yes. And this will remain a fact of human life as long as wicked men rule and the earth remains the cursed planet it is.

When it came forth from the hand of its Maker, it was an unflawed work of perfection—a "good earth." There were no steaming jungles, no frozen wastelands, no barren deserts, no towering mountains burdened with perpetual snow and ice. Such post-fall conditions came about in a series of changes over many centuries. But now Earth is a living testimony to the sins of man. They are written across her face in stark horizons, icy wastelands, brutal deserts, dark jungles, jagged mountains and, in fine, in all of her signs of suffering.

Our Aging Earth

Since God lives in absolute harmony with truth and law, all that he does in nature is positive. Nothing negative can be attributed to him as an arbitrary action on his part. Consequently, mortality (a negative state) with all of its many undesirable aspects, is a product of broken law. Transgression produced the fall and the fall produced mortality. (See Moses 6:57.) This applies to the negative condition of the earth as it is today. The burdens of mortality have taken their toll on our aging planet. She has known many of the symptoms of change and decay characteristic of us humans. The fevers of forest fires and burning deserts, the thirst of drought, the barrenness of lifeless deserts, the vomiting of volcanic eruptions, the sweating of floods and tidal waves, the baldness of denuded woodlands, the convulsions of earthquakes, the organic distresses of inward groanings, the weeping of rains, and even the amputation and separation of portions of her body—all these have been her lot.[47]

Now she is old and tired. Her once smooth skin is withered and pock-marked with craters, canyons, cracks, and fissures. It is wrinkled

---

[47]She is yet to experience dizziness and vertigo, the worst of burning fevers, radical surgery leading to a limited but miraculous rejuvenation, and, finally, death and resurrection.

with craggy hills and high mountain ranges. It is roughened with coarse, stony vistas. It is withered with bleak, barren deserts.

Some of the earth's deterioration can be ascribed to the natural aging process attendant to all living things in a fallen state. However, that process was greatly accelerated and compounded by the judgments of God and the depredations of men. In other words, Mother Earth would be far more lovely in her old age had she not suffered so much in her youth.[48] Man brought about her fall, and he has further dishonored her by his reckless assault on her treasures. Modern technology has made a science of the exploitation of the earth. Man leaves her face scarred and disfigured after extracting the coal, iron, copper, and other valued properties from beneath her peeled back skin. He weakens and unbalances her very being by ceaselessly pumping oil and gas from deep within her bowels. He clogs her veins and arteries—once pure, sparkling oceans, rivers, lakes and streams—with the filth of deadly pollutants. He has invaded the blue aura which surrounds her and contaminated it with the acrid poisonous haze of his commerce and industry. He has brought the life which once teemed in her waters and flourished on her lands and in her forests to the borders of extinction. In brief, man has imposed modern civilization on the earth in an uncivilized manner.

The earth has been plundered with the same thoughtless, unconscionable disregard which characterized the tomb robbers of ancient Egypt. Nothing was sacred, nothing mattered but the treasure itself. The despoilers' one thought was the wealth, ease, gratification, and power the tombs could provide them. In their anxiety to seize the things they esteemed to be of greatest material value, they trampled, smashed, scattered, or carried off as common utensils and household wares, objects of priceless historical interest. And such has been man's treatment of the earth itself; he has betrayed the stewardship God gave him in the beginning.

It may be argued that the gift of dominion justifies man in utilizing the earth's waters, forests, lands, minerals, and animal life as he sees fit. For how can man subdue the earth without using the earth? But the issue is not man's right to use but instead his right use of the planet. "The earth is

---

[48]If Earth is still attractive in spite of being fallen and cursed, how incredibly beautiful it must have been in the beginning! We should remember that we judge the earth by the little we know of the moons and planets in our solar system, not by the cosmic standard of excellence God employs.

the Lord's, and the fulness thereof; the world, and they that dwell therein." (Psalms 24:1, 2; See also D&C 104:14.) It does not belong to anyone else; man is a tenant on another Man's property, a steward over another Man's wealth. As such, man will be obliged to give an accounting of his stewardship over everything placed under his care. (See Luke 16;10-12.)

The earth was prepared for the blessing of all of its inhabitants. The Father never designed that the strong should possess it at the expense of the weak. Had his chidren loved their brothers and sisters as themselves and regarded the earth with gratitude and respect, misery and want would have been unknown to mankind. But because men have sinned grieveously against God, the earth is cursed, and because the earth is cursed, the curses of war, famine, disease, and pestilence continue to stalk the land. We have reaped what we have sown. And the end is not yet.

CHAPTER SEVEN

Earth is Reborn of Water

The history of man was written before it was lived. Three years prior to departing this world, Adam met with his righteous offspring in the valley of Adam-ondi-Ahman and, as patriarch over the human family, he "predicted whatsoever should befall his posterity unto the latest generation."[1] His summary of future events doubtlessly included the prophecy that the first world order would end in a universal flood some seven hundred and twenty-eight years later.

This was not man's first knowledge of the flood; Enoch had seen it in vision more than two hundred years earlier.[2] The occasion was a multi-scened vision of things to come given him on Mount Simeon while

---

[1]D&C 107:56, 57. This assembly took place about B.C. 3070. Apparently Joseph Smith beheld it in a vision for he is quoted as saying: "I saw Adam in the valley of Adam-ondi-Ahman. He called together his children and blessed them with a patriarchal blessing. The Lord appeared in their midst, and he (Adam) blessed them all, and foretold what should befall them to the latest generation." (HC, 3:388.) A similar conference will be held at Adam-ondi-Aham preparatory to the glorious return of Jesus Christ. (See D&C 116; Daniel 7:9, 10 and HC, 3:386, 387.)

[2]Joseph Smith wrote that God's seers and prophets "saw the flood before it came." (HC, 1:283.)

111

meeting face to face with the Lord.[3] The great patriarch was shown that after his "City of Holiness" had fled the earth, the power of Satan would become pandemic: "And he beheld Satan; and he had a great chain in his hand, and it veiled the whole face of the earth with darkness; and he looked up and laughed, and his angels rejoiced." (Moses 7:26.)

Wickedness of Men

By Noah's day the thoughts of men's hearts were "evil continually." (See Moses 8:22.) The plethora of unmitigated wickedness prompted the Lord to tell Enoch:

> Behold these thy brethren; they are the workmanship of mine own hands, and I gave unto them their knowledge, in the day I created them; and in the Garden of Eden gave I unto man his agency;
> And unto thy brethren have I said, and also given commandment, that they should love one another, and that they should choose me, their Father, but behold, they are without affection, and they hate their own blood;
> And the fire of mine indignation is kindled against them; and in my hot displeasure will I send in the floods upon them, for my fierce anger is kindled against them.[4]

Free agency was bestowed upon the human family so that they might voluntarily choose God as their Father. This opportunity was to be afforded all of his children in both their first and second estates. A third portion of the "host" chose to follow rebellious Lucifer in his primal war against Heaven; they became his sons. Enoch beheld that many of those who had remained relatively faithful to the Father in their first estate would, in mortality, reject him in favor of the father of lies. In

---

[3]See Moses 7:2, 3. Enoch was born 622 years after the fall. He was over three hundred years old at the time of his meeting with Adam. His "Zion" had been established for more than two centuries. (See Moses 5:10-25, 68; 8:5-12; D&C 107:39-52.)

[4]Moses 7:32-34. Enoch may well have been the first mortal to learn of a future universal flood since this is the most ancient extant scriptural reference to it. (See Alma 10:22.)

imitating the devil's works, they would become the devil's children. (See John 8:39-44.) Having renounced the God who gave them life, they became, by adoption, the children of death. Hence the Father's lament: "They hate their own blood."

While men are free to destroy themselves, they are not free to destroy others. (See Alma 36:9.) The contagious nature of the evil practices of Noah's generation took an unacceptable toll among the innocent and the young. To allow a world ripened in iniquity to continue to exist by the grace of God would have been a mockery of that grace and an inevitable defeat for the unborn.

President John Taylor defended God's moral integrity in sweeping the race from the earth, when he explained that it was done for the eternal welfare of both the living and the unborn:

> The Lord as a great cosmogonist, took in the various stages of man's existence and operated for the general benefit of the whole. But was it not cruel to destroy them? I think God understood precisely what He was doing. They were His offspring, and He knowing things better than they did, and they having placed themselves under the power and dominion of Satan, He thought they had better be removed and another class of men be introduced. Why? There were other persons concerned besides them. There were millions of spirits in the eternal worlds who would shrink from being contaminated by the wicked and corrupt, the debauched, the dishonest, the fraudulent, the hypocrite, and men who trampled upon the ordinances of God. It might seem harsh for these men to be swept off from the face of the earth, and not allowed to perpetuate their species thereon; but what about the justice of forcing these pure spirits to come and inhabit tabernacles begotten by debauched corrupt reprobates, the imagination of whose heart was only evil, and that continually—what about them? Had they no rights that God was bound to respect? Certainly they had, and He respected them. He cut off the wicked. (JD, 26:35. See also JD, 24:290, 291; 17:205, 206; 18:330, 331 and 19:158, 159.)

Adam's world had to die so that Noah's world might live.

However, the Almighty was also mindful of the eternal welfare of the wicked; divine mercy seasoned divine justice. As Orson F. Whitney observed: "This is the Gospel of salvation, not a Gospel of damnation." He continued:

God does not punish except to save, He never chastens except to purify. In sweeping the antediluvian races from the earth, it was an act of mercy to them, that they might not add sin to sin and heap up iniquity until they could not have been pardoned. He swept them off when their cup was full, and imprisoned their spirits while their bodies mouldered in the grave. Jesus, however, while His body was lying in the tomb, went and preached to the spirits in prison; those who rejected the message that was offered to them by Noah, and were swept away by the flood. (JD, 26:268.)

But before the arm of the Lord was revealed in watery judgment, he made one final effort to save all that would be saved. His patient and longsuffering character was demonstrated by his decision to have Noah and his fellow prophets continue to raise the warning voice of repentance: "My Spirit shall not always strive with man, for he shall know that all flesh shall die; yet his days shall be an hundred and twenty years; and if men do not repent, I will send in the floods upon them." (Moses 8:17. See also Genesis 6:3.) Consequently, Noah and his righteous sons and associates spent the 120-year period immediately preceding the flood, in raising the voice of warning to a mocking, unlistening generation. As it was in Noah's day, so shall it be at the time of the coming of the Son of Man.

The repentance the Lord called for entailed much more than the limited moral reformation of a minority of mankind. The antediluvian world was not a Sodom-and-Gomorrah situation wherein a corrupt majority might be saved from destruction by as few as ten righteous souls. (See Genesis 18.) God's repentance required nothing less than the sincere acceptance of his fatherhood coupled with strict obedience to gospel law on the part of the human family as such. Mankind was enslaved to sin on so vast and pervasive a scale as to render inadequate any repentance that did not bring men to the Savior. It is so today. (See D&C 88:49-53.) Our world faces a certain destruction that no righteous minority—though it number in the many millions—can forestall. (See D&C 5:18, 19; 33:2-4; 38:11, 12; 86:4-7.)

A common misconception about Noah's generation is that almost everyone was viciously wicked. Such was not the case. While we are not informed as to the number who responded favorably to the prophetic message, some surely did. Recall that Enoch saw generation after generation come upon the earth *after* his city was translated. Satan's power grew, angels testified, and "the Holy Ghost fell on *many*, and they were caught up by the powers of heaven into Zion." (Moses 7:27.)

Consequently all of the righteous—other than Noah's family—had either died or been translated before the flood began. Then too, among the candidates for the terrestrial kingdom are those honorable men of the earth who rejected the gospel message and perished in the flood but repented of their sins in the spirit world where they finally accepted Christ as their Lord and Savior. (See Moses 7:38, 39, 57; 1 Peter 3:18; 4:6; and D&C 76:73-75; 88:89; 138:7-10, 28-35.)

As it was in the days of Noah, so shall it be when Christ returns: there will be millions of honorable men and women on the earth who, while not numbered with the saints, will be living lives far above the character and conduct of the truly wicked. The basically decent men, women, and children of Noah's generation fell victim to the moral sickness of many of their fellowmen. For like a deadly disease, the flood did not discriminate between one soul and another—death came to the entire body of mankind. We must not forget that divine judgment is largely self-imposed by man; man dictates his own eternal destiny and pronounces his own eternal fate. The Lord's responses to man are but the harvest of man's will. God is ever free of the blood and sins of his children.

End of the First World

The one hundred and twenty years of grace had passed; the warning voice of Noah fell silent. The ark of deliverance had been prepared,[5] and the parent animals and Noah's family (the eight human survivors of the first world order) were all aboard—and the Lord shut them in.[6] The closing of the ark's portal sounded the death knell of all living things that walked upon the earth or flew through the heavens.

———————————

[5]See Genesis 7:16; Matt. 25:10. Wrote Joseph Smith: "The construction of the first vessel was given to Noah, by revelation. The design of the ark was given by God, 'a pattern of heavenly things.'" (HC, 5:63. Orson Pratt opined: "He [Noah] had a Urim and Thummim by which he was enabled to discern all things pertaining to the ark and its pattern." (JD, 16:50.)

[6]The ark was approximately 450 feet long, 75 feet wide, and 45 feet high. Its draft was probably in excess of 20 feet—hence the need for the flood waters to cover the highest mountains more than 22 feet. (See Genesis 6:15; 7:20.)

Were there mocking onlookers? Did their derisive laughter fill the air? In all probability there was no precedent for even localized flooding much less the universal deluge predicted by Noah. Surely the man was mad! Experience was seemingly on their side. There is no scriptural reference to rain up to that time—not even in the morn of creation. Instead, "there went up a *mist from the earth*, and *watered the whole face of the ground*." (Genesis 2:6. See Moses 3:6; Abraham 5:5, 6; and Ether 2:24.) Thus, the first recorded rains occurred almost two millennia after the earth's fall. But on the seventeenth day of the second month—1656 years after the fall—when Noah was 599 years old, "were all the fountains of the great deep broken up, and the windows of heaven were opened." (Genesis 7:11.) The rain came—but not as we know it today. No tropical downpour, however heavy, can compare with it. The sky became, as it were, a vast upper ocean, its waters crashing against the face of the planet in wave after unrelenting wave, day after day and night after night. The heavens declared the wrath of God.[7]

And the earth bore a second witness. The poised subterranean waters, freed of their rocky chains by the mighty tremblings and tearings of the earth, burst from their hiding places in the great deep in swelling, surging, roaring tidal waves and ever-mounting seas. The waters above and the waters beneath became as one in a confluence of witness and judgment. Heaven and earth bore a common testimony of the corruption of mankind.

Imagine the growing terror which must have gripped all mankind as the deluge rose up and flung itself over the land: screams drowning screams as the dying futilely cried out for nonexistent help and heaven itself assaulted with the fear-born prayers of men driven by extremity to seek in death the God they mocked in life. All was chaos as man and beast struggled for life in the smothering arms of the swiftly rising waters. Escape! But where? Death was waiting in every direction. The flood had

---

[7]It has been suggested that the withdrawal of the Spirit of the Lord triggered the flood: "When the Spirit was partly withdrawn in the days of Noah, the immense masses of water confined below in 'the fountains of the great deep' broke their fetters and overflowed the Earth, while, at the same time, the vapors in the atmosphere condensed and fell down in torrents as if the 'windows of heaven' had been opened (Genesis 7:11), and the result was the destruction of every living creature, except those in the ark." (Hyrum M. Smith and Janne M. Sjodahl, *The Doctrine and Covenants Commentary*, p. 380.)

no single point of origin; it encompassed the globe. Even those who managed to flee to higher ground were quickly smothered beneath a seething, twisting sea of mud, falling rocks, and crashing trees. The watery juggernaut swept all before it in a convulsion of furious power. There was no place to hide; the wrath of God was omnipresent.

The consequence of mankind's offenses were visited on the animal kingdom when the unfaithful stewards of life on this planet brought death to their stewardships:[8]

> And all flesh died that moved upon the earth, both of fowl, and of cattle, and of beast, and of every creeping thing that creepeth upon the earth, and every man:
> All in whose nostrils was the breath of life, of all that was in the dry land, died.
> And every living substance was destroyed which was upon the face of the ground, both man, and cattle, and the creeping things, and the fowl of the heaven; and they were destroyed from the earth: and Noah only remained alive, and they that were with him in the ark.[9]

---

[8]While the animals Noah saved were of both the clean and unclean varieties (Genesis 7:1-3, 8, 9, 14, 15), all were worthy to be perpetuated for as the apostle Peter was told: "What God hath cleased, that call thou not common." (Acts 10:15.)

[9]Genesis 7:21-23. Although Noah filled the ark with a host of creatures representative of the animal kingdom, not every prediluvian species was destined for a place in the second world order. Some creatures—such as those giant reptiles comprising the dinosaur family of the so-called Mesozoic period, either failed to survive the fall or, as their remains indicate, were swept from the earth in the cataclysmic events associated with the deluge. Be that as it may, the many varieties known today comprise the posterity of those animals preserved by Noah. The assumption that he gathered literally every creature from the merest insect to the largest mammoths need not have been the case. Within the micro-evolutionary bounds set by the Almighty, the surviving species have doubtlessly proliferated into a number of subspecies via genetic variation, cross-breeding, and environmental modification.

Virtually every living thing experienced a merciful sudden death.[10] The Lord is not cruel. He did not torture his creatures with a slowly rising, creeping destruction. The waters rose rapidly so that within little more than a month, from its lowest valleys to its highest elevations, the earth disappeared beneath a shoreless global sea unchallenged by even the smallest tip of land.[11]

Whence the Waters?

> And the Gods also said: Let there be an expanse in the midst of the waters, and it shall divide the waters from the waters.
> And the Gods ordered the expanse, so that it divided the waters which were under the expanse from the waters which were above the expanse; and it was so, even as they ordered.
> And the Gods called the expanse, Heaven.[12]

When the physical earth was organized two vast aqueous bodies were also formed. One, the planetary ocean, was in a highly condensed, liquid state. The other was diffused in a gaseous state throughout many thousands, if not millions, of miles of the sidereal heavens surrounding the earth.[13] This watery shroud was apparently so thinly dispersed as to make it undetectable from the earth. The sun, moon, and stars eventually appeared much as they do today, and the skies were no less clear. Yet an invisible veil of water vapor distantly enveloped the unsuspecting planet.

But why do the creation accounts tell of waters above and waters below the expanse or firmament? A man-conceived fantasy of earth's beginnings would hardly include such a notion. Is it not passing strange

---

[10]Marine life, as such, was not destroyed.

[11]See Genesis 7:19; 20; 8:5. The psalmist wrote: "Thou coverest it [the earth] with the deep as with a garment: *the waters stood above the mountains*." (Psalm 104;6.)

[12]Abraham 4:6-8. Moses' account refers to the "expanse" as "a firmament." (See Genesis 1:6-8.)

[13]Hydrogen, the dominant ingredient in water, is the most common of all the known elements.

Length of the Flood

How long did the flood last? The following chart summarizes the information found in Genesis 7 and 8:

Event	Date 600th Year of Noah	Elapsed Days Between Events
A. Flood begins (7:11)	2nd mo., 17 d.	0
B. Period of rising waters ends. Flood level apparently reached. (7:12, 17-23)	3rd mo., 27th d.	40
C. Waters maintain level for additional 110 days. All rain and flooding stops. Wind rises. Waters begin to recede. Ark grounded on Mt. Ararat. (7:24; 8:1-4)	7th mo., 17th d.	110
D. Mountain tops reappear. (8:5)	10th mo., 1st d.	74
E. Raven released. Flys until earth dries up. (8:6, 7)	11th mo., 11th d.	40
F. Dove released. Returns. (8:8, 9)	11th mo., 18th d.	7
G. Dove released again. Returns with olive leaf. (8:10, 11)	11th mo., 25th d.	7
H. Dove released third time. Does not return. (8:12)	12th mo., 2nd d.	7
I. Waters completely recede. Covering of Ark removed. (8:13)	1st mo., 1st d.	29
J. Earth dry. Noah leaves ark. (8:14-18)	2nd mo., 27th d.	56
Total elapsed time from entry to departure from ark was one year and ten days or approximately:		370 days*

This summary is based on a thirty day month. When the additional five days are added, the total elapsed time from entry to departure from the ark is 375 days.

that so odd an element should have found its way into the accounts of both Abraham and Moses? There can be but one reason: It was an important fact the Lord wanted to have included in the divine narratives—one which was not only essential to the basic details of the earth's birth, but of its rebirth as well. Because these waters were an integral part of the earth's creation, there is no reason to doubt that they were an integral part of its fall. Indeed, the fall seems to have made their presence mandatory. Why? Because the great deluge was anticipated from the beginning; the baptism of the earth was foreordained! And the means were prepared. All that was to befall the earth throughout its pre-celestial career was incorporated into its design and organization by its divine architects.

Although the Lord opened the windows of both the sidereal and atmospheric heavens in raining down judgment on mankind, it seems evident that it was the upper waters and not those precipitated from the earth's sparse atmospheric cloud system that constituted the primary source of those rains which fell relentlessly for forty days and forty nights.[14]

Universal Flood

While most geologists reject the Genesis account of a global flood, there are those who, not wishing to discount scripture entirely, favor a small miracle—a regional deluge.[15] However, this is an intellectual luxury Moses' account, combined with other inspired testimony, simply will not allow. Contrary to the egocentric thinking of some Bible critics,

---

[14]The simultaneous precipitation of all the water vapor in the earth's present atmosphere would not cover the ground with two inches of rainfall. (See *The Genesis Flood*, p. 121. Compare Genesis 7:11 and Malachi 3:10.)

[15]The Babylonian Gilgamesh Epic and, to a lesser extent, the Sumerian legend contain a number of elements similar to those found in Genesis, but they are clearly distorted heathen versions of the original account. Their value does not lie in their content but in their very existence. The fact that the basic story was so widespread in the ancient world is a strong argument against the theory of a limited flood. Jesus spoke of Noah and the flood. (See Matthew 24:37-39. Other New Testament references to it are: Luke 17:26, 27; Hebrews 11:7; 1 Peter 3:20 and 2 Peter 3:5-7.)

the ancient prophets were not naive simpletons. A local flood would hardly have covered the highest hills from twenty-two to twenty-seven feet! Nor would it have required five months to the day for the waters to recede sufficiently for the ark to ground itself on the mountains of Ararat. Thereafter, on the first day of the tenth month, the tops of the mountains finally reappeared. (See Genesis 7:11-24.) Regardless of the accuracy of the details found in Genesis, no one can honestly question Moses' *intent* to describe the flood as an unprecedented universal phenomenon.[16]

It would have been ludicrous for Noah to build—or Moses to describe—so mammoth a ship in terms of a regional disaster. The ark's size was dictated primarily by its animal cargo. Why preserve a few representative animals in one limited locality when the same species were to be found virtually everywhere else?[17] And why should Noah— who had been warning of the impending flood for 120 years—build even a rowboat rather than remove his family to higher ground or to another land if that calamity was to be confined to a given people in a given area? Noah was not a madman, he was a prophet of God, who "stands next in authority to Adam in the Priesthood." (HC, 3:386; Luke 1:19, 26.) In all likelihood he was translated at the age of 950, for he is Gabriel, the angel who appeared to Zacharias in the temple and to Mary in Nazareth. Would such a man have been so destitute of reason as to be incapable of distinguishing between a global deluge and a regional flooding? And would Moses?

But, most importantly, if the flood was not universal in character, God has broken his immutable word—given first to Enoch (Moses 7:50, 51) and reconfirmed to Noah (Genesis 9:15)—that the earth would "never more be covered by the floods." For if the flood was not global, then it was local, and if it was local, then the Lord has foresworn himself since such floodings have remained an annual occurence throughout recorded history. However, God is trustworthy; he honors his word perfectly. His promise to never again "destroy *all* flesh" by a global deluge did not preclude the loss of *some* life in subsequent floods of a

---

[16]The *Book of Mormon* disputes the notion of a purely local flood by declaring that "after the waters had receded from off the face of this land it [America] became a choice land above all other lands." (Ether 13:2.)

[17]Joseph Smith's translation of Genesis 9:10, 11 indicates that because of the creatures saved in the ark, the animal kingdom "shall not altogether perish." (JST Genesis 9:16.)

limited nature. God's oath-bound assurances to Enoch and Noah, combined with the fact that localized floodings continue to occur, rules out the possibility that the Noachian deluge was but another in a series of ongoing natural disasters. As with so many other things pertaining to the workings of God, integrity demands that we either accept the flood account as revealed or reject it *in toto*.

Like the Sadducees who rejected the doctrine of the resurrection, those who deny the flood outright, or who seek to carry its waters on both shoulders by maintaining that it was a localized phenomenon, "err, not knowing the scriptures, *nor the power of God.*" (Matthew 22:29.) He who organized this globe and covered it with a universal sea from whence its land masses eventually emerged, was fully capable of returning it to that watery state at his pleasure.

Ancient Mountains

It is admittedly difficult for our finite minds to envision water rising high enough to cover a mountain such as Everest, the summit of which is nearly six miles above the surface of the sea! However, the submersion of the highest mountains might not have required as great a volume of water in Noah's time as would be necessary today.[18] The extent to which the "dry land" had emerged from the earth's primordial sea prior to the flood is unknown. And also unknown is the maximum elevation above sea level of any portion of that land. The assumption that the continents

----

[18]In responding to the question, "Did the flood cover the highest mountains of earth?", Elder John A. Widtsoe wrote: "All parts of the earth were under water at the same time. In some places the layer of water might have been twenty-six feet deep or more; in others, as on sloping hillsides, it might have been only a fraction of an inch in depth." *Evidences and Reconciliations*, p. 111. In other words, a torrential rain would have been sufficient to cover the highest mountains with enough water to immerse the entire earth at a given time. While this is certainly possible, Genesis 8:5 states that "the tops of the mountains" were not seen until over eight months after the rains began, and over six months after they ended.

and their mountain ranges were much the same ages ago as they are today is only that, an assumption.[19]

There is strong scriptural evidence that earth's major mountain ranges (such as the Himalayas, the Andes, the Alps, and the Rockies) did not exist when it was first organized, nor, in all likelihood, before the flood.[20] The first was as the last shall be. Prophecies concerning conditions in the end of time are actually revelations of conditions in the beginning of time. Thus, we know that the primeval earth was characterized by vast plains and relatively low, rolling hills because such will be the general topography of the earth in the millennium. Both ancient and modern revelation declare that Christ's second coming will climax the restoration of all things wherein the earth will be renewed and receive its paradisiacal glory—the glory it had prior to its fall.[21] At that time, the Lord will cause the mountains to be lowered and the valleys to be raised. Thus, the present great mountain ranges will not be found on the millennial earth—an earth characterized by Edenic conditions.

This view suggests that these ranges were produced in connection with the earth's water baptism and will pass away at the time of its spirit baptism. They will no longer be necessary from either a spiritual or a physical standpoint. In a sense, they are blemishes on the earth's face which symbolize its fallen condition; when it rises to a terrestrial estate, these "blemishes" will no longer be appropriate. The term, "mountain," is quite relative and has been applied to large hills as well as towering

------

[19]Fossil evidence indicates that "all the major mountain ranges of the present world evidently were uplifted within the *most recent* eras of geologic history." (*The Genesis Flood*, Morris and Whitcomb, p. 142.) Geologists now believe that "continental drift" has been the dominant element in the mountain building process. If the continents began their "drifting" in the days of Peleg, the great mountain ranges can only be a few thousand years old.

[20]The period of the flood, including the division of the earth into separate hemispheres and continents, was probably the earth's great mountain-building period.

[21]Speaking of this, Parley P. Pratt wrote: "When a Prophet speaks of the restoration of all things, he means that all things have undergone a change, and are to be again restored to their primitive order, even as they first existed." (*A Voice of Warning*, p. 85.)

124   *The Footstool of God*

peaks.²² For example, both the traditional "mount of temptation" (west of Jericho) and the traditional site of the Sermon on the Mount (northwest of the sea of Galilee) are scarcely above sea level. Indeed, there are very few scriptural references to high mountains.

The book of Ether tells of the brother of Jared quarrying sixteen stones from a mountain "called the mount Shelem, because of its exceeding height." (Ether 3:1.) Nephi writes of being caught away in the Spirit of the Lord "into an exceeding high mountain, which I never had before seen, and upon which I never had before set my foot." (1 Nephi 11:1. See also 2 Nephi 4:25.) Neither of these mountains is locatable so that there is no way we can determine just what was meant by "exceeding high." Moses was "caught up into an exceedingly high mountain" when the Lord God commissioned him to return to Egypt and deliver Israel from slavery.²³ The parallel account found in Exodus identifies the mountain as Horeb (or Sinai)—"the mountain of God." (The precise location of which is conjectural.)²⁴ Horeb is almost certainly to be found somewhere in the Sinai range of the Sinai peninsula where the

---

²²It has even been applied to manmade structures. For example, the ziggurats (of which the tower of Babel is the best known) of ancient Mesopotamia were artificial mounds of earth thrown up to simulate mountains and were, in fact, designated as such: "The significance of the ziggurats is revealed by the names which many of them bear, names which identify them as mountains. That of the god Enlil at Nippur, for example, was called 'House of the Mountain, Mountain of the Storm, Bond between Heaven and Earth.'" (Henry Frankfort, *The Birth of Civilization in the Near East*, p. 56.)

²³Moses 1:1, 2, 26. The phrase "an exceedingly high mountain" may be a metaphor for the presence of the Lord. Moses 1:46 tells us that the name of the mount on which Moses stood "shall not be known among the children of men." This would seem to rule out Horeb or Sinai. God is a mountain man and where he is, there is the spiritual mountain. His temple is a symbolic mountain: "the mountain of the Lord's house shall be established in the top of the mountains." (Isaiah 2:2.) Zion becomes "mount Zion" when it is glorified by the presence of the Lord. (See Isaiah 8:18; 55:20; D&C 76:66 and HC, 6:254.)

²⁴See Exodus 3:1. It has been suggested that the names Sinai and Horeb are not to be identified with any one mountain, being conceptual terms denoting emptiness or desolation.

mountains—which vary in height from about 6700 to 9000 feet above sea level—rise only 1800 to 4000 feet above the desert floor.

While such mountains may have been considered "exceeding high" by men whose lives were largely spent in the desert's hills and lowlands, they would hardly compare with ranges in other parts of the world having elevations approaching 30,000 feet. Then too, in every instance where a mountain is described as being "exceeding high," the passage pertains to events *after* the flood.[25] In all likelihood, the great ranges of the world were thrown up in astonishingly brief mountain-building periods partly concurrent with and partly subsquent to the flood. Such profound topographical changes would have been entirely consistent with and supportive of God's postdiluvian division of the earth whereby he separated the human family linguistically, culturally, and geographically.

The time required to bring about major geologic changes is dependent upon the forces involved. When the Almighty exercises his power, time ceases to be a factor. For example, in a matter of hours, a "great mountain" was formed to occupy the site where the Nephite city of Moronihah had stood. The death of Christ was accompanied by other extensive changes in the geology and topography of portions of the western hemisphere—and probably other regions as well. (See 3 Nephi 8:10; 9:5, 8 and Helaman 14:23.) The earth was never the same after the crucifixion of her Creator. (See Helaman 14:21-23; 3 Nephi 9:12-19; 9:5-8.) Multiple catastrophism has been the lot of the earth from its beginning.

Even discounting the foregoing and assuming that the mountains of Noah's time were of formidable height, it would have been a simple matter fo the Lord to cause the land—which floats, as it were, upon a cushion of plastic subterranean materials[26]—to partially sink into the flood waters and then rise again, much as a person is lowered into the waters of baptism and then raised up out of them. Earth—as with any recipient of baptism—would thus have been a willing and an active

---

[25]Enoch, who lived before the flood, talked with God on mount Simeon, but no reference is made to its height. (See Moses 7:2-4.)

[26]Current geophysical research indicates that the relatively thin outer crust of the earth (comprising the continents and ocean basins) is supported by a number of massive, moving plates of layered materials which are, in turn, floating on the molten matter, called magma, found in the core, or mantle, of the earth.

participant in its own immersion. Baptism is not employed as simply a convenient metaphor to argue the case for a universal deluge: its use is deliberate. The flood is a witness for baptism and baptism is a witness for the flood.[27]

Baptismal Covenant of Earth

The earth is a living soul, a dual organism composed of spirit and elementary matter. The measure—or design—of its creation is nothing less than celestial glory: "And again, verily I say unto you, the earth abideth the law of a celestial kingdom, for it filleth the measure of its creation, and transgresseth not the law." (D&C 88:25.) The law it obeys is the law of Christ, the new and everlasting covenant by which men and worlds are sanctified in immortal glory. (See D&C, 88:21.) Basic to that covenant law is the ordinance of baptism—the dual or two-part ordinance corresponding to the dual nature of a living soul—the spirit joined to its physical counterpart. (See D&C, 88:15.) Thus baptism both symbolizes and serves the dual nature of a living soul in that it entails the immersion of the physical body in water and the subsequent immersion of the spirit body in Spirit. For this reason Jesus told Nicodemus: "Except a man be born of water and of the Spirit, he cannot enter into the kingdom of God." (John 3:5.) The baptismal requirement applied with equal force to the earth: it cannot enter the celestial order of kingdoms without being born again of water and of the Spirit.

Like Jesus, Mother Earth had to be baptized to fulfill all righteousness. (See Matthew 3:13-15.) And, like Jesus, she was baptized for her perfecting, not for her sins. Such was not the case with her human children; mankind had defiled her with their abominations. In the wisdom of God it was decreed that she should be freed of her human burden so that both she and her unborn children might have a new beginning." Orson Pratt declared Christ to be Earth's Redeemer when he stated:

> The first ordinance instituted for the cleansing of the earth, was that of immersion in water; it was buried in the liquid element, and all things sinful upon the face of it were washed

---

[27]The apostle Peter understood this point and equated the ark which saved Noah's family from physical death to baptism which saves men from spiritual death. (See 1 Peter 3:20, 21.)

away . . .As man cannot be born again of water, without an administrator, so the earth required an agency independent of itself, to administer this grand cleansing ordinance, and restore it to its infant purity. That administrator was the Redeemer himself.[28]

Brigham Young bluntly stated that the earth was baptized for the remission of sins:

> The Lord said, 'I will deluge (or immerse) the earth in water for the remission of the sins of the people; or if you will allow me to express myself in a familiar style, to kill all the vermin that were nitting, and breeding, and polluting its body; it was cleansed of its filthiness; and soaked in the water, as long as some of our people ought to soak. The Lord baptized the earth for the remission of sins, and it has been once cleansed from the filthiness that has gone out of it, which was in the inhabitants who dwelt upon its face. (JD, 1:274.)

The very nature, purpose, and symbolism of baptism necessitates the total immersion of the entire body; sprinkling or pouring water on the head or some other part of the body is not baptism. The ordinance signifies the remission of *all* sins via a complete immersion in the blood of Christ. Other modes of baptism violate its divine symbolism. (See John 3:23; Romans 6:4; D&C 20:72-74; Mormon 9:6; Moses 6:64 and TPJS, pp. 12, 198, 360.) This fact alone should be enough to convince any one having faith in the scriptures—ancient and modern—that the waters of the flood covered every particle of land on the globe. As with her repentant children, Mother Earth came forth from the womb, with its global sea, at her physical birth only to symbolically return to the womb via the flood. She was immersed therein by the power of the Holy Priesthood.

---

[28]JD, 1:331. See also 1:291-293; 16:313, 314; and 21:323, 324. While Orson Pratt calls baptism "the first ordinance instituted for the cleansing of the earth," its validity depended upon the atonement. Since the atonement retroactively freed both earth and mankind of the burden of original sin, it may be said that it was the divine ordinance of salvation. Thus, as Orson Pratt observed, "Both man and the earth are redeemed from the original sin without ordinances." (JD, 1:291.)

She was born again of water having received the first ordinance of salvation at the hands of her Creator-Savior.

This ordinance was pre-requisite to and symbolic of the conversion, the spiritual renewal, yet to be. For the earth's longed-for "day of righteousness" would not come until the baptismal ordinance had been completed; as with us all, the earth has to be baptized with fire and with the Holy Ghost. (See Matthew 3:11; 3 Nephi 11:35; 12:1, 2; D&C 33:11.) That culminating ordinance has to await the dawning of the millennial day. (See Moses 7:48, 54-61; JD, 1:292.)

Sign of an Oath

Having once received the baptism of water, the earth was never to experience the ordinance again. The flood, like the atonement, would not be repeated. Enoch had pled "that the earth might never more be covered by the floods" and the Lord had sworn with an oath that such would be the case. (Moses 7:50.) Isaiah likened this immutable promise of a single world deluge to Jehovah's promise of a single scattering of the house of Israel ending in the eventual redemption of Zion: "For this is as the waters of Noah unto me: for as I have sworn that the waters of Noah should no more go over the earth; so have I sworn that I would not be wroth with thee, nor rebuke thee."[29]

Following the flood, the Lord comforted Noah—and his posterity down through time—with the same assurance: "And I will establish my covenant with you; neither shall *all* flesh be cut off anymore by the waters of a flood; neither shall there any more be a flood to destroy the earth." (Genesis 9:11. See also 8:21; 9:15.) The sign of that immutable promise was to be the rainbow—a token which was to join all of the other signs the Lord had previously appointed for man's comfort and guidance.[30] "And God made a covenant with Noah, and said, This shall be the token of the covenant I make between me and you, and for every living creature with

---

[29]Isaiah 54:9. Israel's redemption includes the establishment of a latter-day Zion which will be joined to Enoch's city when it returns to the earth. (See JST Genesis 9:21-24.) Orson Pratt said: "The bow that was set in the clouds was to be a token, between God and the inhabitants of the earth, of the bringing again of Zion, and of the assembling of the Saints of all dispensations." (JD, 16:49.)

[30]Joseph Smith taught that "God has set many signs on the earth, as well as in the heavens." (HC, 4:554.)

you, for perpetual generations; I *will* set my bow in the cloud; and it shall be for a token of a covenant between me and the earth." (JST Genesis 9:18, 19.)

The rainbow also betokens the fact that Enoch and his City of Holiness will return in that day when righteousness prevails on the earth: "And the bow shall be in the cloud; and I will look upon it, that I may remember the everlasting covenant, which I made unto thy father Enoch; that, when men should keep all my commandments, Zion should again come on the earth, the city of Enoch which I have caught up unto myself." (JST Genesis 9:21.)

The rainbow is a heavenly sign of God's mercy. When justice replaces that mercy, the token of the rainbow will disappear from earth's skies. This will portend further tribulations and signify the imminent coming of Christ. Joseph Smith explained the significance of the rainbow in this connection:

> I have asked the Lord concerning His coming; and while asking the Lord, He gave a sign and said, 'In the days of Noah I set a bow in the heavens as a sign and token that in any year that the bow should be seen the Lord would not come; but there should be seed time and harvest during that year: but whenever you see the bow withdrawn, it shall be a token that there shall be famine, pestilence, and great distress among the nations, and that the coming of the Messiah is not far distant. (HC, 6:254. See also 5:402.)

The Lord, through Joseph Smith, not only confirmed the basic historicity of the flood account, he also confirmed Moses' testimony that the bow originated "in the days of Noah." Whether it had previously rained or not, no rainbow had ever graced the sky. Had the rainbow been a prediluvian phenomenon, it would not have been employed as a sign. A divine sign is never self-contradictory; it never repudiates its own fixed meaning. The bow—which signifies security from a universal flood— could hardly have been observed before the very catastrophe its presence was to prevent! God is faithful; he does not bear a false witness at any time or in any manner. Then too, the designated sign does not exist prior to the thing it represents. The reality precedes its symbol even as the substance precedes its shadow. The "lights in the firmament of the heaven" were organized to "be for signs" of an already existent God and his glory. Sacrifice—the sign of the atonement—followed the appointment of the Savior. Baptism—the sign of rebirth—follows the acceptance of the covenant which makes rebirth possible. (See John 3:1-8; Romans 6:3-11 and

HC, 4:555.) The gifts of the Spirit—the signs of adoption—follow faith, they do not precede them. (See Mark 16:17; D&C 63:7-12; 68:10-13; 84:65-72.) Examples could be multiplied of this principle.

Finally, the very nature of a divine sign requires its close proximity to the principle, event, or ordinance it symbolizes. A sign remote in time or concept from its object (or referent) would be logically meaningless, being unidentifiable with that object. For example, blood sacrifice—the foreordained sign of the foreordained atonement—was not so recognized by Adam until it was directly identified with the Savior's sacrifice by an angel. (See Moses 5:5-7.) The "sign of the Son of Man" as well as the other cosmic signs mentioned in connection with Christ's return will be given just prior to that great event so that their meaning might be unmistakable to the elect of God. (See Matthew 24:30; D&C 88:93-95.) The rainbow met all three conditions for a valid divine sign.

A unique catastrophe had befallen the earth; a unique sign was instituted for a three-fold purpose: 1) to memorialize the event, 2) to give divine assurance that it would not be repeated, and 3) to warn mankind—by its subsequent withdrawal—of the impending return of Christ and of the earth's fiery baptism associated therewith. The night of God's justice was signified by the flood, the day of his mercy by the rainbow. As that day passes and the sun sets, the bow will be seen no more; darkness will creep across the world and the blessed rains—which the Lord has patiently sent upon the just and the unjust—will cease.

Having rejected the divine invitation to life (as signified by the rainbow) mankind will be given a new sign, a sign of judgment, in the form of drought with its grim attendants—famine, pestilence and death. As it was in the days of Noah, so shall it be in that day—with one great exception: men will not look up to flood-laden heavens, instead they will look up to a cloudless sky with its merciless sun beating down upon a scorched and blistered land.[31] The appropriate portent of the burning to come will have been given.

The Aftermath

Almost four months after the flood waters began to recede, Noah began a series of probings to ascertain conditons beyond the immediate vicinity of the ark. His scout was the raven, a strong, indelicate bird

---

[31]Isaiah prophesied that in the time of Israel's latter-day redemption "the light of the sun shall be sevenfold, as the light of seven days." (Isaiah 30:26.)

eminently suited for the assignment. As Noah doubtlessly expected, the raven never returned. It found refuge on the rapidly emerging mountains from whence it could fly forth in search of carrion and the like. It was a bird of death that lived off of the dead. A week later Noah released a dove, only to have it quickly return to the safety of the ark. Upon being released the following week, it returned again; but this time with an olive leaf in its beak. Noah knew that all would be well. The olive tree, so hardy and enduring, so capable of surviving under severe conditions of abuse and neglect, was coming alive.

How appropriate were the signs! The olive tree was designated the divine symbol of Israel, the Father's family in time and eternity. From it sprang the olive leaf—the symbol of the Lord's message of peace and salvation which Israel was chosen and ordained to bring to the nations of the earth.[32] And just as the dove brought the olive leaf to Noah, so was the message of salvation through Jesus Christ to be brought to mankind by the power of the Holy Ghost—of which the dove is the divine and incorruptible symbol.[33] How marvelous are the ways of the Lord! What has been long regarded as the incidental trappings of an ancient tale prove to be nothing less than symbolic prophecies of God's postdiluvian work in bringing to pass the immortality and eternal life of man!

When the dove was released for the third time it did not return. There was no need to. Hope was no longer confined to the ark. The dove's flight back into the world signaled the return of the Spirit of God to the earth. The Lord had not forsaken his children; life and peace were again proffered them.

And so the second world order began with eight human souls. (See 1 Peter 3:20.) Noah and his little family left the ark and entered a rain-washed world where all was fresh and clean and promising. The animals were released to run upon the land, the birds to restore life and song to the heavens. Ancient words were repeated as God renewed the commandment: "Be fruitful, and multiply, and replenish the earth." (See Genesis 8:17; 9:1, 7.) Life was to be given a second chance; man and creature were to go on.

———————

[32]Referring to D&C 88, the Prophet Joseph Smith wrote W.W. Phelps: "I send you the 'olive leaf' which we have plucked from the Tree of Paradise, the Lord's message of peace to us." (HC, 1:316.)

[33]Joseph Smith said: "The sign of the dove was instituted before the creation of the world, a witness for the Holy Ghost, and the devil cannot come in the sign of a dove." (HC, 5:261.)

But a shadow fell across the day; a portent marred the moment. Whereas man, through Adam, had been designated the steward and protector of lesser life in that earlier Eden, now man, through Noah, became its enemy and destroyer: "And the fear of you and the dread of you shall be upon every beast of the earth, and upon every fowl of the air, upon all that moveth upon the earth, and upon all the fishes of the sea; into your hand are they delivered. Every moving thing that liveth shall be meat for you; even as the green herb have I given you all things."[34] If Adam's world—sired as it was by the noblest of men and founded upon the highest principles of truth, mercy and peace—eventually fell to ignominy before a satanic assault, what real hope was there for Noah's world when its very birth was a product of death and its infant beginnings were stained by blood? Truly, there had been a descending; the higher law of reverence for life had been replaced by a lesser law of conflict and death.

Would man limit the taking of life to the animal kingdom? Would he stay his hand from striking down his fellows? He had not done so in a better day, would he do so now? The distinction between the greater and the lesser life became so blurred in the minds of men as to somehow merge all life into one life. Knowing it, the Lord testified to the sanctity of all life by making men accountable for all life.

> And surely your blood of your lives will I require; at the hand of every beast will I require it, and at the hand of man; at the hand of every man's brother will I require the life of man.
> Whoso sheddeth man's blood, by man shall his blood be shed: for in the image of God made he man. (Genesis 9:5, 6. See D&C 49:21.)

Another fall had taken place; the earth was not what it had been in the beginning, nor what it was when Adam and Eve left the Garden. It was a new, but not a better world. For one thing the longevity of man was greatly diminished. Whereas the antediluvian patriarchs lived for many centuries, the lifespan of those enumerated in scripture rapidly declined thereafter. For example, the average lifespan of the nine patriarchs (Enoch being excluded) from Adam to Noah was 912 years, while that of

---

[34]Genesis 9:2, 3. Man and beast were herbiverous before the fall. (Genesis 1:29, 30.) While divine authorization to eat flesh may have been given prior to Noah's time, this passage contains the first known scriptural approval for so doing.

the first nine patriarchs born after the flood was 285 years—a sixty-nine percent drop in life expectancy. Why so drastic a decline? No one knows. The eating of meat has been suggested as a possible contributing cause. However, a more likely explanation may be found in the drastic modification of the environment which attended the flood. Prior to that cataclysm, the upper waters may well have served as a protective screen against the bombardment of cosmic and solar rays to which the earth's surface is constantly subjected. The removal of that screen—whether in whole or in part—when those waters were used in the deluge would have exposed the earth and its denizens to higher levels of radiation therafter. This would have resulted in a decline in longevity more or less proportionate to the increased amounts of natural radiation reaching the earth.[35]

Thus, as the fall set in motion those processes of change and decay which inevitably end in death, the flood—with its attendant modification of the global environment—accelerated those processes of change and decay operative today. Whether this proves correct or not, the fact remains that the heavens and the earth that were "of old" were replaced by "the heavens and the earth, which are now." If this planet's present atmosphere is essentially the same as it has always been, Peter used meaningless terms. (2 Peter 3:5-7.) Geologists do acknowledge that the earth's present disparate climate—ranging from polar frigidity to equatorial heat—is far different from the virtually global tropicality which characterized the primeval planet. Indeed, just such a climate was necessary in order to produce the lush vegetation, dense forests and teeming life forms from which the earth's vast deposits of coal, oil, and gas were subsequently formed.

The world that had been was not the world that emerged from the second global sea. Something had happened to this planet's external character, something profound enough to move the apostle Peter to refer to its antediluvian period as "the old world." (2 Peter 2:5.) Commenting on those who scoff at the doctrine of Christ's eventual return, he wrote:

---

[35]Research into the effects of radiation at *all* levels of intensity, no matter how sublethal, has demonstrated that radiation does "appreciably reduce the life span." Commenting on this fact, Morris and Whitcomb wrote: "If such effects can be observed in a short lifetime as a result of artificial radiations, it is certainly possible that much greater effects on longevity would have been produced over the millenniums by the natural background radiation." (Morris and Whitcomb, *The Genesis Flood*, p. 401.)

For this they willingly are ignorant of, that by the word of God the heavens were of old, and the earth standing out of the water and in the water:

Whereby *the world that then was, being overflowed with water,* perished:

But *the heavens and the earth, which are now,,* by the same word are kept in store, reserved unto fire against the day of judgment and perdition of ungodly men. (2 Peter 3:5-7.)

The "heavens and the earth, which are now" await the coming of creation's Redeemer. He will baptize them in his sanctifying Spirit, thereby completing the saving ordinance begun in the days of Noah. So that while the "wisdom of the world" relegates the immersion of the earth in baptismal waters to the realm of fantasy, it was nonetheless, a magnificent reality, an essential act of preparation for even more wondrous things to come.

CHAPTER EIGHT

Earth is Divided

Mother Earth has grown old; although still beautiful to mortal eyes, the magnificence with which she was originally endowed by her Creator is only dimly perceptible now. She has been shorn of her pristine glory, not only because of her previously cited sufferings but also because of disfigurement and dismemberment. From time to time certain regions of the earth have been radically modified while others have been literally severed from the planet and relocated elsewhere in the heavens.

The Primal Land

The "dry land" that first rose up out of the earth's primordial sea was essentially an island of unknown size. The present continents did not exist. Parley P. Pratt, speaking of Genesis 1:9, declared that "the waters, which are now divided into oceans, seas, and lakes, were then all gathered into *one* vast ocean; and consequently, [the] land which is now torn asunder, and divided into continents and islands almost innumerable, was then one vast continent or body, not separated as it now is.[1]

---

[1]Pratt, *A Voice of Warning*, p. 85. (Italics in the original.) For citations of this statement by John Taylor and Joseph Fielding Smith, see Joseph Fielding Smith, *Man, His Origin and Destiny*, pp. 381-382.

The earth continued to grow as more and more land emerged from the global sea. An example of this growth process occurred less than a thousand years after the fall in the days of the patriarch Enoch: "There also came up a land out of the depth of the sea, and so great was the fear of the enemies of the people of God, that they fled and stood afar off and went upon the land which came up out of the depth of the sea." (Moses 7:14.) The dimensions of this new land are not revealed, but it appears to have been of considerable size.

Enoch's City of Holiness

Enoch, the seventh partriarch,[2] was blessed with a wise and righteous father who taught him "in all the ways of God." (Moses 6:21.) At the age of twenty-five, this remarkable young man was ordained a patriarch (an evangelist) by Adam himself. (See D&C 107:48.) It seems that at about the same time he responded to a divine call to take the message of repentance to the outside world with such zeal that he eventually established a church of God (See Moses 6:26-36; D&C 76:67; JD, 16:48; 21:242; 26:24.) This great prophet, seer and revelator was mighty in word and deed, and his priesthood powers were awesome:

> And so great was the faith of Enoch, that he led the people of God, and their enemies came to battle against them; and he spake the word of the Lord, and the earth trembled, and the mountains fled, even according to his command; and the rivers of water were turned out of their course; and the roar of the lions was heard out of the wilderness; and all nations feared greatly, so powerful was the word of Enoch, and so great was the power of the language which God had given him. (Moses 7:13. See JST Genesis 14:30, 31.)

The church of Enoch grew in both numbers and righteousness to such an extent that, at age sixty-five, he formally established "the City of Holiness, even ZION.[3] It was a spiritual ark wherein the antediluvian

---

[2]Enoch lived *circa* 3378 to 2948 B.C.—430 years before being translated. (See D&C 107:48, 49.)

[3]See Moses 7:19. Adam's blessing upon Enoch may well have been in connection with the establishment of Enoch's city. (See D&C 107:48.)

saints found safety from the wickedness and warfare of the outside world. God "dwelt with his people" thus transforming the city into a microcosm of Christ's world-wide millennial reign. (See Moses 7:16.) So glorious was the City of Holiness that Enoch thought that Zion would "dwell in safety forever." (Moses 7:20.) However, the righteousness of Zion could not save a world drowning in its own carnality. Indeed, the moral degenerecy of the children of men made it impossible for the city to long remain among them. Wilford Woodruff said that Enoch's Zion did not remain on the earth because "wickedness prevailed." Elder Woodruff explained that the "majority of the human family in that generation were wicked; they were not ruled over by the Lord; and, hence, there were not men enough on the face of the earth, in that generation, who were willing to receive the Gospel, keep the commandments of God, and work the works of righteousness, for Enoch to have power to remain on the earth." (JD, 11:242. See also 26:34.) Zion was to endure, but not on this earth. After 365 years, Enoch and his city were taken into the bosom of the Lord, translated to a terrestrial sphere where they remain unto this day. (See Moses 7:21. See also JD, 3:320; 16:49.)

> And Enoch and all his people walked with God, and he dwelt in the midst of Zion; and it came to pass that Zion was not, for God received it up into his own bosom; and from thence went forth the saying, ZION IS FLED. (Moses 7:69. See HC, 5:64.)

Two other scriptural witnesses confirm the reality of this unprecedented event. The writer of Hebrews testified that "by faith Enoch was translated that he should not see death; and was not found, because God had translated him: for before his translation he had this testimony, that he pleased God." (Hebrews 11:5. See Genesis 5:22.) The second witness is found in the Doctrine and Covenants wherein the Savior declared: "I am the same which have taken the Zion of Enoch into mine own bosom. (D&C 38:4.) That his "bosom" is not on this globe was made explicit by the Savior when he identified Enoch and his brethren as those "who were separated from the earth, and were received unto myself."(D&C 45:12.)

Righteous antediluvians were translated to Enoch's city *after* it was removed from earth. "The Holy Ghost fell on many, and they were caught up by the powers of heaven into Zion." (Moses 7:27.) Thus, the City of Holiness became a gathering place for the saints of God in Enoch's generation; they constituted the "general assembly and church of Enoch" gleaned from the nations of the first world order. (See D&C 76:67.)

In her poem, "Address To Earth," Eliza R. Snow wrote:

When Enoch could no longer stay
Amid corruption here,
Part of thyself was borne away
To form another sphere:

That portion where his City stood
He gain'd by right approv'd;
And nearer to the throne of God
His planet upward mov'd.

Wandle Mace quoted Joseph Smith as saying that "when Enoch and his City was taken away, a portion of earth was taken and would again be restored." (Journal of Wandle Mace, Brigham Young University Library, p. 48.)

Thus, it appears that not only were Enoch and his people translated from the earth, but that their city was also literally spirited away![4] Enoch's Zion was not limited to a few square miles of urban streets and buildings; it encompassed a vast rural hinterland as well; for "the Lord blessed the land, and they were blessed upon the mountains, and upon the high places, and did flourish." (Moses 7:17.) Speaking of Enoch's priesthood powers, Brigham Young said: "He obtained power to translate himself and his people, with the region they inhabited, their houses, gardens, fields, cattle, and all their possessions. He had learned enough from Adam and his associates to know how to handle the elements, and those who would not listen to his teachings were so wicked that they were fit to be destroyed, and he obtained power to take his portion of the earth and move out a little while, where he remains to this day." (JD, 3:320. Compare JD, 8:279.)

We may judge something of the dimensions of Enoch's city from its location which was apparently revealed to the Prophet Joseph Smith. Joseph Young (brother of Brigham Young and one of the first seven presidents of Seventies) summarized what he had heard Joseph Smith teach in a discourse given in Nauvoo:

---

[4]This was the understanding of John Taylor (JD, 21:157; 26:34, 89, 90), Wilford Woodruff (JD, 11:242), and Orson Pratt who said that Enoch's people "having learned the doctrine of translation, were caught up into the heavens, the whole city, the people and their habitations." (JD, 17:147. Compare also JD, 8:51; 15:263; 16:49, 50.

The people, and the city, and the foundations of the earth on which it stood, had partaken so much of the immortal elements, bestowed upon them by God through the teachings of Enoch, that it became philosophically impossible for them to remain any longer upon the earth; consequently Enoch and his people, with the city which they occupied, and the foundations on which it stood, with a large piece of earth immediately connected with the foundations and the city, had assumed an aerial position within the limits of our solar system; and this in consequence of their faith. (Joseph Young, Sr., *History of the Organization of the Seventies* [Salt Lake City: Deseret News, 1878], p. 11.

According to Joseph Young, Joseph Smith stated publicly that "the City of Enoch would again take its place in the identical spot from which it had been detached, now forming that chasm of the earth, filled with water, called the Gulf of Mexico." (*Ibid.*, p. 12.)

Whether this statement was based upon personal knowledge or hearsay is unclear. Neither is it clear that Young meant to suggest that Enoch's city occupied the entire Gulf of Mexico. The Prophet may have had in mind a limited region contiguous with the present southern gulf coast of the United States. In time the facts will be known.

The loss of so extensive a portion of the earth did not go unnoticed. While men may have been prevented from observing Zion's actual departure, they certainly became aware of its disappearance. The word went forth: "Zion is fled."[5] Such incredible news must have set atingle the souls of the God-fearing who had been left behind. The more vicious elements of society would have received the news with unalloyed rejoicing. The City of Holiness stood as a living witness against sin and debauchery. Now that witness was no more. Little did men know that the flight of Zion spelled the doom of their dark world: scarcely six hundred years later that world was swept from under heaven in a planet-wide deluge.

But even as Enoch's Zion was taken from among men in a time of spiritual darkness, so will it return in a time of spiritual enlightenment to

---

[5]Moses 7:69. The verb, "fled," is noteworthy. Men did not say that the city had simply sunk into the earth or the sea, they apparently realized that it had actually taken flight. This suggests that there may well have been eye-witnesses to the event. (See JD, 2:212; 21:157 and 26:34.)

add its glory to that of the latter-day Zion of redeemed Israel.[6] Such was the assurance given to both Enoch and Noah by the Lord.

Post-Earth Ministry of Enoch

The Prophet Joseph Smith revealed the astonishing fact that Enoch and his people, having achieved a terrestrial condition, became ministers to peoples of like glory on other worlds of this eternity:

> Now this Enoch God reserved unto Himself, that he should not die at that time, and appointed unto him a ministry unto terrestial bodies...He is reserved also unto the Presidency of a dispensation...He is a ministering angel, to minister to those who shall be heirs of salvation...Their place of habitation [of translated beings] is that of the terrestrial order, and a place prepared for such characters He held in reserve to be ministering angels unto many planets. (HC, 4:209, 210. See also HC, 4:425.)

Since the dwelling place of translated beings is of a terrestial order, it may be that such men as the apostle John and the three Nephite disciples are associating with Enoch and his people in labors that extend to the "outmost parts of heaven." (See HC, 2:261; Deuteronomy 30:4.)

When shown the future sufferings of those who would perish in the flood, Enoch's "heart swelled wide as eternity; and his bowels yearned; and all eternity shook." (Moses 7:41.) His mission as a translated being took him into that eternity for which he had been spiritually prepared. Since he had established a terrestrial Zion on earth and had been appointed to minister to other terrestrial bodies, his mission seems to be centered in the progress of other Zion-like societies on other worlds. Indeed, he knew that God had always gathered such Zions unto himself out of these worlds. (See Moses 7:31.)

Ultimately, this multiplicity of Zions constitutes the one Zion of God even as the New Jerusalem is to be a complex of many Zion-like stakes or

---

[6]The beautiful psalm in D&C 84:100 describes earth's millennial glory and declares: "The Lord hath brought down Zion from above. The Lord hath brought up Zion from beneath." (See also Moses 7:63, 64 and D&C 101:17-23.)

as the three Gods constitute the one God. (See Moses 7:64 and D&C 20:28.) Oneness has ever been the grand objective of the plan of salvation. Christ has said: "If ye are not one ye are not mine." (D&C 38:27.) This principle is universal; all men and all worlds must become one in Christ if he is to claim them as his own. Enoch's mission to "many planets" surely has this object in view. President John Taylor wrote that "the translated residents of Enoch's city are under the direction of Jesus, who is the Creator of worlds; and that He, holding the keys of the government of other worlds, could, in His administrations to them, select the translated people of Enoch's Zion, if He thought proper, to perform a mission to these various planets, and as death had not passed upon them, they could be prepared by Him and made use of through the medium of the Holy Priesthood to act as ambassadors, teachers, or messengers to those worlds over which Jesus holds the authority."(*The Mediation and Atonement*, p. 76.)

Melchizedek and His People

Melchizedek was a high priest after the order of the Son of God, a man of great righeousness and, therefore, of mighty faith.[7] This combination of virtue and authority endowed him with the priesthood power possessed by men who "were translated and taken up into heaven." The text implies that he, together with his people, eventually joined Enoch's Zion which had been translated some fifteen hundred years earlier.

> And his people wrought righteousness, and obtained heaven, and sought for the city of Enoch which God had before taken, separating it from the earth, having reserved it unto the latter days, or the end of the world...
> And this Melchizedek, having thus established righteousness, was called the king of heaven by his people, or, in other words, the King of peace.[8]

---

[7]Melchizedek bestowed the Holy Priesthood upon Abraham and blessed him with all of the riches of eternity. (See JST Genesis 14:40 and D&C 84:14.)

[8]JST Genesis 14:34, 36. A precedent for such translations to Enoch's city was established prior to the flood when worthy saints "were caught up by the powers of heaven into Zion." (Moses 7:27.)

In the Days of Peleg

Ninety years after the flood, a man was born who is identified with one of the most remarkable events in geologic history. His name was Peleg. Genesis rather casually explains that "in his days was the earth divided."[9] The Joseph Smith Translation reads: "And Peleg was a mighty man, for in his days was the earth divided."[10] The use of the preposition "for" suggests that Peleg's mightiness had something to do with the miraculous division of the earth into its present continents—a miracle accomplished through the power of the Holy Priesthood which Peleg held. Such mighty acts have been associated with righteous priesthood bearers from the beginning of time: "For God having sworn unto Enoch and unto his seed with an oath by himself; that every one being ordained after this order and calling should have power, by faith, to break mountains, *to divide the seas*, to dry up waters, to turn them out of their course." (JST Genesis 14:30.) There is no reason to doubt that Peleg, Enoch's descendant, was just such a man.

Regardless of the impact of the fall and the flood on the earth's primal land mass, its division into two separate hemispheres with their distinct islands and continents began, and was apparently completed, during Peleg's lifetime—a period of 239 years.

Orson Pratt believed that whereas the flood had undoubtedly "produced some changes on the surface of our globe," the divison of "the one great antediluvian continent" into the various islands and continents did not occur at that time, but in the days of Peleg. (JD, 18:317. See also JD, 8:195; 17:187 and Pratt, *A Voice of Warning*, p. 87.)

Most scholars believe that Genesis 10:25 refers to a cultural or linguistic rather than to a physical division of the earth. While this viewpoint is certainly more acceptable to the rational mind, it does not square with

---

[9]Genesis 10:25. Peleg means "division" in Hebrew. Referring to Adam's possible dwelling place after his fall, Orson Pratt said: "It might have been upon what we now term the great eastern hemisphere, for in those days the eastern and western hemispheres were one, and were not divided asunder till the days of Peleg." (JD, 16:48.)

[10]JST Genesis 10:16. Peleg lived from 1746 to 1985 years after the fall, or between *circa* B.C. 2254 and 2015. These dates are based on the geneologies found in the books of Genesis and Moses. Abraham may have been alive when the earth was divided since he was about 48 years old when Peleg died.

either scripture or modern revelation. For one thing, Genesis 10:32 states that the descendants of the three sons of Noah comprised the nations which were "divided in the earth after the flood." This is in contradistinction to the division which occurred during the lifetime of Peleg. Then too, Genesis 11 begins with the building of the tower of Babel, goes on to the confounding of man's universal language (with its consequent scattering of the peoples), and then pauses to provide a second abbreviated genealogy of the house of Shem ending with Abraham. This genealogy lists Peleg without restating the explanation given in Genesis 10:25 for his being so named. (See Genesis 11:16.) The parenthetical placement of this modified genealogy of Shem's posterity—coming as it does after the account of the events associated with the tower of Babel—strongly suggests that the earth's division not only followed these events but was a direct result of them!

Continental Drift

Time is vindicating Genesis. The theory that the earth's continents were originally joined together has been confirmed within the last decade. Francis Bacon is credited with advancing the theory four hundred years ago. It was ignored until 1915 when Alfred Wegener, a German scientist-explorer, published a paper in which he asserted that the continents originally consisted of two great land masses which eventually broke up and began drifting apart. Like Bacon, Wegener, was disbelieved. However, in the last fifteen years, marine geologists have amassed a body of irrefutable evidence to the effect that all of the earth's land masses were once fused together into one supercontinent.

In time, this "ur-continent" divided into what is now called Gondwanaland[11] and Laurasia.[12] Then, about 200 million years ago[13] (due to further increasing pressures within the earth's interior) these two

---

[11]Gondwanaland (the Southern Hemisphere) formed Antarctica, Australia, South America, India, and Africa.

[12]Laurasia (the Northern Hemisphere) formed North America Greenland, Europe, and most of Asia.

[13]Given the present distance between the continents and the present rate (two centimeters per year) at which the ocean floor appears to be expanding, geologists have concluded that the continents began moving apart some 200 million years ago.

land masses began breaking up and drifting apart, thereby forming the continents as they exist today. America once joined Europe and Africa at a point about midway in what is now the Atlantic Ocean. America was, therefore, at least three thousand miles closer to Palestine than it is now!

The suggestion that the formation of the major mountain ranges occurred in conjunction with the Flood and the division of the earth in the days of Peleg is supported by current geologic research. It is reasoned that the crust of the earth (about ten miles deep), being composed of comparatively light materials, is "floating" on the heavier materials comprising the earth's mantle (about 2200 miles deep). The upper mantle has broken up into a number of relatively shallow sub-sections called "plates" that are about sixty miles thick and, in some instances, thousands of miles wide. The earth's internal pressures cause these plates to move about, sometimes slipping and sliding over one another. On occasion, in their random movements, the plates have caused their passengers—the continents—to collide with one another, thereby causing them to buckle in the general vicinities of their points of contact. In this way, the Alps, the Andes, the Himalayas, etc., came into being.[14]

The fact that the breakup of the earth's original land mass is causally identified with mountain-building lends much credence to the declaration of Moses in Genesis. That the earth was divided is now the testimony of both scripture and science. Characteristically, the point at issue is not *what* happened, but *when* and *how* it happened.

While it is desirable to receive scientific confirmation of scriptural claims, their ultimate validity is not determined by the position men take on them, whether pro or con. Modern scripture provides a second witness to Genesis 10:25 in an unmistakeable allusion found in the *Doctrine and Covenants*. In a revelation given to the Prophet Joseph Smith in 1831, the Lord declared that when he comes again "the earth shall be like as it was in the days *before it was divided*."[15]

---

[14]The presence of marine fossils at the top of such peaks as Everest is believed to be an evidence that the Himalayas were formed from materials forced up from the ocean floor when the plate carrying India and Australia ground into the Eurasian landmass.

[15]D&C 133:24. Joseph Smith accepted the literalness of Earth's division. (See HC, 1:275.)

Purpose of the Division

The Lord's wisdom in separating the Americas from the eastern continents becomes apparent in the light of postdiluvian history. Doing so has enabled him to apportion the earth among his spirit children according to his eternal purposes relative to the house of Israel. Thus Moses declared that "when the Most High divided to the nations their inheritance, when he separated the sons of Adam, he *set the bounds* of the people according to the number of the children of Israel. For the Lord's portion is his people; Jacob is the lot of his inheritance." (Deuteronomy 32:8,9.) Paul, mindful of Moses' words, told the Athenians that God "hath made of one blood all nations of men for to dwell on all the face of the earth, and hath determined the times before appointed, and the *bounds of their habitation.*" (Acts 17:26.)

It would appear that the Lord did not "set the bounds" of the nations until after the Deluge and the division of the earth in the time of Peleg: the house of Israel did not come into being until a number of centuries after those spectacular events. This suggests that these "bounds" involved more than the mere assignment of different peoples to different portions of the earth. They were actually geologic demarcations designed to control and direct the flow of humanity from one portion of the globe to another! Israel's several lands of promise were scattered across the earth, being preserved behind natural barriers formed of mountains, deserts, jungles, and vast stretches of open sea. (See 1 Nephi 17:38; 2 Nephi 24:2 and Isaiah 24:1,2.) This allowed the Shepherd of Israel to divide and/or isolate his flock as circumstance required. In time all shall realize that the earth was divided (as it was cursed) because of—and for the good of—mankind.

The division of this planet's original land mass is symbolic of the spiritual alienation which presently exists between God and mankind. The Almighty was much closer, in fact and in Spirit, to the antediluvians than he has been to Noah's posterity. [16] It is significant that the glorious reunion of the Creator, Jesus Christ, with the millennial earth will be

---

[16]Brigham Young taught: "The things that pertain to God and to heaven were as familiar among mankind, in the first ages of their existence on the earth, as these mountains are to our mountain boys, as our gardens are to our wives and children, or as the road to the Western Ocean is to the experienced traveller. From this source mankind have received their religious traditions." (JD 9:148.)

accompanied by a like reunion of the earth's land masses. They will be "married" as they were in the beginning—before their "divorce" in the days of Peleg. (See Isaiah 62:1-4; HC, 1:275.)

The Lost Tribes of Israel

Israel's Beginnings

It was more than five hundred years after the flood before the family of Israel came into being. Although Abraham is rightly regarded as the father of the Hebrews, the Israelitish wing of that clan was founded by his grandson, Jacob.[17] His four wives (Leah, Rachel, Bilhah and Zilpah) bore him twelve sons; their descendents comprise the "twelve tribes" of Israel.

The house of Israel was conceived in Mesopotamia, born in Canaan, and attained adolescence in Egypt where it became a slave people with slave ways. Jehovah raised up Moses to offer them the truth that would make them free. They accepted only a portion of that truth and obtained only a portion of the physical and spiritual freedom they might have enjoyed. Subsequent to their exodus from Egypt and the passing of Moses and Joshua, they broke up into a loose-knit confederation of independent tribes held together as much by the constant threat of their alien neighbors as by any common commitment to the law of Jehovah. In time, however, their desire for the security and for the political status enjoyed by neighboring monarchies saw the period of the judges give way to the United Kingdom under Saul, David, and Solomon.

Solomon's death sparked a civil revolt which ended in the division of the monarchy into the Southern kingdom of Judah and the Northern kingdom of Israel or Ephraim. The tribes of Benjamin and Simeon were generally absorbed into Judah, while the remaining tribes identified with Israel. (See I Kings 11:29-36.) The two kingdoms existed side by side in an unstable peace for about two hundred years until, in a period of less than twenty years, the Northern kingdom was vanquished. By 738 it had become a mere vassal of Assyria. Six years later, Tiglath-pileser III (Pul) subdued much of Israel (Gilead, Galilee and the Plain of Sharon) and transported a number of the people to various localities in the empire.

---

[17]The name, Israel, was bestowed upon Jacob when he returned to Canaan after his twenty-year sojourn in Haran. (See Genesis 32:24-28 and 35:10.)

(See 2 Kings 15:29.) Finally, in 721, a three year siege of Samaria,[18] the capital city of Israel, ended in victory for Sargon II who "carried Israel away into Assyria, and placed them in Halah and in Habor by the river of Gozan, and in the cities of the Medes."[19]

Such was the origin of the so-called lost ten tribes.[20] They had been driven from their promised land because they had rejected Jehovah; they had betrayed their ancient covenants and descended to the grossest iniquities. Moses had warned Israel in clear and unmistakeable terms that the breaking of its covenant with Jehovah would result in their expulsion from Canaan and their dispersion among the heathens: "Ye shall be plucked from off the land whither thou goest to possess it. And the Lord shall scatter thee among all people, from the one end of the earth even unto the other." (Deuteronomy 28:63,64. See also 4:25-28; 28:25-37, and Joshua 23:15.) Similar warnings were repeated by Israel's later prophets such as Amos: "For, lo, I will command, and I will sift the house of Israel among all nations, like as corn [wheat] is sifted in a sieve, yet shall not the least grain fall upon the earth." (Amos 9:9.) Commenting on the words of Isaiah, Nephi explained to his brothers that "the house of Israel, sooner or later, will be scattered upon all the face of the earth, and also among all nations."

> Behold, there are many who are already lost from the knowledge of those who are at Jerusalem. Yea, the more part of all the tribes have been led away; and they are scattered to and fro upon the isles of the sea; and whither they are none of us knoweth, save that we know that they have been led away.[21]

---

[18] The siege was prompted by Israel's rebellion against Assyria following an ill-advised treaty with Egypt which Isaiah had warned against.

[19] 2 Kings 17:6. The annals of Sargon II state that 27,290 Israelites were taken captive. However, this figure is probably limited to those more prominent citizens taken in the fall of Samaria; the actual number exiled to Assyria through the years was undoubtedly much larger.

[20] Neither in the Bible or the *Doctrine and Covenants* are these tribes referred to as "lost." However, the term does appear in the *Book of Mormon*. (See 2 Nephi 29:13; 3 Nephi 17:4 and 21:26.) The designation "ten" is found only in 1 Kings 11:31-35 and D&C 110:11.)

[21] 1 Nephi 22:3, 4. See Isaiah 49. The allegory of Zenos (Jacob 5) deals with the varied scatterings of Israel among the nations.

The fullfillment of such prophecies began with the Northern Kingdom, the fate of which was declared by Ahijah more than two hundred years prior to the fall of Samaria: "For the Lord shall smite Israel, as a reed is shaken in the water, and he shall root up Israel out of this good land, which he gave to their fathers, and shall scatter them *beyond the river*, because they have made their groves, provoking the Lord to anger." (1 Kings 14:15. See also 1 Kings 11:31-36.) Although the phrase "beyond the river" is sometimes applied to the Jordan river system, the localities mentioned in 2 Kings 17 suggest that the writer had reference to the Euphrates—the river beyond which lay Halah and Harbor and the cities of the Medes.[22] Indeed, they were the very areas from which Sargon II selected those who were to replace the Israelites in Samaria.

The Samaritans

Honoring the principle of divide and conquer, Sargon II made it a policy to exile a considerable portion of each captive people to distant regions of the empire where they could be assimilated into other minorities. This policy was followed with the Israelites: "People from the lands which I had conquered I settled there." Thus many thousands of Israelites were uprooted and driven from their promised land, and their places were taken by idolaters: "And the king of Assyria brought men from Babylon, and from Cuthah,[23] and from Ava, and from Hamath, and from Sepharvaim, and placed them in the cities of Samaria instead of the children of Israel: and they possessed Samaria, and dwelt in the cities thereof." (2 Kings 17:24.)

In time, many of those Israelites left behind in northern Palestine intermarried with their heathen neighbors, thereby producing a racially and religiously mixed people—the Samaritans. Regarded as mongrelized inferiors, the Samaritans were despised by the Jews even in the days of

---

[22]H. Agrippa warned the Jews not to look for assistance even from their compatriots "beyond the Euphrates" in Parthia should they attempt to revolt. (See F. Josephus, *Wars of the Jews*, Book II, chap. 16:4.) The apocryphal writing, 2 Esdras, states that the ten tribes were carried "over the waters" into another land from whence they eventually crossed the Euphrates in search of "a further country." (See 2 Esdras 13:39, 42.)

[23]Josephus, the first century Jewish historian, wrote that the Assyrians replaced the Israelitish exiles with idol worshippers from Cuthah in Persia. (See F. Josephus, *Antiquities of the Jews*, Book IX, chap. 14.)

Jesus. However, not all of the tribal members had remained in the north; some had moved to Judah even before the fall of the Northern Kingdom, and, in time, others followed.[24] This was easily done since free movement from place to place had never been challenged. Indeed, there was considerable travel and commerce both within and between nations of the ancient world. The number of Israelites who left their homeland and immigrated to other lands—whether voluntarily or otherwise—must have been quite large. Thus a process of dispersion spanning many centuries resulted in the sprinkling of the blood of all twelve tribes throughout the earth. The sheep of the Holy One of Israel were scattered on a thousand hills.

A Remnant Led Away

Scripture indicates that the scattering of Israel was to be of a dual character. On the one hand it involved the assimilation of some Israelites into various ethnic groups to such an extent that their Israelitish origins were lost and they became, for all intents and purposes, Gentiles.[25] On the other hand it involved the preservation of selected remnants from the different tribes by means of geographic and/or cultural isolation or insulation.[26] Such was the case with ancient Israel; Jehovah reserved a remnant of those taken captive to Assyria for himself—"even the tribes

---

[24] See 1 Chronicles 11, 15. Note that although Lehi lived in Jerusalem, he was from the tribe of Manessah. Ishmael, a fellow resident, was from the tribe of Ephraim. (See JD, 23:184; 1 Chronicles 9:3 and Luke 2:36.)

[25] This process had been underway long before the fall of the kingdom of Israel and has continued to the present day. Note the marriage of Judah (Genesis 38) and the fact that a "mixed-multitude" accompanied Israel out of Egypt (Exodus 12:38. See also Numbers 11:4; Leviticus 24:10; Hosea 7:8 and Nehemiah 13:3. The Restored Church is described in Gentile terms even though its members are primarily descendents of Jacob. (See 1 Nephi 10:14; 13:35-40; 15:13; 21:22; 22:8; 2 Nephi 30:2, 3; 3 Nephi 16:6, 7; Ether 12:22; Mormon 5:10, 15; D&C 14:10 and 109:60.)

[26] An example of cultural insulation are the Jews who have retained their fundamental ethnic identity in spite of their worldwide dispersion. Examples of geographic isolation are the people of Enoch, the Jaredites, the Lehites, and the Mulekites.

which have been lost, which the Father hath led away out of Jerusalem."[27]
The Savior seems to distinguish between those Israelites *carried* away by
Sargon II to the *known* land of Assyria and those Israelites *led* away by the
Father to an *unknown* land described by the Savior as being "neither of the
land of Jerusalem, neither in any parts of that land round about whither I
have been to minister." (3 Nephi 16:1.) That land was unknown to
everyone but God—"for they are not lost unto the Father, for he knoweth
whither he hath taken them."[28] Thus, the lost tribes of prophecy were
drawn from the main body of exiles not long after their forced emigration
from the promised land. They are a choice remnant of that remnant of
the Northern Kingdom of Israel which faded from religious history
almost three thousand years ago.[29]

Although there is no extant scriptural record of the exodus of the lost
tribes from Assyria, the apocryphal book, 2 Esdras, provides an account
compatible with all that has been revealed on the subject:

> The ten tribes, which were carried away prisoners out of their
> own land in the time of Osea [Hosea] the king, whom Sal-
> manasar the king of Assyria led away captive, and he carried
> them over the waters, and so came they into another land. But
> they took this counsel among themselves, that they would leave
> the multitude of the heathen, and go forth into *a further country,
> where never mankind dwelt,* that they might there keep their
> statutes, which they never kept in their own land. And they
> entered into Euphrates by the narrow passages of the river.
> For the Most High then shewed signs for them, and held still

---

[27]3 Nephi 21:26. The redemption of the lost tribes is but one phase of
the "work of the Father" in the latter days. (See also 3 Nephi 15:15-17;
16:1-3 and 17:4.)

[28] Nephi 17:4. The whereabouts of the main body of the ten tribes
was supposedly known to the ancient world, as is attested by Flavius
Josephus (*Wars*, Book II, ch. 16, par. 4) and the fifth century church
scholar, Jerome, who wrote that the ten tribes dwelt in the land of the
Medes where they were still subject to Persian rule. (*Commentaries*, vi, pp.
7, 30.)

[29]It is noteworthy that the *Book of Mormon* never refers to the lost tribes as
the *ten* tribes. The actual composition of the lost tribes as they exist today is
conjectural.

the flood, till they were passed over. For through that country there was a great way to go, namely, of a year and a half: and the same region is called Arsareth. (2 Esdras 13:39-45.)

Commenting on this passage, George Reynolds suggested that the only place the tribes could go and be free of all contaminating influences lay to the north "toward the polar star." He believed that they crossed the river Euphrates at a gorge far to the north "so narrow that it is bridged at the top." Reynolds concludes: "How accurately this portion of the river answers to the description of Esdras of the 'narrows' where the Israelites crossed!"[30] In his imaginative description of the further travels of Israel "toward the polar star," Reynolds wrote that, "inasmuch as they had turned to the Lord and were seeking a new home wherein they could the better serve Him, they were doubtless guided by inspired leaders....But what must have been their sensations when they came in view of the limitless Arctic Ocean....The prospect must have been appalling to the bravest heart not sustained by the strongest and most undeviating faith in the promises of Jehovah....No wonder if some turned aside, declared they would go no further and gradually wandered back through northern Europe to more congenial climes." (Reynolds, *Are We of Israel*, pp. 31-33. See also *Juvenile Instructor*, 18 (January 15, 1883), p. 28.)

That there were those of the Northern Kingdom who repented of their past follies and sought to isolate themselves from the heathen world which had been so instrumental in bringing about their downfall is altogether consistent with the ways of the Lord.[31] He has endeavored to remove his people from among the cultures of the world on several occasions. Enoch isolated his people in his City of Holiness. The Jaredites were separated from the people of Babel and brought to a virgin America. Moses and Joshua were instructed to utterly destroy the Canaanites from among them. A remnant of Joseph was led away from Palestine so that they could be isolated from the corrupting influences of the Jews in a land where God could "raise up unto me a righteous branch from the fruit of

---

[30]George Reynolds, *Are We of Israel?*, p. 27, 28. This work is based in part on Reynolds' articles appearing much earlier in the *Juvenile Instructor* and was copyrighted by Joseph F. Smith for the Church's Deseret Sunday School Union.

[31]Orson Pratt wrote: "They must have repented of their sins or God would not have miraculously divided the river for them to pass over." (*Millennial Star*, 29 (March 30, 1867), p. 200.)

the loins of Joseph." And a remnant of that people was led away by Mosiah I prior to the first destruction of the Nephite nation. It is a common scriptural motif.

Jehovah's Other Sheep

There is scriptural evidence that the lost tribes did repent and become faithful to the law of Moses and even worthy of receiving the higher gospel law. It is provided in a prophecy of Zenos. He predicted that in due time the Lord God would manifest himself to all the house of Israel and that he would visit "some with his voice, because of their righteousness." (1 Nephi 19:11.) The Savior fulfilled this prophecy by personally teaching those of the house of Joseph in America who were spared in the destructions associated with his crucifixion because they were "more righteous" than those who perished. He explained to them that he had "other sheep" which were not located either in America or in Palestine who had never heard his voice nor received his ministrations.

By command of the Father, Christ was going to visit them so that they might be "numbered among my sheep." (See 3 Nephi 16:1-3.) That he was referring specifically to the lost tribes is made clear by his announcement to the Nephites: "But now I go unto the Father, and also to show myself unto the lost tribes of Israel, for they are not lost unto the Father, for he knoweth whither he hath taken them." (See 3 Nephi 17:4. See also 3 Nephi 21:26-29.) Thus, the very day on which the resurrected God of Israel first appeared to the house of Joseph in America, his "other sheep"—the lost ten tribes—beheld his face and heard his voice because, as Zenos had prophecied, "of their righteousness."

Although the Messiah ministered to the gathered, but rebellious, sheep of his Jewish fold, they neither heard his voice nor beheld him in his glory. Only the more righteous were so privileged. Nor did he visit any sheep that were intermingled with the Gentiles. The fold of Joseph in America and the fold of the lost tribes in their unknown hiding place were each assembled in one place apart from the known nations of the earth. While the servants of the Lord are obliged to cover the world as fishers and hunters of men, the Shepherd of Israel has not and will not do so. His personal mission is always limited to a physically gathered people.

Parenthetically, there is no reliable evidence whatsoever that the Savior visited any of the scattered blood of Israel in the nations of Europe in 34 A.D. or at any other time subsequent thereto. The pagans of Europe in the first and later centuries were just that, pagans; they did not worship the God of Israel, they did not know of—much less obey—the law of Moses which would have been necessary were they to be considered "righteous" in the legal sense of the word. (See Romans 9:31-10:5.) The identification of Jesus Christ with such pagan deities as Odin, the supreme god of Norse mythology, is quite unsupportable. Nor are there any worthy grounds for the claim that Christ actually visited Britain or any other known country after his resurrection.[32]

Their inhabitants were Gentiles who were ineligible for a personal visitation from the resurrected Christ. For he had told the Nephites that "the Gentiles should not at any time hear my voice—that I should not manifest myself unto them save it were by the Holy Ghost." (3 Nephi 15:23.) Whatever the presence of the blood of Israel among the Gentile peoples of Europe and Great Britain may be, it does not solve the mystery of the whereabouts of those "other sheep" whom the Shepherd of Israel visited following his initial appearance to his fold in America. (See 3 Nephi 16:1-3; 17:4.)

A Single Body

The divine purpose which the Lord had in confounding his chosen people will become increasingly apparent as the end draws near. Israel is the spiritual "salt" of the human family (see Matthew 5:13 and D&C 101:39, 40)—the means by which God's covenant with Abraham will be fulfilled. (See Abraham 2:8-11 and Genesis 12:1-3.) However, in seasoning the earth with the blood of Israel, it was neither necessary nor desirable that all of God's "salt" be poured into the spiritual food of the nations. The needed Gentile-Israelite mixture required only a partial scattering; a remnant of Israel was to be preserved. Parley P. Pratt, a leading nineteenth-century apostle and scriptorian, distinguished between the condition of the Jews and that of the ten tribes. He wrote that the Jews

---

[32]In speaking affirmatively of the British-Israel movement and certain of its concepts, Anthony W. Ivins (of the First Presidency), expressed his belief that Israel was in the British Isles "where we have always known them to be." (CR, (Oct. 3, 1926), pp. 16-18.) However, Elder Mark E. Petersen, in rejecting the British-Israel doctrine, added: "I do not believe we should accept the current views that the lost ten tribes have been found in the northern nations of Europe, or that they have been named, indexed, and classified. I do not believe that we can accept the peculiar notion that the mythical Odin of the North was in reality the Savior of the world performing his work among the northern nations of Europe or the ten tribes." (*CR*, April 5, 1953, p. 83.)

were said to be dispersed because they had been "scattered among the nations." In contrast, Pratt said that the ten tribes are "outcasts because they are cast out from the knowledge of the nations into a land by themselves." (*A Voice of Warning*, p. 29.)

The dispersion of Judah was prophecied in terms almost identical to those used in connection with the scattering of the ten tribes. Speaking of those Palestinian Jews who had not been taken captive into Babylon, the Lord said that he would, "persecute them with the sword, with the famine, and with the pestilence, and will deliver them to be removed to all the kingdoms of the earth, to be a curse, and an astonishment, and a hissing, and a reproach, among all the nations whither I have driven them." (Jeremiah 29:18. See also 7:15; 13:19.)

Jesus also prophecied the world-wide dispersion of the Jews (which followed the fall of Jerusalem in 70 A.D.): "And they shall fall by the edge of the sword, and shall be led away captive into all nations: and Jerusalem shall be trodden down of the Gentiles, until the times of the Gentiles be fulfilled." (Luke 21:24.) And so we see that eventually remnants of all twelve tribes were scattered among the nations. Today, Jews can be found in virtually every country under the sun, yet they are also gathered in the modern state of Israel. So too, while the ten tribes were dispersed throughout the heathen world, yet there is good reason to believe that, in the wisdom of God, a remnant was hidden away in splendid isolation.

This is the plain implication of Joseph Smith's declaration in the tenth Article of Faith: "We believe in the literal gathering of Israel *and* in the restoration of the Ten Tribes." In refuting the belief that Israel exists "only in a scattered condition," Apostle Orson F. Whitney wrote:

> If this be true, and those tribes were not intact at the time Joseph and Oliver received the keys of the gathering, why did they make so pointed a reference to 'the leading of the ten tribes from the land of the north?' This, too, after a general allusion to 'the gathering of Israel from the four parts of the earth.' What need to particularize as to the Ten Tribes, if they were no longer a distinct people? And why do our Articles of Faith give those tribes a special mention? (Whitney, *Saturday Night Thoughts*, p. 174.)

Joseph Fielding Smith wrote: "That they are intact we must believe, else how shall the scriptures be fulfilled? There are too many prophecies concerning them and their return in a body, for us to ignore this fact." (Smith, *Way to Perfection*, p. 130.) James E. Talmage took a like position: "while many of those belonging to the Ten Tribes were diffused among

the nations, a sufficient number to justify the retention of the original
name were led away as a body and are now in existence in some place
where the Lord has hidden them."[33]

With but few exceptions (such as B. H. Roberts), most Church authorities of the past held the belief that the lost tribes were an isolated,
integral body. However, their location has been a matter of much conjecture.

Views on Location of Lost Tribes

Scattered Among Nations

The present whereabouts of the lost tribes has intrigued scriptorians
for centuries. Where are they? The question has produced a number of
answers ranging from the rationally plausible to the seemingly impossible.

The most widely-held view among scholars—being the most
naturalistic—is that the tribes are not lost *to* the world but lost *in* the
world.[34] This is not without apparent scriptural support.[35] They were
gradually, but inevitably, scattered among and assimilated into the
nations and cultures of the Near East and became lost as a recognizable
ethnic society.

---

[33]Talmage, *Articles of Faith*, p. 340. The chapter on the dispersion of
Israel justifies Elder Talmage's statement and is recommended for study.

[34]B. H. Roberts, of the First Council of Seventy, subscribed to this
viewpoint: "I believe, for myself, that within the known regions of the
earth, where the children of men are located, it is quite possible for God to
fulfill all of his predictions in relation to the return of Israel....[They
could not] be lost to the knowledge of God, though now lost to men. And
as it was possible to lose these tribes of Israel among the nations of the
earth, so is it possible for God to recover them from their scattered
condition from among these nations, with a display of the divine power."
Defense of the Faith and the Saints, vol. II, p. 479, 480. A similar view is
advocated in extensive treatments of the subject by two other LDS writers:
James H. Anderson, *God's Covenant Race* and Earnest L. Whitehead, *The
House of Israel*.

[35](See Psalm 44:11; Jeremiah 7:15; 9:16; 16:13; 30:11; 31:10;
Ezekiel 11:16; 12:15; 20:23; 36:17-19; Zechariah 10:9; Daniel 12:7.)

A modification of this view holds that a considerable number of Israelites drifted into Northern Europe and Britain where they eventually merged with the various Teutonic tribes. The fact that the ancestries of most members of the LDS Church are traceable to those areas and that they have been declared to be descendents of Joseph's son, Ephraim, is considered highly supportive of this viewpoint.[36]

However, the arguments advanced in support of the dispersion theory are, in the writer's opinion, unconvincing. When all relevent scriptures—together with the pronouncements of a number of latter-day prophets and apostles—are taken into account, the conclusion seems almost inescapable that one portion of the ten tribes is dispersed among the nations while another portion has been segregated from the rest of mankind.

But for this to be the case, God—a miracle—must be introduced into the matter. For, it is argued, how can there be a civilization numbering in the hundreds of thousands, if not millions, somewhere on the earth unknown to the rest of mankind? Granted, occasionally a small group of primitives has been discovered in some remote corner of the globe, but that is a far cry from the sort of thing envisioned for the lost tribes.

Polar Regions

In his previously cited work, *Are We of Israel?* George Reynolds took the position that the location of the ten tribes in the "frozen regions of the north" was the belief of the Latter-day Saints. (See Reynolds, *Are We of Israel?* pp. 8, 10, 23, 24, 33.) This idea has not been publicly supported by other Church leaders for more than a quarter of a century.

Jeremiah prophesied that the lost tribes would come from (or out of) the "land of the north" or "the north country." (See Jeremiah 3:18; 16:15; 23:8; 31:8.) He is supported by Moroni who, in summarizing the teachings of a more ancient prophet, Ether, wrote that the inhabitants of old Jerusalem will be "gathered in from the four quarters of the earth, *and* from the north countries." (Ether 13:11.) Two modern revelations received by Joseph Smith also affirm that the lost tribes are in "the north countries" and that they will be led "from the land of the north." (See D&C 110:11; 133:26.)

The phrase "land of the north" has been generally understood to refer to the unpopulated regions of the globe beyond the arctic circle.

---

[36]Brigham Young taught that the Anglo-Saxons were the descendents of Ephraim. (See JD, 10:188.)

Consequently most of those who adhere to the unified body concept have argued that the lost tribes are hidden away somewhere in the northern polar regions. However, not one of the passages bearing on the subject explicitly supports such an interpretation. This did not prevent the notion from gaining a foothold both in and out of the Church among some exegetes. Several theories involving that general locale have been advanced; two of them were attributed to the Prophet Joseph Smith in second or third-hand testimony.

Benjamin F. Johnson asked the Prophet Joseph Smith "where the nine and a half tribes of Israel were" and was told that "they are in the north pole in a concave just the shape of that kettle. And John the Revelator is with them, preparing them for their return." (Benjamin F. Johnson, *My Life's Review* (Independence, Mo.: Zion's Printing & Publishing Co., 1947), p. 93.)

A variation on the "concave" location had the ten tribes dwelling inside the earth. This theory was ridiculed in the old *Deseret Weekly*:

> Some think the earth hollow and that at the northern end of the earth there is a great hole. They fancy that the earth is inhabited inside with a race of people, said by some to be what is called the ten tribes, as the statement is made that they journeyed to the north for many days and it seems impossible to many to account for them on the land that they now live on....I cannot believe that they are in any such a locality. (W.J.R., "The North Pole." *The Deseret Weekly*, (June 20, 1896), p. 20, 21.)

The second theory attributed to Joseph Smith is based upon the claimed testimony of his body guard, Philo Dibble.[37] According to the hearsay account, a small sphere lies above and beyond each of the poles on a line with the earth's inclined axis. These two spheres constitute, as it were, the wings of the earth, with the lost tribes supposedly located on the

---

[37] It is a third person account insofar as Philo Dibble is concerned. His son, Sidney Dibble, signed a notarized affidavit in 1906 to the effect that a drawing shown him by M. W. Dalton was a reasonably accurate facsimile of a diagram shown him by his father. He further attested that his father told him that Joseph Smith had given him the diagram in about 1842. However, Sidney did not attest as to any explanation of the diagram. (See M. W. Dalton, *A Key To This Earth*, [Willard, Utah] 1906, p. 86.)

north "wing."[38] A "narrow neck of land" connects each of the spheres to the earth.[39]

Both Johnson and Dibble were men of recognized integrity; there are no grounds on which to question their veracity. However, their accounts appear to be garbled versions of the Prophet's remarks. As such, they are valuable, not for their details, but because they substantiate all other statements attributed to Joseph Smith on the unity and isolation of the tribes.

Among the earliest LDS thinkers known to have advocated a polar setting for the lost tribes were W. W. Phelps and Orson Pratt. After theorizing that there might be more than three and a half billion souls living in unknown parts of the earth, W. W. Phelps continued: "Let no man marvel at this statement, because there may be a continent at the north pole, of more than 1300 square miles, containing thousands of millions of Israelites." He further suggested that they were the branches referred to in the allegóry of Zenos (see Jacob 5) which were planted in the nethermost parts of the earth which brought forth much fruit—since "no man that pretends to have pure religion, can find 'much fruit' among the Gentiles, or heathen of this generation."[40]

Orson Pratt shared Phelps' expansive notion of an arctic civilization "around the pole" not unlike the Shangri-la of Hilton's *Lost Horizon*. He described it as being an unknown region "seven or eight hundred miles in diameter" encircled by "great mountain ranges" and characterized by "deep and extensive valleys" having comparatively mild temperatures. (JD, 18:26. See also JD, 19:171, 173.)

Others, while denying that a polar location for the tribes was either scriptural or doctrinal, have expressed the belief that they could still be hidden from men somewhere in the arctic. In commenting on *Doctrine & Covenants* 133:27, Smith and Sjodahl wrote that Peary's discovery of the

---

[38]The inhabitants, if any, of the south sphere were not identified. It has been speculated that Enoch's city is located there.

[39]A similar diagram was produced by another intimate friend of Joseph Smith, Oliver B. Huntington. The Huntington diagram shows the two objects to be more like bulges or elongations of the earth than separate spheres. (See *The Young Woman's Journal*, 3 [March 1892], p. 264.)

[40]Letter of W. W. Phelps to Oliver Cowdery, *Messenger and Advocate*, Vol. II, No. 1, (October, 1835), p. 194. Unlike Antarctica, there is no land beneath the polar ice cap.

north pole did not prove that the lost tribes were not hidden away in the arctic because "there is a great deal of country in the north that no man, to our knowledge, has visited." Consequently the Lord can "keep them hidden...until it is time for them to be revealed." (Hyrum M. Smith, and Janne M. Sjodahl, *Doctrine And Covenants Commentary*, revised ed., 1950, p. 844.)

Elder Orson F. Whitney expressed a somewhat similar view in writing that "the fact that Arctic explorers have found no such people at the North Pole—where some theorists have persisted in placing them—does not prove that the 'Ten Tribes' have lost their identity. It was tradition, not revelation, that located them at the North Pole...Those tribes could still be intact, and yet much of their blood be found among the northern nations." (Whitney, *Saturday Night Thoughts*, p. 174, note "s".)

Such are the more prominent theories as to the whereabouts of the ten tribes. They virtually exhaust all possibilities: the tribes are either on the earth, above the earth or in the earth; they are either at the pole, near the pole or somewhere beyond the pole. As with the "flat earth" theory, the more we learn about this planet, the less tenable these possibilities become.

The extensive mapping and settlement of the arctic, together with the advanced state of modern geology, renders the idea of a northern hiding place for the lost tribes increasingly unlikely. The whole zone is subject to constant exploration and research. Satellites equipped with cameras capable of photographing virtually any and all objects on the land below are constantly sweeping across the entire earth. Thanks to such technology, probing eyes are everywhere; there is no place to hide even one man, much less an entire civilization. From a rational standpoint it is most improbable that the lost tribes are presently living anywhere in the arctic zone.

Another Sphere

So far as the Church is concerned, the lost tribes are lost: "Where they went and where they are, we do not know." (Smith, *Way to Perfection*, p. 130.) Consequently, while no authoritative answer can be given as to their location, hopefully it will not be amiss to briefly consider one more possibility. Since they are apparently not to be found among the inhabited regions of our globe, and since they are consistently referred to as being in or coming from the north, the only feasible area would seem to lie beyond the arctic circle.

But, as was previously noted, the arctic zone has been well-charted and subjected to ever-increasing development. For a population numbering in the many thousands, if not millions, to be hidden away there, either on or within the earth, would require an unprecedented and uncharacteristic miracle on the Lord's part.[41]

Although scripture is emphatic in declaring that the lost tribes will *come from* the north, nowhere is it written that they actually dwell in the frozen reaches of this planet. Indeed, another possible location is based upon respectable testimony to the effect that they do not. This testimony places them on a portion of this earth among the stars.

Although the extra-terrestial theory is generally ridiculed, being considered the height of credulity by the empirically-minded, the fact remains that a number of Joseph Smith's associates quoted him as teaching it.[42]

Moses assured his people that, although they would be scattered, in a day of repentance they would be "gathered from all the nations." He added: "If any of thine be driven out unto the outmost parts of heaven, from thence will the Lord thy God gather thee, and from thence will he fetch thee."[43] Was this mere hyperbole? Was Moses simply underscoring the certainty of the Lord's promise? Or was he alluding to another segment of Israel that would not be gathered out of the nations but brought back from the "outmost parts of heaven"?[44] Has a remnant of Israel followed the precedent of Enoch and been translated from the earth?

---

[41]It would be unprecedented because a similar miracle is nowhere recorded in scripture. It would be uncharacteristic because it would interfere with the prevailing natural order *over an extended period of time* and constitute a control over human activities on a scale inconsistent with the Lord's established ways.

[42]On the other hand, there is not a single, explicit statement by, or attributed to, Joseph Smith to the effect that the ten tribes are scattered among the nations. All of the Prophet's remarks—direct and hearsay— sustain the view that they are an integral unit lost to the world.

[43]Deuteronomy 30:4. In commenting on this passage, Joseph Smith wrote: "It has been conjectured. . .[that] the ten tribes have been led away into some unknown regions of the north. Let this be as it may, the prophecy I have just quoted 'will fetch them,' in the last days, and place them in the land which their fathers possessed." (HC 2:261.)

[44]Joseph Smith defined "outmost parts of heaven" as being "the breadth of the earth." Both phrases are ambiguous.

Several such testimonies were recorded in his private journal by Charles L. Walker. On 18 October 1880, he heard Addison Everett testify to having heard Joseph Smith say that "the earth had been divided and parts taken away, but the time would come when all would be restored and the earth again would revolve in its original orbit next to Kolob and would be second in size to it. (Walker, vol. II, p. 505.)

On 6 March 1881, Walker records that Jacob Gates gave a sermon in which he told of hearing Joseph Smith in Far West, Missouri, declare that the lost tribes "are hid from us by land and air." Said Bishop [Edward] Partridge: "I guess they are by land and water," in a doubting manner as if Joseph did not know what he was talking about. "Yes," said Joseph, "by land and air they are hid from us in such a manner and at such an angle that the astronomers cannot get their telescopes to bear on them from this earth." (Walker, vol. II, p. 539.)

Daniel Allen's first hand testimony identifed the apostle John with the lost tribes:

> I heard Joseph the Prophet say that he had seen John the Revelator and had a long conversation with him, who told him that he John was their leader, Prophet, Priest and King, and said that he was preparing that people to return and further said there is a mighty host of us. And Joseph further said that men might hunt for them but they could not find them for *they were upon a portion of this planet that had been broken off and which was taken away* and the sea rushed in between Europe and America, and that when that piece returns there would be a great shake; the sea would then move to the north where it belonged in the morning of creation. (Minutes of the "School of the Prophets," (17 August 1872) Parowan, Utah, pp. 156, 157.)

Bathsheba W. Smith testified that she was about twenty years old when she heard Joseph Smith preach that "Peradventure, the Ten Tribes were not on this globe, but a portion of this earth cleaved off with them, went flying into space, and when the earth reels to and fro like a drunken man, and the stars from heaven fall, it would join on again."[45]

After praising Joseph Smith's ability to clarify and expand the meaning of scripture, Wandle Mace cited an occasion when he had reached an

---

[45]"Recollections of the Prophet Joseph Smith," *Juvenile Instructor*, (June 1, 1892), 27:344. Bathsheba was the wife of George A. Smith.

impasse as to the whereabouts of the lost tribes since—if they had multiplied proportionately to the Jews—"where is there habitable earth for this vast amount of people who are hidden from the rest of mankind?" His question was answered by the Prophet in a Sunday morning discourse on the restitution of all things:

> In the course of his remarks he spoke of the earth being divided at various times. He said, 'When Enoch and his City were taken away, a portion of earth was taken and would again be restored. Also in the days of Peleg, the earth was divided...' He then referred to the Ten Tribes, saying, 'You know a long time ago in the days of Shalmaneser, king of Assyria, the Ten Tribes were taken away, and have never been heard of since.' He said, 'The earth will be restored as at the beginning, and the last taken away will be the first to return, for the last shall be first, and the first shall be last in all things.' ...These remarks satisfied me, it was no longer necessary to hunt the place on this earth where the Ten Tribes were so long hidden, for the earth was divided and taken away, and will be the first to return, as it was the last taken away. (Journal of Wandle Mace, pp. 38, 39. Brigham Young University Library.)

Writing in the *Millennial Star*, Parley P. Pratt expressed the same basic idea: fragments of the earth have been broken off—"Some in the days of Enoch, some perhaps in the days of Peleg, some with the ten tribes, and some at the crucifixion of the Messiah." (*Millennial Star*, I (February, 1841), p. 258.)

Among other notable persons who gave similar testimony was Eliza Roxcey Snow, sister of Lorenzo Snow and a plural wife of both Joseph Smith, and after his death, Brigham Young. One stanza of her poem, "Address to Earth," reflects her understanding of the subject:

> And when the Lord saw fit to hide
>   The *"ten lost tribes"* away,
> Thou, earth, wast sever'd to provide
>   The orb on which they stay.

In view of the fact that the poem was included in Church hymnals for some fifty years, it would appear that its doctrinal validity was acknowledged during the administrations of Brigham Young, John Taylor, Wilford Woodruff, and Lorenzo Snow.

There is good reason to believe that Eliza R. Snow obtained her views on the lost tribes—and other matters as well—from Joseph Smith. In a signed statement, Homer M. Brown described an experience had by his grandfather, Benjamin Brown:

> "Brother Brown, will you give us some light and explanation of the 5th verse on page 386 of the Hymn Book which speaks of the Ten Tribes of Israel, or the part of this earth which formed another planet, according to the Hymn of Eliza R. Snow?"
>
> "Yes, sir, I think I can answer your question. Sister Eliza R. Snow, in visiting my grandparents, was asked by my grandmother: 'Eliza, where did you get your ideas about the Ten Lost Tribes being taken away as you explain it in your wonderful hymn?'
>
> "She answered as follows: 'Why, my husband (The Prophet Joseph) told me about it."[46]

In confirmation of Sister Snow's testimony, Patriarch Brown then told of a conversation between his grandfather and the Prophet concerning the ten tribes. Responding to the question of their location, Joseph Smith is said to have taken Benjamin Brown and his wife outside and, pointing to the north star, asked them: "Now do you discern a little twinkler to the right and below the Polar Star, which we would judge to be about the distance of 20 feet from here?" They answered in the affirmative and then returned to the house. (Smith, *The Last Days*, pp. 211-213.)

Brown's testimony is corroborated in two entries in the private journal of Charles L. Walker, a friend of Eliza R. Snow. He reports that in a prayer meeting on 11 February 1881, a "Sister Green" told of hearing Eliza R. Snow "speak of the 9 and 1/2 lost tribes being on an orb and would eventually come back to the(i)r former place and we should know when they came by certain signs etc., etc." (Walker, vol. 2, p. 532.) These remarks may have prompted Walker's visit to Eliza R. Snow a month later during which the division of the earth was discussed:

----

[46]Robert W. Smith, *The Last Days*, p. 77. The statement of Homer M. Brown was made in the presence of Theodore Tobiason and Israel Call. Elder Brown was serving as a patriarch in the Granite Stake of the LDS Church in Salt Lake City, Utah at the time.

She told me that she heard the Prophet Joseph say that when the 10 tribes were taken away the Lord cut the earth in two, Joseph striking his left hand in the center with the edge of his right to illustrate the idea and that they (the 10 tribes) were on an orb or planet by themselves and when they returned with the portion of this earth that was taken away with them the coming together of these 2 bodies or orbs would cause a shock and make the 'earth reel to and fro like a drunken man.' She also stated that he said the earth was now ninety times smaller now than when first created or organized.[47]

Wilford Woodruff's journal entry for September 8, 1867 explicitly states that Brigham Young also attributed the extraterrestrial concept to Joseph Smith: "We had social conversation in the evening. President Young said *he heard Joseph Smith say* that the Ten Tribes of Israel were on a portion of land separated from this earth." (Church Archives, Salt Lake City, Utah. Spelling and punctuation corrected.) In his biography of Wilford Woodruff, Matthias Cowley summarizes the foregoing journal entry thusly: "The leaders on their return from Provo made a visit to Logan. Here, President Young is quoted as saying that the ten tribes of Israel are on a portion of the earth, —a portion separated from the main land." (Cowley, *Wilford Woodruff*, p. 448.)

A Possible Reconciliation

It might be argued that the three theories attributed to Joseph Smith, being contradictory, negate one another, making it unnecessary to seriously consider any one of them. However, the combined testimonies of such responsible persons as Brigham Young, Wilford Woodruff, Parley P. Pratt, Eliza R. Snow, Bathsheba W. Smith, and Wandle Mace cannot be lightly dismissed. They obviously carry greater weight than the less supported declarations of Benjamin F. Johnson and Philo T. Dibble. Even so, the contradiction between the three theories may be more apparent than

---

[47] Walker, vol. 2, p. 540. The statement that the earth is now ninety times smaller than its original size may have been a misunderstanding on Walker's part since another account indicates Eliza R. Snow said it was nine times smaller. Parley P. Pratt declared it to be several times smaller.

real. The lost tribes *did* journey northward and they did not do so capriciously—they must have had a destination in mind. That destination may well have been the type of climatically-tempered region Johnson claimed the Prophet described. If such were the case, then a land mass of considerable size once existed in that now frigid zone—a lost continent.

This brings us to the second theory which is based upon the supposed testimony of Dibble to his son, Sidney. The notion of a sphere joined to the earth at or near its northern axis by a narrow causeway of land is manifestly ludicrous. At best it can only be regarded as a garbled version of the Prophet's actual statement. He may have poetically described the two spheres as the "wings" of the earth which—when they return—will be folded much as a bird's wings are folded against its body. (See D&C 88:45.) Dibble may have assumed that the two spheres were, therefore, literally connected to the earth in wing-like fashion. By so qualifying this aspect of the Dibble account it ceases to differ materially from the better-attested extra-terrestrial theory. Both views place the tribes beyond the earth; the major point at issue would be the distance involved.

If the tribes are hidden in space, they must have undergone a change similar to that which will come upon those saints living at Christ's return who will "be quickened and be caught up to meet him." (D&C 88:96. See 1 Thessalonians 4:17.) While no vehicle would have been required to transport the Israelites, their departure could have involved a portion of the earth like Enoch's city. That portion could have been the "concave" of Johnson's testimony—the "north country" of scripture which was originally a part of the polar regions but later "broken off" and conveyed to a distant point in space, probably near the north or polar star. (This might explain Joseph Smith's instructions to Benjamin Brown.)

Why is there no land around the north pole? Antarctica covers the south pole, but a frozen sea covers the north pole. Has it always been this way, or were both poles once covered by land? If they were, what happened to the land around the north pole? Was that land the "north country" of the lost tribes? Was it the vehicle used in removing them to a distant location in space? Will it return to its former location in due time? Is this the reason the tribes will come from the north? Is this how a highway will be cast up in the midst of the great deep? Is the polar sea that "great deep?" Is this why the ice will flow down at their presence?

If we answer with a guarded "yes" to these questions, then the tribes could have traveled to that region, dwelt in an area characterized by a temperate climate for a time and then been transported from the earth. While this is admittedly conjecture, still it does reconcile the various statements attributed to Joseph Smith by all of those previously quoted.

Conclusion

If the present whereabouts of the lost tribes were to be made known to anyone it would most likely be the Lord's own prophet. But so far as we know, none of Joseph Smith's successors claimed personal revelation on the matter. This prompts two questions. First, did Joseph Smith actually teach the extra-terrestrial theory ascribed to him by such prominent personalities as Brigham Young, Wilford Woodruff, and Eliza R. Snow? One's answer to this query depends upon the credence given their statements. Certainly they were persons of responsible character who were closely associated with Joseph Smith for a number of years. Although minor elements in their respective testimonies may be at variance, all agreed on the essential points. On what basis can we impugn their word? The accuracy of their testimonies is accepted on other items of history, why challenge their reliability or integrity on this issue?

Still, granting that the Prophet Joseph Smith did so teach, a second question must be asked: What was the source of his views? Were they based upon divine revelation, or were they simply his own speculations on the subject? This question is presently unanswerable. The statements attributed to him were made in comparatively private conversations rather than in known public discourses. But whether in private or in public, their prophetic validity remains a matter of opinion. Lacking any solid evidence to the contrary, it appears that the God of Israel did reveal the general stellar location of the lost tribes to Joseph Smith—the prophet who was given the keys for the gathering and the leading back of all twelve tribes.

The teaching that Enoch's city was literally translated to a terrestial sphere is also attributed to Joseph Smith by some of the same persons who testified that he taught an extra-terrestrial locale for the lost tribes. Therefore, the same two questions posed about these tribes must be asked in connection with Enoch's city as well. It is the writer's opinion that Enoch's Zion was literally and miraculously removed from the earth. The God of miracles can repeat his miracles; the lost tribes could have likewise "fled" into space. For if they are not hidden on the earth, they must be hidden in the heavens—otherwise, as Joseph Fielding Smith asked, "How shall the scriptures be fulfilled?"

CHAPTER NINE

Earth in the Meridian of Time

Signs of the Savior's Birth

The birth of the Creator caused the heavens to rejoice and to be further glorified by the presence of a new star unlike any that had been seen before. It was observed on both the eastern and the western hemispheres and was altogether a fitting sign of Jesus Christ, that "bright and morning star" who will usher in the perfect day of peace when he ascends his millennial throne.[1] Its appearance was accompanied by a most remarkable phenomenon in America: a period of over thirty hours of unbroken daylight.[2] The skies were filled with light even though the sun had set as usual. Samuel, the Lamanite, had prophecied this miracle five years earlier: "There shall be great lights in heaven, insomuch that in the

---

[1]See Helaman 14:5; Matthew 1:10; 3 Nephi 1:21 and Revelation 22:16. The heavenly signs seem to have been prepared for the scattered house of Israel rather than for the Gentile nations. Appropriate signs were undoubtedly given to peoples on other earths as well.

[2]This daylight may have lasted thirty-three-hours—one hour for each year of the Savior's life.

167

night before he cometh there shall be no darkness, insomuch that it shall appear unto man as if it were day." (Helaman 14:3.)

The "light of the world" had come among men so that no one need walk in darkness or be in bondage to their fallen natures in a fallen world. He had come to free mankind from the penalties, the curses, pronounced in the "first judgment" (see 2 Nephi 9:7) when the earth's fall reduced man to laboring for his daily bread.[3]

The Creator Suffers

Nullifying a cause results in nullifying its effects[4]; in atoning for Adam's transgression, the Savior ultimately freed mankind from its negative consequences as well.[5] He met the law's demands sweat for sweat—the sweat of the Son of God for the sweat of Adam, the sweat of spiritual agony for the sweat of physical exertion. Jesus had told his disciples: "But I have a baptism to be baptized with; and how am I straitened till it be accomplished!" (Luke 12:50) Although he had previously been baptized by John in the gentle waters of Jordan, he endured a second, infinitely painful immersion when he descended below all things in Gethsemane. It was there that he laid down his very soul for mankind. Trembling under the combined weight of humanity's guilt, he bled at every pore in the bloody baptism of his incomprehensible atonement. (See Luke 22:44; and D&C 19:18.) He sweated his life's blood so that—whether for Adam's transgression or for their own sins—no one need sweat without hope again. The sacrifice that was to lift the ancient curse from both man and creation had been made.

In an ironic, poignant act of gratuitous savagery, the thorns that marred the earth following Adam's transgression were fashioned into a mock crown by Jesus' tormentors and viciously crushed down upon his brow. Thus, as he hung upon the cross of Golgotha, he wore the cruel

---

[3]Moses 4:23-25. This judgment is still in force; indeed, it became increasingly severe as additional curses befell later generations because of their own abominations.

[4]See, for example, Mark 2:9.

[5]Although Jesus Christ has atoned for the fall, its natural consequences will not be reversed until the earth is regenerated in connection with his latter-day return. He will come with healing in his wings so that the earth can, once more, yield of her strength. (See Malachi 4:2; Ezekiel 34:27 and D&C 59:3.)

symbol of that fallen world he had come to redeem! Jesus' impalement on the "tree" provided the visible tokens of his spiritual crucifixion, and of God's all-encompassing love—spirit and element, the soul of the Redeemer, had been offered upon the altar of sacrifice to the law's demands. He had made himself "a curse for us." (Galatians 3:13.) Therefore the cry: "Eli, Eli, lama sabachthani"—"My God, my God, why hast thou forsaken me?"—was not his alone, rather it was the cumulative cry of a mankind that, in forsaking God, had also been forsaken.[6] The sinless Son of God not only personified the pains of all men, but he bore a lost testimony to his own redemptive mission in their behalf.

Creation's Compassion

The Spirit of God envelops and permeates all his creations, uniting them as one organism. (See D&C 88:41.) It is in him that all things live and move and have their being. (See Acts 17:28.) Therefore, each part of the cosmic body affects, however minutely, that body as a whole. Each life is a qualification of all life; for life is locked into life. And the greater the life, the more it influences every other life. The Creator is the preeminent example of this truth. Jesus Christ, the embodiment of the Spirit of God, is in all and through all things. When he trembled under the agonies of Gethsemane and Golgotha, all nature responded with empathic pain. This statement is not intended as poetic hyperbole. So perfectly attuned is the Creator to his creations that when certain Pharisees objected to Jesus' disciples shouting, *Blessed be the king that cometh in the name of the Lord,* Jesus responded: "I tell you that, if these should hold their peace, the stones would immediately cry out." (Luke 19:40.) If failure to witness to the kingship of Christ would have provoked the very stones to break their silence, would nature have remained indifferent to his death?

Indeed, the Creator's sufferings evoked a lament from earth that could not be suppressed—a lament that could only be discerned by the most spiritual of men. The superb prophet Enoch was such a man; he enjoyed the gift of interpretation of tongues where nature was concerned. He heard the earth cry: "Wo, wo is me, the mother of men; I am pained, I am weary, because of the wickedness of my children. When shall I rest, and be cleansed from the filthiness which is gone forth out of me? When will my Creator sanctify me, that I may rest, and righteousness for a

---

[6]Psalm 22:1 and Matthew 27:46. Psalm 22 is messianic in nature, being a prophecy of the redemptive mission of Jesus Christ.

170   *The Footstool of God*

season abide upon my face?"[7] Enoch's whole being comprehended and empathized with the emotions of Mother Earth: "And when Enoch *heard* the earth mourn, he wept, and cried unto the Lord, saying: O Lord, wilt thou not have compassion upon the earth?" (Moses 7:49.) Jesus' crucifixion was the supreme offense against the earth whose elements had provided his very flesh and blood. Is it any wonder she reacted to this outrage as to no other? Enoch saw the Son of Man lifted up on the cross and "he heard a loud voice; and the heavens were veiled; and all the creations of God mourned; and the earth groaned and the rocks were rent." (Moses 7:56.) The prophet Zenos confirmed Enoch's vision when he wrote that "the rocks of the earth must rend; and because of the groanings of the earth, many of the kings of the isles of the sea shall be wrought upon by the Spirit of God, to exclaim: The God of nature suffers." (1 Nephi 19:12. See also Romans 8:19-23.)

Signs of the Atonement

As Jesus hung upon the cross, the different parts of the earth (as with any body) responded with greater or lesser agitation to the trauma it was experiencing. (See 3 Nephi 8:19.) In Jerusalem there was three hours of darkness followed by a mild earthquake during which the heavy veils (or curtains) of the temple were torn from top to bottom. The significance of

---

[7]Moses 7:48. The earth speaks with the voice of the Spirit of God which permeates its being. The mind and heart of the Father are, in turn, the source of the voice and passions of his Spirit. (See D&C 88:6-13.) Orson Pratt said: "When that Spirit, which is thus diffused through all the materials of nature, undertakes to converse with the minds of men, it converses in a different kind of language from that we use in our imperfect state. It communicates ideas more rapidly—more fully, and unfolds a world of knowledge in a moment." (JD, 3:102, 103.) Brigham Young asked: "What filthiness has gone forth out of her? You and I, and all the inhabitants of the earth; the human body, and all earthly bodies, both animal and vegetable." (JD, 1:274.) Even as the earth is defiled by that which emanates from her, so is man defiled by that which comes out of him. (See Mark 7:15.)

this event was undoubtedly lost at that time to all but the most discerning of Jesus' disciples.[8]

Such was not the case with the house of Israel in America.[9] The sign given them was both graphic and unforgettable, taking the form of unparalleled natural disasters in those lands inhabited by the Nephite-Mulekite nation. However, these calamities did not come unannounced; they were predicted nearly fifty years in advance by Samuel, the Lamanite prophet.[10] He prophecied that at the time that Christ "yielded up the ghost," the sun and the moon and the stars would "refuse to give light" for three days (until the resurrection). Samuel further declared that there would be "thunderings and lightnings" for many hours, that the "earth would shake and tremble," and that rocks, above and beneath the earth, would be "broken up." Also, there were to be "great tempests" and "many mountains" were to become as valleys while many valleys were to "become

---

[8]The ripping of the massive curtains which separated the outer holy place from the inner holy of holies was surely a deliberate act of the Lord by which he signified several things. Foremost was the fact that God's eternal High Priest had, by the sacrifice of his own life, entered the presence of the Majesty on High once and for all—thereby ending forever the need for, or the legitimacy of, the annual ritual of the levitical high priest on the day of atonement. (See Hebrews 9.) It also marked the end, as prophecied by Jacob, of Judah's spiritual primacy over Israel. (See Genesis 49:10.) Further, it symbolized the end of the Mosaic covenant. Even as Moses' smashing of the original tablets containing the higher law ended Israel's ancient abortive gospel dispensation, so did the tearing of the temple curtains signify the end of Israel's subjection to the lesser law of carnal commandments. (See Matthew 27:51; Mark 15:33; Luke 23:44; and JST Exodus 34:1,2.)

[9]Upheavels were experienced even on the isles of the sea. (See 1 Nephi 19:11, 12.)

[10]Nephi had forseen these destructions in a vision given him over five hundred years earlier. (See 1 Nephi 12:4, 5.)

mountains." Finally, highways were to be "broken up," and many cities were to be destroyed.[11]

The prophet Mormon provides us with a graphic summary of the divine judgments which overtook Israel in America. A storm of unheard of fury lashed the land. There was "a great and terrible tempest; and there was terrible thunder, insomuch that it did shake the whole earth as if it was about to divide asunder. And there were exceeding sharp lightnings, such as never had been known in all the land." (3 Nephi 8:6, 7.) Cities were hurled into the angry maw of the sea or inundated as its waters poured in upon them. Others disappeared when the earth parted to swallow them up. Still others became fiery ruins or were leveled to dust-laden rubble by the violence of rock grinding on rock. A great mountain was formed as a natural tombstone over one city when an incredible mass of earth was carried up and over it in one gigantic surge. Northward, the "whole face of the land was changed," making it impossible to determine its original geologic features. All of this in three hours! Then came the darkness— darkness so thick, so impenetrable as to defy every effort to produce light. (See 3 Nephi 8:21, 22.) The darkness which blanketed those ancient lands for three days was both a symbol of the spiritual darkness of those who perished and a reminder to us all of what our fate would be were it not for Jesus Christ, the Light of the world.

The severity of the judgments which befell American-Israel were not equaled elsewhere in the known world. This was due in part to the fact that they had been blessed with greater spiritual enlightenment than any of their contemporaries.[12] They had been led by prophets for six centuries. They had been given a heaven-inspired government. The church of God had been among them for more than a hundred years. They had known of Christ and made solemn covenants with him. In fine, much had been given; much was expected. Yet apostasy was rampant among them.

---

[11]Helaman 14:20-24. The chaos which accompanied the death of the Creator is symbolic of the chaotic state all nature would be in were it not for him.

[12]God's labor was with Israel, not the Gentile nations whose opportunity to receive the Gospel was yet in the future. The calamities associated with Christ's death were, therefore, directed against the rebellious of Israel, not the world at large. (See 1 Nephi 19:11.)

And so they had brought the heavy judgments of God upon themselves—for judgment begins at the house of the Lord.[13]

However, the calamities which befell the Nephite-Mulekite nation were not merely punitive in nature: they also served to purge the land of those who were hardened in sin and rebellion against God. Thus, only the more righteous survived the holocaust. (See 3 Nephi 9:11-13.) The cleansing of that society of its living abominations paved the way for the personal visitation of the resurrected Christ some months later. Further, by removing the incorrigibles, it became possible for the Lord to establish his Church and kingdom among the Nephites in greater fulness than ever before. A new foundation was laid in righteousness upon which a Zion-like order was built which thrived for more than a century and a half.[14] The spirit of the Priesthood dictated all that Christ did: in using the forces of nature against them he reproved American-Israel with sharpness; but in blessing them with his presence and his kingdom, he showed forth an increase of love.

The Scandal of Eternity

In crucifying their Messiah, Jesus' enemies among the Jews did what no other men would have done; for as the prophet Jacob noted, "there [was] none other nation on earth that would crucify their God."[15] Jesus came to Jerusalem—the one place on earth where his life would be taken. But more than this, he seemingly came to the one world that could have provided a Golgotha! It appears that no other earth harbors such appalling wickedness, such incredible insensitivity to the Spirit of God as does

---

[13]See 1 Peter 4:17; D&C 112:24-26. Judah also suffered grievously after their rejection of Jesus as the Christ. (See Matthew 24:1-22 and 1 Nephi 19:13, 14.)

[14]The destruction which preceded the coming of Christ to Israel in ancient America is prophetic of the last days. Prior to the world coming of Christ, the wicked will be decimated with natural calamities and then utterly destroyed when he comes in glory to establish the kingdom of God in its millennial fulness.

[15]2 Nephi 10:3. This indictment applies to the religious leaders and hierarchy who actually plotted his death, not to the Jewish people as a whole.

our beleagured planet. Sin plummeted to its nadir on this earth; it has
fallen as no other creation has fallen. Glorious and beautiful in the
beginning, it gave birth to the best and the worst of men—Christ and his
saints, and Cain and the murderers of God. The judge of all things
handed down the ultimate indictment of this world when he told Enoch
that of "all the workmanship of mine hands there has not been so great
wickedness as among thy brethren." (Moses 7:36.) "Perhaps this is the
reason Jesus Christ was sent here instead of some other world," wrote
Joseph Fielding Smith, "for in some other world they would not have
crucified Him, and His presence was needed here because of the extreme
wickedness of the inhabitants of this earth." (Smith, *The Signs of the Times*,
p. 12.)

What an ignominious distinction! Man has turned this planet into the
scandal of eternity. He has made it a moral slum, unworthy of even the
feet of an angel in his glory.[16] Yet, it seems to be a truism that neither men
nor worlds can rise higher than they are capable of descending. The
power to do good is proportionate to the power to do evil. Thus, Earth,
having been capacitated to fall to the depths of degredation, will rise to the
heights of glory. For as Brigham Young supposed, "God never organized
an earth and peopled it that was ever reduced to a lower state of darkness,
sin and ignorance than this. I suppose this is one of the lowest kingdoms
that ever the Lord Almighty created, and on that account is capable of
becoming exalted to be one of the highest kingdoms that has ever had an
exaltation in all the eternities." (JD, 10:175.)

Creation Travails

Earth, like an aging widow, mourned the death of her Creator. She
was in the dark hours before her deliverance. In prophesying of these
latter-days, Isaiah wrote: "The earth mourneth and fadeth away, the
world languisheth and fadeth away, the haughty people of the earth do
languish." (Isaiah 24:4.) Neither Earth nor the Lord's people can be truly
happy with the status quo.[17] Both man and Earth were created in glory for

---

[16]This appears to be literally true since no authentic account of a
glorious angelic visitation describes the messenger as touching the
ground. (See D&C 110:2; JS-History 2:17, 30 and Revelation 1:15.)

[17]Brigham Young maintained that "happiness that is real and lasting
in its nature cannot be enjoyed by mortals, for it is altogether out of
keeping with this transitory state." (JD, 1:2. See also D&C 101:36 and
Alma 37:45.)

glory. Both fell to achieve a greater glory. For this reason, Earth and the sons and daughters of God who dwell on her are in a state of anxious anticipation.[18] The apostle Paul felt that all creation was poised on the hope of Christ's emancipating return: "For we know that the whole creation groaneth and travaileth in pain together until now." (Romans 8:22.) Creation's pain, suffered in consequence of the fall and the atonement, reached its zenith in the meridian of time—the spiritual crossroads of human history.

Earth has not forgotten the sacrifice of its Lord. It not only bears record of him as Creator, but it also testifies of him as Redeemer and Savior. The atonement is written upon the face of this planet in the language of nature. It is memorialized by the scarred earth. It is witnessed by the agonized formations of fragmented rock and twisted mountains. It is spoken of by divided lands and lands beneath the sea. The testimony is there for every seeing eye and every discerning heart. It was meant to be so; the most momentous event since the fall was not to go un-memorialized.

[18]Only those who have been overcome by the world are fully content in it. (See John 17:14-17; Hebrew 11:13-16; D&C 45:11-14.)

CHAPTER TEN

Earth in Latter Days

Time is running out for our world. We are living in the closing moments of Earth's sixth temporal day—the day before the day on which the Savior will return and the world as we know it will be no more.

> Behold, now it is called today until the coming of the Son of Man....For after today cometh the burning—this is speaking after the manner of the Lord—for verily I say, tomorrow all the proud and they that do wickedly shall be as stubble; and I will burn them up, for I am the Lord of Hosts; and I will not spare any that remain in Babylon. (D&C 64:23, 24. See also D&C 45:6.)

The Creator divided the mortal lifespan of this earth into seven periods, or days, of a thousand years each. (See D&C 77:6; HC, 5:64 and JD, 26:200.) The period from Adam to Christ consumed approximately the first four thousand years—or the first four days of the earth's week. Earth's "last days" (or weekend) began two thousand years ago in the meridian of time, or, in other words, on Friday. (See Hebrews 1:2; 2 Timothy 3:1 and 2 Peter 3:3.) This is that period of human history termed "the Saturday evening of time." (Whitney, *Saturday Night Thoughts*, pp.

9-13 and JD, 26:200.) Soon there will be "time no longer."[1] For the beginning of Earth's second sabbath marks the end of telestial time insofar as this fallen world and Satan (its alien god) are concerned.

Mighty events are prophesied in connection with the return of Earth's creator and rightful King. The heavens and the earth will unite in a common testimony of unprecedented majesty and power as sign upon sign trumpets the fall of the kingdom of the devil and the end of his world. (See D&C 88:87-94.) These portents will begin on the earth and end in the heavens. Although droughts, famines, pestilences, earthquakes, volcanic eruptions, tidal waves, etc., are strewn through the history of mankind, their climactic forms have been reserved for the judgments of the last days; the worst is yet to come!

Withdrawal of the Spirit

The invisible sign of the approaching end of Earth's telestial days is the withdrawal of the Spirit of the Lord, the fading of the light of Christ. The Spirit of the Lord is the fountainhead of those natural forces man has identified. It is the ultimate power from which all lesser powers derive. It is the divine mortar which binds all creation together in one orderly, harmonious structure. It is the organizing, governing, and sustaining principle in all things. In the total absence of the Spirit, there can only be aimless chaos. Indeed, where the Spirit is not, there will be a certain madness—the insanity of meaningless, uncomprehending existence. To the extent that the Spirit is manifest to less than an optimum degree, there will be proportionately greater disorder and decay. Simply stated, the less the light, the greater the darkness. This law of life applies everywhere and to everything throughout the dominions of God. Where God is not, life is not. His Spirit flows forth from his presence to infuse life into life. (See D&C 88:11-13.) However, man's retention of the Spirit requires that he live his life in harmony with the will of the Giver of that life.

Relative death is the wage of those who refuse to live their life in harmony with God's will. The greater their deviation from the divine standard, the greater their damnation and spiritual death. The world with its myriad varieties of contrasting ethical, moral, and religious types is a kaleidoscope of the degrees of glory to be found in both time and eternity. The Almighty's patience is not limitless; there comes a time when his Spirit will no longer strive (labor) with men. (See Genesis 6:3; I Nephi

---

[1]See D&C 84:110; Revelation 10:6. Time as such, being a concommitant of matter, never ends; it is eternal. (See HC, 6:474.)

7:14; Moroni 8:27, 28, 9:34; Ether 2:15 and D&C 1:33.) When men knowingly and willfully reject him to the spiritual point of no return—the point where their cup of iniquity is hopelessly full—God has no choice but to reject them. Satan has claimed them for his own and "he doth seal you his." (Alma 34:35.) Thus we have the agency to drive the Lord out of our lives, (see Moses 7:32-37) but we do so at the inevitable peril of enslavement to the enemy of our souls.

There is no third road for mankind; like it or not, we will be ruled either by the powers of peace and happiness of by those of strife and misery. While in this vacillating life, our inconstancy brings us under the influence of both God and Satan, in the life to come we will faithfully serve either the one or the other.[2] Satan rewardeth "no good thing." (Alma 34:39; 30:60.) When he is allowed to prevail the consequence is always destructive. Nephi warned that the "Spirit of the Lord will not always strive with man. And when the Spirit ceaseth to strive with man then cometh speedy destruction, and this grieveth my soul." (2 Nephi 26:11.) The flood, Sodom and Gomorrah, and the ancient civilizations in America are testimonies to this truth. The prophet Mormon encapsulated the foregoing when he summarized the downfall of the Jaredite nation: "The Spirit of the Lord had ceased striving with them, and Satan had full power over the hearts of the people; for they were given up unto the hardness of their hearts, and the blindness of their minds." (Ether 15:19.) The Jaredite tragedy was but another example of the eternal truth that two opposing principles can no more rule the human soul than can two separate physical bodies occupy the same given space.

The brilliance with which the Spirit—the light of Christ—bathed the primeval earth in glory faded with the fall and has generally continued to diminish thereafter. This lessening of spiritual light is quite undetectable to a world already groping in a darkness of its own making, but it is readily perceptible to the people of the Most High—"the children of the day." (See I Thessalonians 5:5.) They know that we are living in the twilight of the Spirit—a twilight produced by man's persistent rebellion against those principles of intelligence the Almighty ordained for human progress and happiness. In August, 1831, Jesus Christ told Joseph Smith: "I, the Lord, am angry with the wicked; I am holding my Spirit from the inhabitants of the earth." (D&C 63:32.) In January 1833 the Prophet alluded to this revelation and said that the withdrawal of the Spirit was an obvious fact:

---

[2]Most of mankind will eventually repent and be delivered from Satan's influence.

"The governments of the earth are thrown into confusion and division; and *Destruction*, to the eye of the spiritual beholder, seems to be written by the finger of an invisible hand, in large capitals, upon almost every thing we behold."[3]

Our generation is witnessing the acceleration of this withdrawal process. The decline in genuine moral and religious commitment has become a cliche of the times. Newspapers, books, magazines, motion pictures, television, and lecture halls spew forth an endless barrage of commentary, analyses, and examples of this retreat from righteousness—few and far between are those who decry it. The loss of the Spirit is the death of love. The pitiful, drunken mourners at its wake are ever the same: pride, lust, jealousy, fear, strife, and division. They will be out in force as the last days come to an end; men "will be drunken with iniquity and all manner of abominations." (2 Nephi 27:1.) Sin is a spiritual intoxicant, and it will cause love in all of its manifestations to "wax cold." (See Matthew 24:12 and D&C 45:27.) As it was in Paul's generation, so shall it be in our own: "Men shall be lovers of their own selves, covetous, boasters, proud, blasphemers, disobedient to parents, unthankful, unholy, without natural affection, truce breakers, false accusers, incontinent, fierce, despisers of those that are good, traitors, heady, highminded, lovers of pleasures more than lovers of God; having a form of godliness, but denying the power thereof: from such turn away." (2 Timothy 3:2-5.)

The Lord's indictment of this generation becomes more unassailable with each passing day: "Every man walketh in his own way, and after the image of his own god, whose image is in the likeness of the world." (D&C 1:16.) This apostasy from the true god is the basic cause of the moral and social deterioration of our race. We are afflicted with such man-engendered plagues as sexual license, infidelity, divorce, delinquency, crime, strife, and war. These social diseases have, in turn, begotten nearly all of the pain, misery, and suffering to which flesh is heir.

Man-Made Calamities

As the violation of moral law inevitably results in social upheaval, so does the violation of physical law produce natural upheavals. Our inability

---

[3]HC, 1:314. (Italic in original.) While the Spirit is being withdrawn from the nations, it will not depart from those who love the Lord and keep his commandments. (See *ibid.*, p. 231.)

to discern the causal relationship between human behavior and the predicted judgments of the last days does not preclude the possibilitiy of such a relationship. The divine dictum that we reap as we sow is not limited to any given time, place, or circumstance. This generation is experiencing some of the natural consequences of our long and increasing misuse of the earth's resources. In many places, the land has been denuded of its forests and woodlands, subjected to relentless planting and overgrazing, and otherwise abused. The varying wages of these sins have been the devastating erosion of vital top soil, the formation of vast new deserts, and widespread flooding. The gravest human concomitants of these disasters are famine, disease, and death for literally millions, especially in the backward nations of Asia and Africa.

The earth's waters have been similarly mistreated. The much-publicized overharvesting of its great fishing grounds is but one example. Oil drilling rigs, tanker ships and, surprisingly, automobile exhaust emissions combine to blanket the sea with millions of tons of petroleum pollutants yearly. To this may be added more millions of tons of industrial and human waste—along with the rest of civilization's trash—which has been callously discharged for many decades into the earth's once clear and pure waters. For some time, competent marine biologists have been expressing growing alarm over the logarithmic speed with which the marine life cycle is being disrupted with a resultant loss of from 30 to 50 percent of both plant and fish life in the last twenty-odd years alone! These authorities warn that the waters, which cover 70 percent of the globe's surface, are relatively shallow when compared to the total bulk of the planet. Being so, they cannot be considered a "bottomless sewer." Indeed, the sea's ability to cleanse itself has long since been overwhelmed by staggering amounts of man-originating pollutants. Unless this dumping practice is stopped, it is believed that a few more decades will bring death to the earth's dying oceans.

The impact of chemical pollutants on the quality of our air and water is readily apparent; they are part of the visual environment. Such is not the case with the unseen dimension of the environment which lies beneath the earth's surface. It is from these regions that man has obtained the richest plunder of all, petroleum and natural gas. A few short years have seen this vast treasure greedily depleted. This plundering has been compounded by another: the pumping of billions of gallons of water from the planet's aquifers to make arid land productive, to provide for steadily growing and proliferating communities, and to meet the enormous demands of heavy industry. The result has been a steady and, in some places, alarming drop in the water table. As with the rest of earth's bounties, there is only a finite amount.

What will be the long range effects of these losses? Were these vast quantities of gas, oil, and water more closely associated with the earth's dynamics than we have supposed? Did they somehow serve to stabilize its internal forces? Is there a causal relationship between the relentless emptying of the earth's veins and arteries and the predicted future upsurge of earthquakes, tidal waves, and volcanic eruptions in "diverse places?"[4] Whatever the facts prove to be, one thing appears certain: our greedy consumption of these precious resources portends more than an inconvenience for future generations. It is a sign of the times. Would it not be ironic if man's very efforts to plunder the earth in the name of progress should become a key factor in the destruction of his vaunted civilization?

It is also significant that the world's last epoch should be the repository of all the genius, knowledge, power, and accomplishment of the race—the grand summation of the works of man, good and bad, for the past six thousand years. This epoch has its divine counterpart in the dispensation of the fulness of times in which all of the knowledge, keys, powers, principles, and ordinances of all previous dispensations are being gathered in one. Thus, this is the climactic age of confrontation between the two, great opposing kingdoms of God and Satan. (See D&C 1:35, 36, and 38:12.) Only one will survive.

The Wrath of God

Man's immoral treatment of the earth, with its attendant disastrous results, is but one more evidence of the fact that we are punished as much by our sins as we are for them. Consequently, the prophecies concerning the last days should not be regarded as the petulant, arbitrary threats of a vengeful deity, but as the concerned forewarnings of an omniscient Father. The phrase, "wrath of God," engenders the image of a furiously offended Being. However, the term is simply an impressive way of personalizing the natural effects of broken law. Disobedience is the real precursor of the divine judgments which will be meted out by a just Father upon his rebellious children with ever-

---

[4]A number of articles and books have been published on the "Gaia hypothesis" by a group of earth scientists who maintain that the earth is not a neutral, impassive entity, but a living body with the equivalence of senses, intelligence, and the capacity to act. "If men continue to antagonize it, the earth will become the most dangerous opponent ever to face the human race."

increasing frequency and force. Their wickedness has resulted in imposing God's wrath on themselves by imposing it on him.

Because God is obliged to honor the law he represents, his hands are tied; he cannot forever ignore the persistent defiance of the law and retain his own integrity. Divine justice could only be denied at the expense of God's position as God. (See Alma 42:13, 22, 25.) His fall would bring all organized creation crashing down around him like Samson in the temple of Dagon. But our merciful Father has never willed pain and misery for his children. He has ever been the innocent victim of their guilt. How infinitely gracious he has been in accepting the necessary suffering which that guilt has imposed upon him and his Beloved Son.

The Lord's Sermons

The *Doctrine and Covenants* contains the Lord's "voice of warning" to this generation—a contemporary prophecy of things to come in the not-too-distant future. As such, it speaks plainly and not in parables, allegory, or metaphor as is the case with most of the prophetic writings of the Bible.[5] It tells us that the voice of judgment will grow intermittently louder and louder until it falls silent "for the space of half an hour" and then rises to a climax in the unveiling of the face of Jesus Christ.[6]

Now is the day of mercy, the day when the Lord's servants are carrying his invitation to the wedding feast of salvation to the nations. (See Matthew 22:1-14.) Unfortunately, few are accepting their message; the voice of warning is generally ignored. Consequently, the testimonies of the servants will soon be replaced by that of their Master: "And after your testimony cometh wrath and indignation upon the people." (D&C 88:88.) At that time the Lord will deliver his own sermons; not in words but in awesome deeds whereby he will raise his voice in a last call to repentance—a call that will send the heavens and the earth into

---

[5] The *Doctrine and Covenants* provides the plainest and most detailed information regarding the last days and subsequent events to be found in all scripture. It is the key to the book of Revelation and those works of a similar nature found in the Old Testament, much as the *Book of Mormon* is the key to an understanding of the gospel of Jesus Christ as found in the New Testament.

[6] See D&C 88:95; Revelation 8:1 and JD, 7:51.

unprecedented commotion.[7] Tempests in the form of tornadoes, hurricanes (typhoons), and the like will be unleashed with mounting frequency and fury. Shattering electrical storms will rock the heavens with ear-tingling thunders and vivid lightnings. (See D&C 43:22, 25; 87:6 and 88:90.) These will trigger widespread fires and devastating hailstorms. (See D&C 43:25 and 109:30.) One in particular—the last?— will apparently be world-wide in scope: "There shall be a great hailstorm sent forth to destroy the crops of the earth." (D&C 29:16. Compare Revelation 16:21.) All these calamities, together with engulfing tidal waves, land-smothering volcanic eruptions, and deadly earthquakes, will combine their voices in crying, "Repent! Repent!" (See D&C 29:13, 16; 43:18-25; 45:33, 41; 87:6, 88:89-91; and 2 Nephi 6:15; 27:2 and Mormon 8:29, 30.) This cry will be heard by all peoples; most of whom will be suffering, in varying degrees, the natural consequences of the forenamed disasters: drought, famine, disease, and pestilence. (See D&C 43:25; 84:97; 87:6; Revelation 15:16; 18 and JST Matthew 24:30.) But in addition to these historic plagues, the *Doctrine and Covenants* predicts "an overflowing scourge; for a desolating sickness shall cover the land" so painfully lethal that men will "lift up their voices and curse God and die." (D&C 45:31, 32. See *Ibid.*, 5:19 and Revelation 9:6.)

It has been suggested that the above is actually a description of the symptoms of exposure to lethal amounts of radiation, the by-product of an atomic war. Perhaps. The journal of Wilford Woodruff contains an account of a vision given John Taylor the night of December 16, 1877, in which he was shown latter-day conditions reminiscent of those depicted in Zechariah and the *Doctrine and Covenants*. President Taylor described the effects of some strange malady which swept the world producing agonizing death for apparently millions. A grisly account of conditions in New York City in which he referred to men hiding in cellars or "coverts" is especially noteworthy:

> I found myself in Broadway New York and here it seemed the people had done their best to overcome the disease. But in wandering down Broadway I saw the bodies of beautiful women lying stone dead, and others in a dying condition on the sidewalk. I saw men crawl out of the cellers and rob the dead bodies of the valuables they had on and before they could return to their coverts in the cellars they themselves would roll over a time or two and die in agony. On some of the

---

[7]The judgments of the last days will differ more in degree than in kind from those which have been meted out to the present time.

back streets I saw mothers kill their own children and eat raw flesh and and then in a few minutes die themselves. Wherever I went I saw the same scenes of horror and desolation rapine and death. (Journal of Wilford Woodruff, June 15, 1878. Church Archives.)

A chillingly graphic passage in an earlier revelation received by Joseph Smith seems to provide a word picture of this "desolating sickness":

Wherefore, I the Lord God will send forth flies upon the face of the earth, which shall take hold of the inhabitants thereof, and shall eat their flesh, and shall cause maggots to come in upon them; And their tongues shall be stayed that they shall not utter against me; and their flesh shall fall from off their bones, and their eyes from their sockets; And it shall come to pass that the beasts of the forest and the fowls of the air shall devour them up. (D&C 29:18-20.)

The prophet Zechariah described the fate of the latter-day enemies of the Jews in almost identical terms when he wrote that "their flesh shall consume away while they stand upon their feet, and their eyes shall consume away in their holes, and their tongue shall consume away in their mouth."[8]

In 1950, President George Albert Smith warned that "it is only a question of time, unless they repent of their sins and turn to God, that war will come, and not only war, but pestilence and other destruction, until the human family will disappear from the earth . . .It will not be long until calamities will overtake the human family unless there is speedy repentance. It will not be long before those who are scattered over the face of the earth by millions will die like flies because of what will come." (CR, April 5, 9, 1950, pp. 5, 169.)

These statements are not prophetic hyperbole; the categorical prophecies which deal with the end of the world will be fulfilled. (See D&C 1:7, 37, 38; 101:64; 109:44-47.) And all will be accomplished speedily: "For thus saith the Lord, I will cut short my work in righteousness, for the days come that I will send forth judgment unto victory." (D&C 52:11)

---

[8]Zechariah 14:12. (See JD, 14:351.) Orson Pratt identified this passage with the millennium rather than the last days. (See JD, 21:325.)

Why Latter-day Calamities?

We reiterate, the calamities of the last days should not be regarded as merely the vengeful responses of an offended God; their purposes are multiple and essential to the salvation of mankind. In the very beginning, Adam learned that creation is a witness for God: "All things have their likeness, and are created and made to bear record of me." (Moses 6:63.) Creation not only testifies of the Creator's existence, but also of his attributes, not the least of which are mercy and justice. The former is seen in the smiling, life-sustaining ways of nature; the latter in its dark, threatening moods. The sun that blesses, also burns; the rains that bring life can sweep it away. Both reveal God; both are valid expressions of his holy nature; both exemplify the two roads which lie before all men. Joseph Smith wrote that "our heavenly Father is more liberal in His views, and boundless in His mercies and blessings, than we are ready to believe or receive; and, at the same time, is more terrible to the workers of iniquity, more awful in the executions of His punishments, and more ready to detect every false way, than we are apt to suppose Him to be." (HC, 5:136.)

Man's experiences with God and nature are of his own making. If they appear inconstant and perverse, it is only because we, by our inconstant and perverse lives, have elected to have them so.[9] The calamities of the last days constitute the Almighty's last reminder to the world of this fact. In addition to provoking at least some of the wicked to repent, the judgments are also designed to accelerate the sifting process which will transfer the morally bankrupt element of society to the spirit world where they will be prepared for eventual resurrection into a kingdom of glory.[10] Then too, while the earth's upheavals are one of the means by which this separation will be accomplished, their ultimate purpose is to bring about the restoration of the planet's primeval form and character. Thus, by ridding it of those who persist in defiling it with their pollutions, and by restoring it to its Edenic condition, the earth will be made ready for the rule of her Creator and King.

---

[9] Recall Paul's words to the rebellious saints in Corinth: "What will ye? Shall I come unto you with a rod, or in love, and in the spirit of meekness?" (1 Corinthians 4:21.)

[10] Only those qualified to dwell upon the earth in its millennial (paradisaical) state will survive the judgments preceding and attending the return of Christ.

Return of the Lost Ten Tribes

One of the most awesome events to occur in the not-too-distant future is the descent of the lost tribes from their hiding place in the land of the north. They will return as part of the great in-gathering of Israel in anticipation of the Holy One's pre-advent appearance to his people in Zion, the New Jerusalem.[11] Thus, there will be "one fold and one shepherd" before the Lord is manifest to the Gentiles at the time of his world coming. (See 3 Nephi 15:17.) The place of the lost tribes in the prophetic scheme was pinpointed by the angel Moroni at the time of his instructions to young Joseph Smith in 1823. After prophesying of the coming forth of the Book of Mormon, of the rise of the Church, and of the persecution which would attend the latter-day work, Moroni continued:

> Then will persecution rage more and more, for the iniquities of men shall be revealed, and those who are not built upon the rock will seek to overthrow this church; but it will increase the more opposed, and spread farther and farther, increasing in knowledge till they shall be sanctified and receive an inheritance where the glory of God will rest upon them; and when this takes place, and all things are prepared, the ten tribes of Israel will be revealed in the north country, whither they have been for a long season; and when this is fulfilled will be brought to pass that saying of the prophet— 'And the Redeemer shall come to Zion, and unto them that turn from transgression in Jacob, saith the Lord.'[12]

Keys for Leading Tribes

Israel's ingathering is a vital part of the restitution of all things wherein, as Joseph Smith wrote: "a whole and complete and perfect union, and welding together of dispensations, and keys, and powers, and glories should take place, and be revealed from the days of Adam even to the present time." (D&C 128:18. See also Ephesians 1:9, 10.) This great harvest must include the redemption of righteous Israel,

---

[11]Orson Pratt taught that the lost tribes would come to America *after* the latter-day Zion had been built. (See JD, 18:22-25, 68 and 16:325.)

[12]*Messenger and Advocate*, 2 (October, 1835), p. 199. (Excerpt from account of early history of Joseph Smith by Oliver Cowdery.) See also Isaiah 59:20.

both physically and spiritually. The authority for Ephraim, the elder brother of Israel, (see Jeremiah 31:9) to accomplish this labor was given to Joseph Smith and Oliver Cowdery in the Kirtland Temple on April 3, 1836, by Moses himself: "Moses appeared before us, and committed unto us the keys of the gathering of Israel from the four parts of the earth, and the leading of the ten tribes from the land of the north."[13] Note that the *gathering* of Israel from the four parts of the earth is distinct from—and apparently preliminary to—the *leading* of the tribes from the land of the north. Clearly, the two activities, while related, are not to be equated as one. (See, Smith, *Way to Perfection*, p. 130.)

John the Revelator

John the apostle's desire to continue to bring souls to Christ until his return was granted so that John might do a greater work and "prophesy before nations, kindreds, tongues and people."[14] And so, in time, John became a translated being, no longer subject to the limitations of mortality.[15] The "greater work" assigned to John included the responsibility for overseeing the "gathering in" and "sealing up" of the twelve tribes of Israel preparatory to Christ's coming. (See Revelation 7:2-4; D&C 77:9, 14.) This mission was symbolized in John's vision by the "little book" which, when he ate it, was sweet in his mouth but bitter in his stomach.[16]

John has been laboring among the nations of the earth for more than nineteen centuries. In doing so he has also ranged far and wide in ministering to the scattered peoples of Israel. In the absence of the Shepherd, John has become the guardian of his flock. According to

---

[13]D&C 110:11. It has been conjectured that Joseph Smith, as a resurrected being, will turn the key for the ten tribes and be an active participant in the mighty events associated with their exodus to the land of Zion. (See D&C 133:26.)

[14]D&C 7:3. See John 21:20-23. A similar request was made by three of the Nephite disciples who also became translated beings. (See 3 Nephi 28:4-10.)

[15]The powers of translated beings are defined by Christ himself in 3 Nephi 28:7-9.

[16]See Revelation 10. Note that the Savior's summary of John's labors in D&C 7:3 are restated in Revelation 10:11.

John Whitmer's report of the fourth general conference of the Church held June 3-6, 1831: "The Spirit of the Lord fell upon Joseph in an unusual manner, and he prophesied that John the Revelator was then among the Ten Tribes of Israel who had been led away by Shalmaneser, king of Assyria,[17] to prepare them for their return from their long dispersion, to again possess the land of their fathers." (HC, 1:176.) Orson Pratt said that "John the Revelator will be there, teaching, instructing and preparing them...for to him were given the keys for the gathering of Israel." (JD, 18:25. See Smith, *Way to Perfection*, p. 131.) John's assignment to "minister for those who shall be heirs of salvation who dwell on the earth," does not necessarily preclude a labor to regions beyond the earth. In addressing the general conference of October, 1840, the Prophet Joseph Smith referred to translated beings and said that "their place of habitation is that of the terrestrial order, and a place prepared for such characters He held in reserve to be ministering angels unto many planets." (HC, 4:210.) If a remnant of the ten tribes were transported to another sphere, the mission given John would require that he minister to them on that sphere, and the powers prossessed by him as a translated being would enable him to do so. But regardless of the hiding place of the lost tribes whether it be outer space or some unknown region of the earth—they will be led back with a high hand and the outstretched arm of Jehovah.

The Second Exodus

The exodus of Israel from Egypt involved the mass movement of hundreds of thousands—if not millions—of men, women, and children together with their livestock and other possessions. It was an undertaking of enormous proportions; a miracle in the truest sense of the word. Yet great as it was, the return of the lost tribes will cause it to pale by comparison. Jeremiah prophecied:

> Therefore, behold, the days come, saith the Lord, that it shall no more be said, The Lord liveth, that brought up the children of Israel out of the land of Egypt;
> But, The Lord liveth, that brought up the children of Israel from the land of the north, and from all the lands whither he

---

[17]Shalmaneser V began the siege of Samaria, but died before its fall. His successor, Sargon II, completed the leading away of the ten tribes.

had driven them: and I will bring them again into their land that I gave unto their fathers.[18]

The work of the "fishers and the hunters" in carrying the message of salvation to the nations and gathering out the believing blood of Israel—"one of a city, and two of a family"—is *not* a mass movement comparable to the exodus of ancient Israel. (See Jeremiah 16:16; 3:14.) Only the return of a multitude numbering in the millions can satisfy Jeremiah's prophecy. And such will be the case! The most detailed revelation on the return of the lost ten tribes was appropriately given to Joseph Smith:

> And they who are in the north countries shall come in remembrance before the Lord; and their prophets shall hear his voice, and shall no longer stay themselves; and they shall smite the rocks, and the ice shall flow down at their presence.
> And an highway shall be cast up in the midst of the great deep.
> Their enemies shall become a prey unto them,
> And in the barren deserts there shall come forth pools of living water; and the parched ground shall no longer be a thirsty land.
> And they shall bring forth their rich treasures unto the children of Ephraim, my servants.
> And the boundaries of the everlasting hills shall tremble at their presence.
> And there shall they fall down and be crowned with glory, even in Zion, by the hands of the servants of the Lord, even the children of Ephraim.
> And they shall be filled with songs of everlasting joy.
> Behold, this is the blessing of the everlasting God upon the tribes of Israel, and the richer blessing upon the head of Ephraim and his fellows. (D&C 133:26-34.)

This categorical revelation is explicit on several points. The lost tribes will come from the north. (See Isaiah 43:6; 49:12; Jeremiah 3:18; 6:15; 23:8; 31:8 and D&C 110:11; Ether 13:11.) Their destination is America, the

---

[18]Jeremiah 16:14, 15. See also Jeremiah 23:7, 8; 31:7, 8 and HC, 2:357. The dual redemption of Israel, involving both a gathering in and a leading back, stated so explicitly in D&C 110:11, is also inferred in these and other Old Testament passages.

land of Zion, for "unto it all the tribes of Israel will come."[19] They will be led by "their prophets" who are preparing them to rejoin the rest of the family of Israel and to receive the fulness of the Lord's blessings.[20] In cautioning against the notion that "we are the only people who will have Prophets," Orson Pratt said that only "a portion of the Priesthood will be there." Consequently "the fulness of the blessings of the Priesthood" will be "given to them after they come to Zion." (JD, 18:25. See also JD, 18:38 and 2:201.)

When the divine command is given, their prophets will "stay themselves" no longer in their present hiding place in the "north countries." And even as the mountains shall flow down and the seas boil at the presence of Christ in his glory, so will the glacial rocks melt and their icy waters flow down at the presence of the returning tribes. This suggests that the very manner in which they make their appearance will release an energy force sufficiently great to melt the frozen reaches of the north![21] A land bridge—a highway to Zion (see Isaiah 11:16.)—will miraculously appear in the arctic ocean over which the tribes will then journey southward into America—for has not the Lord "made the depths of the sea a way for the ransomed to pass over?" (Isaiah 51:10.)

Enemies A Prey

The tribes will not be allowed to enter North America without opposition; they will be confronted with "enemies" seeking to repel them as invaders as well as coveting their "rich treasures."[22] But it will be a futile enterprise; Israel will vanquish their "prey" and proceed on to the land of

———————

[19]HC, 1:315. The tribe of Judah will gather to Palestine rather than to America.

[20]See JD, 4:231, 232. The only true prophets in the known world are those associated with the Church of Jesus Christ of Latter-day Saints. The Prophets ministering to the lost tribes will become subject to their keys and authority. (See D&C 133:32.)

[21]It has been theorized that the heat created by the friction produced when the earth's missing fragments are restored will be a factor in melting the frozen wastes of the arctic. (See Smith, *The Last Days*, pp. 79, 80.)

[22]The fact that the tribes will be confronted with enemies clearly suggests that their return will be prior to Christ's coming since all of the remaining wicked will be destroyed by that consuming event.

Zion. (See Isaiah 11:14.) Thus, the return of the ten tribes will occur in a period of social and natural upheaval when "the boundaries of the everlasting hills shall tremble at their presence." For as Orson Pratt said, "this great Rocky Mountain range, extending from the arctic regions south to the central portions of America, will tremble beneath the power of God at the approach of that people." (JD, 18:24. See also Psalm 114.)

America will not then have teeming masses of people crowded into a virtually continent-wide megalopolis such as exists today. The wickedness of men and the judgments of God will have combined to greatly reduce the population. In a letter to the editor of a Rochester, New York, paper in 1833, Joseph Smith prophecied by the "authority of Jesus Christ" that "pestilence, hail, famine, and earthquake will sweep the wicked of this generation from off the face of the land, to open and prepare the way for the return of the lost tribes of Israel from the north country." (HC, 1:315. See also HC, 3:391; JD, 17:4, and 21:301.)

Isaiah prophecied that Israel would "break forth on the right hand and on the left;" and that their "seed" would "inherit the Gentiles and make the desolate cities to be inhabited."[23] It would seem, therefore, that the empty cities of America will become the dwelling places of Joseph and his companions.

Treasures

All Israel, including the ten tribes, was bound by the law of Moses until freed from it by Christ at his death. Thereafter, the resurrected Lord visited the lost tribes and revealed the new and everlasting covenant to them so that they might be gathered unto himself—"one fold and one shepherd." (See 3 Nephi 16:3; 17:4.) Having risen to the saving grace of the gospel of Jesus Christ, the lost tribes have been and are now being prepared to rise even higher to the exalting grace made possible through the holy endowment with its associated sealings and anointings. All Israel is destined to receive the word of the Lord "line upon line" so that they might rise in glory from "grace to grace." Only in this way can the promises made to Abraham be kept perfectly.

Moses prophecied that the house of Joseph would "push the people together to the ends of the earth." (Deuteronomy 33:17.) The Church— predominantly the blood of Joseph through Ephraim and Manasseh—is now engaged in a world-wide missionary effort which will partially fulfill

---

[23]Isaiah 54:3. See 3 Nephi 22:3. The Savior's reference to Isaiah's prophecy was made in the context of the fate of the Gentiles in America, the land of Joseph.

Moses' prophetic charge. Joseph Smith explained that one of the main objects in the gathering effort was to "build unto the Lord a house whereby He could reveal unto His people the ordinances of His house and the glories of His kingdom, and teach the people the way of salvation." (HC, 5:423.)

Consequently, the "rich treasures" of the lost tribes will doubtlessly include essential genealogical, as well as scriptural and historical, records. (See 2 Nephi 29:13; JD, 19:172; 21:301.) In a proclamation to the world in 1845, the quorum of the Twelve declared that "the ten tribes of Israel should also be revealed in the north country, together with their oracles and records, preparatory to their return, and to their union with Judah, no more to be separated." (Issued in New York City, 6 April 1845. See also JD, 21:301 and Talmage, *Articles of Faith*, p. 513.)

The genealogical information provided by their records will enable the tribes to perform the necessary ordinances both for themselves and their kindred dead. As with all men, they cannot be perfect without their dead nor can their dead be perfect without them. A whole and complete union of all those comprising the Father's celestial family must be achieved before he will accept it from the hands of his Only Begotten Son.

It is ordained that the tribes should come to Zion, the New Jerusalem, for it is there that they will receive the culminating ordinances which will make them kings and queens, priests and priestesses unto the Most High. It is there that they will "fall down and be crowned with glory, even in Zion, by the servants of the Lord, even the children of Ephraim." (D&C 133:32. See JD, 18:127.) For only when those who are joint-heirs with Christ in all that the Father possesses have been crowned as eternal kings and lords can the Redeemer rule as King of kings and Lord of lords. Ephraim, the recipient of father Jacob's right-hand blessing, (see Genesis 48:10-22) will have faithfully discharged his calling as the elder brother of and savior to the house of Israel. (See Jeremiah 3:9, 20 and Obadiah 21.) And the dreams of his father will have come eternally true: the sheaves and the stars will bow before the house of Joseph so that they might receive the "blessings of the everlasting God" at the hands of Ephraim and his fellows. (See Genesis 37:5-10 and Ezekiel 37:19.)

Signs on Earth and in Heaven

Prior to the "great day" of the Lord (his world advent), the heavens and the earth will virtually explode with awesome portents. (See D&C 29:14 and 45:9, 10.) The most vivid of these will be associated with the house of Israel: the redemption of Zion, the return of the lost tribes, and the deliverance of a remnant of Judah at Jerusalem. The redemption of Israel which began in the nineteenth century will be fully realized in the twenty-first century. The signs accompanying this final in-gathering will, therefore, span the same time period. As we approach the grand de-nouement of prophecy, these signs will increase both in frequency and intensity until they reach a climax in the very heavens.

The momentous return of the lost tribes will occasion an earthquake of vast proportions, for "the *boundaries* of the everlasting hills shall trem-ble at their presence." (D&C 133:31.) So violent and extensive shall be the upheavels which shake the earth in future days that those conditions which prevailed in the Americas during Christ's crucifixion will be re-peated: "There was thick darkness upon the face of the land." (3 Nephi 8:20.) The lights of heaven will go out for the "stars of heaven and the constellations thereof shall not give their light: the sun shall be darkened in his going forth, and the moon shall not cause her light to shine." (Isaiah 13:10.) This unique prophecy is stated three times by Joel: first—it seems—in connection with the redemption of Zion in America and there-after in connnection with Christ's deliverance of the Jews at Jerusalem.[24] It was in the context of Judah's deliverance that Jesus reiterated the words of Isaiah and Joel: "And immediately after the tribulation of those days, the sun shall be darkened, and the moon shall not give her light, and the stars shall fall from heaven, and the powers of heaven shall be shaken." (JST Matthew 24:34. Compare Mark 13:38 and Luke 21:25.) This prophecy also appears once in the Book of Revelation and four times in the *Doctrine and Covenants*.[25] Most commentators assume that these "stars" will be meteorites. However, meteorites do not constitute a unique sign; meteoric showers or "falling stars" have been observed throughout the ages. Impressive as they are, they are still too prosaic to qualify as distinct signs of the approaching return of Christ. Then, too,

---

[24]See Joel 2:10, 31; 3:15 and Acts 2:20. Zion will be redeemed and the New Jerusalem established before the return of the lost tribes and the selection of the 144,000, which events will occur in the closing period of the sixth seal. (See Revelation 7:1-4; 8:1 and D&C 77:9-11.) The deliver-ance of Judah will occur *after* the opening of the seventh seal and during the final phase of the judgments which will immediately precede Christ's world coming. (See Revelation 8-11.)

[25]See Revelation 6:12, 13; D&C 29:14; 34:9; 45:42 and 88:87. The sun is described as becoming "black as sackcloth of hair" in Revelation, but as being "darkened" or as hiding "his face" in the *Doctrine and Covenants*. In Revelation, the moon is described "as blood," while the *Doctrine and Covenants* states that the moon will be "turned into blood" or "bathed in blood" or, simply, "withhold its light."

he has declared that "the stars shall be hurled from their places." (D&C 133:49.) Meteoroids are, by definition, placeless wanderers in outer space; they have no fixed orbits from which they could be hurled.

Another compelling reason for rejecting the meteoroid theory is the fact that it can only be entertained at the expense of a critical element in the prophecy itself—that of selectivity. Neither the Lord nor his prophets said that *all* of the stars making up the countless galaxies, nor even all of those visible to the naked eye, were going to fall. The prophecy pertains only to a select number of heavenly bodies. This limitation was expressed in John's vivid words when he wrote that the "stars of heaven fell unto the earth, even as a fig tree casteth here untimely figs, when she is shaken of a mighty wind." (Revelation 6:13. See D&C 88:87 and Isaiah 34:4.) Untimely figs are those which ripen in the winter out of "due time". As such, they are comparatively few in number. So too, comparatively few stars will fall in connection with Christ's return. This view is confirmed in a modern revelation which says that only "some" will fall. (D&C 34:9.)

It should also be observed that one version of this prophecy (Revelation 6:13) contains an interesting addition: stars are going to fall *to the earth*. This would seem to support the theory of meteoric showers, since the smallest known star is many times larger than the earth and would engulf it like a whale swallowing plankton.[26]

In responding to Joseph Fielding's question: "How can the stars fall from heaven to earth, when they (as far as we know) are much larger than the earth?", Parley P. Pratt, editor of the *Millennial Star*, wrote:

> We are nowhere given to understand that all the stars will fall or even many of them: but only 'as a fig tree casteth her

---

[26]In scripture, the star is a symbol for man. The morning stars who sang together were the pre-mortal sons of God (Job 38:7 and D&C 128:23), Lucifer, a "son of the morning" sought to exalt himself above "the stars of God" (Isa. 14:12-14), he fell as a star to earth (Rev. 9:1) and a third of the stars with him (Rev. 8:12 and 12:4, 8, 9). Abraham, Isaac and Jacob were promised that their posterity would be as the "stars of heaven" (Gen. 15:5; 22:17; 26:4; Exo. 32:13; Dt. 28:62; 1 Chron. 27:23 and D&C 132:30). Joseph's brothers were the eleven stars who bowed to him (Gen. 39:9, 10). Daniel saw the "little horn" oppress the stars, the Lord's people (Dan. 8:10). It symbolized the seven servants (angels) and twelve apostles (Rev. 1:20; 3:1; 4:5; JST Rev. 5:6; 12:1 and 1 Nephi 1:10). Christ is the "star out of Jacob" (Num. 24:17) and the "bright and morning star" (Rev. 2:28; 22:16; 2 Pet. 1:19).

UNTIMELY figs when she is shaken with a mighty wind.' The stars which fall to the earth, are fragments, which have been broken off from the earth from time to time, in the mighty convulsions of nature. Some in the days of Enoch, some perhaps in the days of Peleg, some with the ten tribes, and *some at the crucifixion of the Messiah*. These all must be restored again at the 'times of restitution of ALL THINGS.' This will restore the ten tribes of Israel; and also bring again Zion, even Enoch's city. (*Millennial Star*, I [February, 1841], p. 258. Italics in original.)

Elder Pratt's statement in no way precludes the participation of true stars in the fulfillment of this prophecy, he does suggest that Enoch's Zion and the lost tribes of Israel will constitute at least two of those "stars" that John saw fall to the earth."[27]

The Earth Shall Reel

A latter-day revelation predicts that "not many days hence and the earth shall tremble and reel to and fro as a drunken man; and the sun shall hide his face, and shall refuse to give light; and the moon shall be bathed in blood; and the stars shall become exceedingly angry, and shall cast themselves down as a fig that falleth from off a fig-tree." (D&C 88:87. See also Isaiah 13:13, 14; 24:18-20; D&C 45:48 and 49:23.) Joseph Smith also put the reeling of the earth in the context of stars falling when he said that "the time is near when the sun will be darkened, and the moon turn to blood, and the stars fall from heaven, and the earth reel to and fro." (HC, 2:52.)

While this unprecedented phenomenon may be repeated, it will definitely take place when the Messiah stands upon the Mount of Olives. Following the resurrection of the celestial dead, the Messiah will gather the wicked to Armageddon, "the battle of that great day of God Almighty." This will fulfill Joel's prophecy: "Multitudes, multitudes in the valley of decision: for the day of the Lord is near in the valley of decision." The destruction of the armies marshalled against the Jews will be accompanied by the mightiest earthquake in the history of man, one that will

---

[27]Indeed, John's very language suggests that stars of great magnitude will be hurled through space as glorious heralds of the Savior's second advent!

devastate the great cities of the world, transform the face of the earth, and result in the "full end of all nations."[28]

> Then shall the arm of the Lord fall upon the nations.
> And then shall the Lord set his foot upon this mount, and it shall cleave in twain, and the earth shall tremble, and reel to and fro, and the heavens also shall shake.
> And the Lord shall utter his voice, and all the ends of the earth shall hear it; and the nations of the earth shall mourn, and they that have laughed shall see their folly. (D&C 45:47-49. See also D&C 84:118.)

While modern revelation likens the earth's movements to those of a drunken man, Isaiah also compared them to those of a frightened animal: "Therefore I will shake the heavens, and the earth shall remove out of her place. . . .And it shall be as the chased roe, and as a sheep that no man taketh up." (Isaiah 13:13, 14.)

The approach of one or more extra-terrestrial bodies of sufficient mass could affect the earth's orbital stability so as to cause it to move erractically and appear to stagger through the heavens. From the standpoint of contemporary science, such a thing would be catastrophic in the extreme. However, the Almighty is fully cognizant of the physics involved; its accomplishment would be a miracle to everyone but himself. The ability of an omnipotent Creator to manipulate his creations cannot be circumscribed.

Wandle Mace heard the Prophet Joseph Smith illustrate how the return of the lost tribes and Enoch's city would affect the earth:

> Some of you brethren have been coming up the river on a steamboat, and while seated at the table, the steamboat runs against a snag which upsets the table and scatters the dishes; so

---

[28]See Revelation 6:12, 13;11:13; 16:14-21 and D&C 87:6. For the brief period then remaining before Christ's world advent, peoples will cluster together in loosely organized tribal arrangements. (See JST Matthew 24:37.) A similar condition existed among the Nephites following the fall of their republic just prior to Jesus' crucifixion. (See 3 Nephi 7.)

it will be when these portions of earth return. It will make the
earth reel to and fro like a drunken man.[29]

The Prophet then went on to quote from Isaiah: "The earth shall reel to
and fro like a drunkard, and shall be removed like a cottage; and the
transgression thereof shall be heavy upon it; and it shall fall, and not rise
again." (Isaiah 24:20.)

Samuel H. Rogers recorded a similar explanation of the phenomenon by Joseph Smith in 1840:

> We also read in the Scriptures that the earth shall reel to and
> fro like a drunken man. What shall cause this earth to reel to
> and fro like a drunken man? We read that the stars shall fall to
> the earth like a fig falling from a fig tree. When these stars
> return to the place where they were taken from, it will cause the
> earth to reel to and fro. Not that the planets will come squarely
> against each other, in such case both planets would be broken
> to pieces. But in their rolling motion they will come together
> where they were taken from which will cause the earth to reel
> to and fro. (Journal of Samuel Holister Rogers, type copy,
> Brigham Young University Library, p. 17.)

Bathsheba W. Smith and Eliza R. Snow also testified to having heard
Joseph Smith teach that the return of the lost tribes would cause, or be in
connection with, the earth reeling like a drunken man. If the testimonies
of these women, together with those of such men as Brigham Young,
Parley P. Pratt, and lesser known associates of Joseph Smith are reliable,
and Enoch's city and the lost tribes were literally Spirited away on separate

---

[29]Mace Journal, p. 39. Daniel Allen reported hearing Joseph Smith
say that the return of that portion of the earth inhabited by the lost tribes
would cause "a great shake." (Minutes of School of the Prophets,
Parowan, Utah, Aug. 17, 1872, p. 157.) Parley P. Pratt wrote: "When the
fragment (some of which are vastly larger than the present earth) are
brought back and joined to this earth, it will cause a convulsion of all
nature; the graves of the Saints will be opened, and they rise from the
dead; while the mountains will flow down, the valleys rise, the sea retire to
its own place, the islands and continents will be removed, and earth be
rolled together as a scroll. The earth will be much larger than it is now."
(*Millenial Star*, 1 [February 1841], p. 258.)

fragments of the earth, there is no doubt but that their reunion with their parent body could trigger just such a phenomenon.

But whatever causes the earth to reel to and fro, it will have to be of an *unprecedented* nature. A force will be suddenly released that will be far more powerful than that of earthquakes, volcanic eruptions, or any-or all-of the *ongoing* geologic upheavals of the last days.

The Half Hour of Silence

The opening of the "seventh seal" will begin with "silence in heaven about the space of half an hour."[30] The social disorders, wars, and natural calamaties which lie ahead of mankind in these closing moments of the time of the sixth seal will be but portents of the final judgments that the Almighty will bring upon the wicked following that silence. For some twenty-odd years, during which the Lord will complete the gathering of his "wheat" into his garner, the "tares" will have a last opportunity to reflect upon and, hopefully, repent of their rebelliousness. (See D&C 43:21-25; 88:88-92 and 101:65, 66.) However, mankind in general will continue to be indifferent to heaven's pleas, being absorbed in its own self-generated pleasures and problems. Jesus compared these times to the closing moments of Noah's world. (See JST Matt. 24:44, 45.)

Thus, following the heaven-granted armistice, the silence will be broken by the successive sounding of the trumpets of the seven angels appointed to mete out the final series of plagues which will culminate in the world-wide appearance of the Son of Man.[31] The Lord will preach his own sermons—not in words, but in power. His arm shall fall upon the nations, saying: "Be still, and know that I am God: I will be exalted among the heathen, I will be exalted in the earth." (Psalm 46:10.)

----

[30]Revelation 8:1. See also D&C 88:95 and JD 8:51. The seventh seal mentioned in the book of Revelation symbolizes the events which are to transpire during the seventh one-thousand-year period of the earth's temporal existence. (See D&C 77:6, 7.) If the data provided in scripture is accurate, this period will begin within the next twenty-odd years or so. In all probability, the "half hour" refers to celestial, not earth, time—a period of about twenty-one years. (See Abraham 3:4; 5:13; 2 Peter 3:8.) Prophecies of an eschatological nature are invarialy couched in the language and time frame of God, not of man. (See, for example, D&C 63:53.)

[31]See Revelation 8:1-10; 7; 11:14, 15; 15:8; 16:1-17 and D&C 88:92-106. Michael is the seventh angel (D&C 88:112); the others also figure prominently in the work of the dispensation of the fulness of times.

Sign of The Son of Man

The final heavenly portent of Christ's world coming will be the sign of the Son of Man which will be miraculously observed in the eastern sky world-wide. Jesus taught his disciples that "after the tribulation of those days, and the powers of the heavens shall be shaken, then shall appear the sign of the Son of Man in heaven; and then shall all the tribes of the earth mourn." (JST Matthew 24:37. See Also D&C 88:93 and 49:23.) The ignorant and unbelieving will attribute it to some natural phenomenon. As Joseph Smith said: they will "say it is a planet, a comet, etc. but the Son of Man will come as the sign of the coming of the Son of Man, which will be as the light of the morning cometh out of the east." (HC, 5:337.)

Wandle Mace heard Joseph Smith teach that the principle of the first being last and the last being first would also apply to the return of Enoch's city and the lost tribes: Because the City of Enoch was the first body to be taken from the earth, it will be the last body to return to it. Perhaps the return of Enoch's city and the sign of the Son of Man are one and the same. Indeed, Mace quoted Joseph Smith as teaching that this climactic sign was "the return of the City of Enoch to the earth." (See "Joseph Smith Papers," Church Archives, Salt Lake City, Utah.) The fact that the sign of the Son of Man and the return of Enoch's Zion are both placed in the same prophetic time frame—being associated with the imminent coming of the Lord—is not conclusive proof, but nevertheless supportive of the argument for their common identification.

The Zion of Enoch is destined to participate in the millennium, that "day of righteousness" which all holy men have sought. And they were promised that they would see it "in their flesh." (See D&C 45:11-14.) For example, the Lord told Enoch that the saints of Latter-days would also build a "Holy City"—Zion, a New Jerusalem—to which the elect would be gathered in anticipation of the Savior's world coming:

> Then shalt thou and all thy city meet them there, and we will receive them into our bosom, and they shall see us; and we will fall upon their necks, and they shall fall upon our necks, and we will kiss each other....and for the space of a thousand years the earth shall rest. (Moses 7:63, 64.)

The use of the pronouns "we," "us" and "our" in this passage suggests the profound union between Jesus Christ and the people of Enoch. They fled to his presence when they left the earth; they will accompany him when he returns.

Would it be inappropriate for ancient Zion to be the sign of him whose people they are? He has been their God and King for some five thousand years. They have walked and talked together. Theirs has been a millennial-like relationship; they bask in terrestrial glory. (Hereafter, they will be united forever as the exalted ones comprising "the church of Enoch, and of the Firstborn.") These same conditions will exist on this earth when it is renewed and receives its paradisaical glory and Jesus Christ claims his rightful position as God and King over all of its inhabitants.[32] The blessings of a city will be magnified into the blessings of an entire world. The peace and happiness enjoyed by relatively few will become the common lot of all mankind. Thus the Zion of Enoch is, by its very nature, a sign of the coming reign of the Son of Man, a visible testimony of what that reign will mean to a desperate, suffering humanity.

According to Joseph Young, the Prophet taught that Enoch's city would return to its original site in the region of the Gulf of Mexico. This would be in harmony with the principle of the restitution of all things. (See Acts 3:21; D&C 128:18.)

Then, too, the sites for the Lord's millennial seats of government were selected in the context of a grand design. The New Jerusalem, the center place of the Zion of the latter-days, will be built upon that consecrated spot of land designated by revelation; it cannot, it will not be built anywhere else. (See D&C 90:37; 97:19; 101:17, 20 and HC, 2:261, 262.)

This land is not far from the Gulf of Mexico; indeed, when the New Jerusalem is fully developed, the two sites will, if Joseph Young is correct, be contiguous. For the original New Jerusalem will be magnified through the establishment of many Zion-like communities—thus expanding into "the regions round about." (See D&C 133:9; 82:14; 101:21; 109:59.) In time, this process would produce a perfect union of the two Zions—the first and the last—as one vast, splendid Holy City:

The Lord hath gathered all things in one.
The Lord hath brought down Zion from above.
The Lord hath brought up Zion from beneath. (D&C 84:100.)

Noah was told that the rainbow would betoken the union of these terrestrial societies:

---

[32]Enoch's Zion and the latter-day Zion of Joseph Smith constitute, in their union, the nucleus of the millennial society which the Savior will establish on a world-wide basis.

And the bow shall be in the cloud; and I will look upon it, that I may remember the everlasting covenant, which I made unto thy father Enoch; that, when men should keep all my commandments, Zion should again come on the earth, the city of Enoch which I have caught up unto myself.

And this is mine everlasting covenant, that when thy posterity shall embrace the truth, and look upward, then shall Zion look downward, and all the heavens shall shake with gladness, and the earth shall tremble with joy;

And the general assembly of the church of the first-born shall come down out of heaven, and possess the earth, and shall have place until the end come. And this is mine everlasting covenant, which I made with thy father Enoch. (JST Genesis 9:21-23.)

But before this grand union occurs the words of Isaiah will be fulfilled: "And the Redeemer shall come to Zion, and unto them that turn from transgression in Jacob, saith the Lord." (Isaiah 59:20.) This he will do that "my covenant people may be *gathered in one* in that day when I shall come to my temple." (D&C 42:36. See Malachi 3:1; D&C 36:8; 133:2; and HC, 6:254.) As he dwelt with his people in Enoch's "City of Holiness" before the earth's watery baptism, so will the Redeemer dwell with his saints in the New Jerusalem before the fiery baptism of the earth at the time of his world coming. (See Moses 7:16; D&C 84:101; 97:19; and 3 Nephi 20:22; 21:22, 23.) Therefore, it will be in Zion and in her stakes that the saints will be dwelling while being prepared in all things—temporally and spiritually, in principle and by ordinance—for the day when the Son of Man comes in his glory, with all of the holy angels, to assume kingship over the entire earth.

CHAPTER ELEVEN

Earth's Day of Righteousness

Enoch heard the earth ask: "When shall I rest, and be cleansed from the filthiness which is gone forth out of me? When will my Creator sanctify me, that I may rest, and righteousness for a season abide upon my face?" (Moses 7:48.) Earth had not been alone in its desire for sanctification and rest; all holy men and women have sought for that day of righteousness without finding it. They have "confessed they were strangers and pilgrims on the earth; but obtained a promise that they should find it and see it in their flesh." (D&C 45:12, 13. Compare Hebrews 11:13-16.) That promise will be kept; for on the earth's second sabbath there will be a millennial day of rest for all creation. Its dark, pre-dawn hours will give way to the brilliance of its Day Star—the Son of Man. Only those who are worthy will abide the rising of that Son; only they will be permitted to keep that long sabbath.

The Great Unveiling

In being cast down to this benighted corner of the universe, the earth, like Adam, was driven from the presence of the Lord and passed through a veil into a state of telestial corruption which marked the beginning of its temporal existence. The Father's spirit children pass through that same spiritual veil when they come to earth and enter their fallen physical bodies; indeed, the body constitutes a second veil between them and their divine Parent.[1]

When the Son of Man came to earth he, too, accepted the limitations imposed by the fall of Adam: "Forasmuch then as the children are partakers of flesh and blood, he also himself likewise took part of the same. . . . For verily he took not on him the nature of angels; but he took on him the seed of Abraham."[2] God incarnate was God veiled. His immortal glory was hidden behind the common facade of humanity; few there were who had the eyes to see what lay behind that facade.

Jesus' petition—"O Father, glorify thou me with thine own self with the glory which I had with thee before the world was" (John 17:5)—was granted in his resurrection. When the veil fell away from the glorified Christ, he could no longer remain with nor be seen by faithless men; only those who receive of his Spirit may behold his glory. (See John 1:14; Luke 9:28-32 and Moses 1:2, 9-14.) "For no man has seen God at any time in the flesh, except quickened by the Spirit of God. Neither can any natural man abide the presence of God, neither after the carnal mind." (D&C 67:11, 12. See also 88:68.)

God is a consuming fire, (Deuteronomy 4:24) and who will "abide the day of his coming? and who shall stand when he appeareth? for he is like a refiner's fire, and like fuller's soap." (Malachi 3:2. Compare D&C 128:24.) The answer is that only the purified and those who have been quickened by a portion of his glory will be able to endure that glory. (See D&C 35:21; 38:8 and 45:57.) Unlike his obscure entrance into this world as the babe of Bethlehem, the Savior's return will not be done in a corner; it will be as public and as universal as the rising of the sun: "For as the light of the morning cometh out of the east, and shineth even unto the west, and covereth the whole earth; so shall also the coming of the Son of Man be." (JST Matthew 24:27.)

---

[1]Brigham Young said: "Because we are encumbered with this flesh, we are in darkness; the flesh is the veil that is over the nations." (JD, 4:134.)

[2]Hebrews 2:14, 16. Although Jesus' divine conception rendered him immortal, still he subjected himself to all of the natural vicissitudes of the flesh. (See Hebrews 4:15; Mosiah 3:7 and Alma 7:11, 12.)

Earth's Spiritual Baptism

As the fall alienated man from God, so did it alienate the earth from its Creator. The ordinance of reconciliation is the same for both—baptism. It was born "of water" when it was immersed in the flood; it will be born "of the Spirit" when it is immersed, first in fire, and then in the Holy Ghost at the Savior's glorious coming. Brigham Young remarked that "this earth, in its present condition and situation, is not a fit habitation for the sanctified; but it abides the law of its creation. [It] has been baptized with water, will be baptized by fire and the Holy Ghost, and by-and-by will be prepared for the faithful to dwell upon."[3]

In quoting Malachi's prophecy that the "day cometh that shall burn as an oven" and that the wicked "shall burn as stubble," Moroni added a significant clause: "for they that come shall burn them." (JS-H 1:37.) The world will not end in an atomic holocaust. It will not perish at the hand of man, but in the judgments of God. It will not pass away in darkness but in light—the light of Christ and that vast concourse of celestial beings who will descend with him. The intense spiritual energy—the glory—eminating from the Savior and the resurrected host accompanying him will be "as the melting fire that burneth, and as the fire which causeth the waters to boil." (D&C 133:41. Compare Isaiah 64:2.)

Every form of life—whether man, animal, or vegetation; whether of land, sea or air—of a corrupt (telestial) nature will be consumed in the day that "shall burn as an oven." (See Malachi 4:1; D&C 64:24 and HC, 1:283.) Not even those inferior forms of marine life which lived through the flood will escape the global firestorm. The very seas will boil so that only those things fit to live in terrestrial waters will survive. (See Isaiah 64:1, 2 and D&C 133:41.)

---

[3]JD, 8:83. See also JD, 26:266. Orson Pratt explained: "As the earth was cleansed from its transgression by baptism in water, so it must again be cleansed, before it is made immortal. It must be cleansed by an element that is stronger and more purifying than that of water, namely, the element of fire...So this earth in due time must be baptized with fire *first*, and *then* the Holy Ghost. Fire will cleanse all the proud and they that do wickedly from its face—disobedient persons, all persons that are corrupt, all sinful persons, all who do not keep the commandments of God; it will cleanse the earth by burning them as stubble, fulfilling the words of the prophet Malachi." (JD, 21:324. See JD, 1:331; 16:319.)

And every corruptible thing, both of man, or of the beasts of
the field, or of the fowls of the heavens, or of the fish of the
sea, that dwells upon all the face of the earth, shall be
consumed;
And also that of element shall melt with fervent heat; and all
things shall become new, that my knowledge and glory may
dwell upon all the earth.[4]

The eternal law of affinities causes like to cleave to like. A holy,
incorrupt God cannot dwell in his glory on a corrupt earth or among a
corrupt people. Hence the necessity of a refining fire that will purge away
all uncleanness. The very elements comprising the face of the earth,
together with every work or action of man by which he has polluted it
physically or morally will come under this fiery judgment; nothing will
escape; everything will be weighed in the Lord's balances. Peter wrote:
"The heavens shall pass away with a great noise, and the elements shall
melt with fervent heat, the earth also and the works that are therein shall
be burned up....Nevertheless we, according to his promise, look for new
heavens and a new earth wherein dwelleth righteousness." (2 Peter 3:10,
13. See also 3 Nephi 26:2; Mormon 9:2 and Isaiah 34:4.)

The fallen, telestial nature of this planet will be consumed to nothingness so that Earth and its heaven might begin the long journey back
into the presence of the Father by rising to the glory of the Son—even a
terrestrial glory. Being thus endowed with paradisaical splendor, Earth
will be so marvelously transfigured that its former state "shall not be
remembered, nor come into mind."[5]

Joseph Smith wrote:

Yea, the righteous shall dwell in the presence of God,
And of Jesus, forever, *from earth's second birth*—

---

[4]D&C 101:24, 25. The destruction of all extant telestial life forms
prior to the earth's renewal is probably the final phase of a process of
elimination that began after the fall and was accelerated by the flood. The
dinosaur was very likely a victim of this weeding out process.

[5]Isaiah 65:17. See *ibid.*, 66:22. The prophet Mormon argued that
Jerusalem in Palestine could not be the *New* Jerusalem "for it had been in a
time of old; but it should be built up again." (Ether 13:5.) So will it be with
the earth in the millennial period; it will be the same *core* planet, but so
gloriously renewed as to constitute a new world.

For when he comes down in the splendour of heav'n,
All those he'll bring with him to reign on the earth.[6]

With the completion of the total ordinance of baptism, Earth will have been sanctified by the Spirit unto the renewing of its body. (See D&C 84:33 and JD, 15:365.) It will be a truly "born again" planet—born into a state of terrestrial glory and into the literal presence of the God of that glory, the Son of Man.[7]

Restitution of All Things

The Father's wondrous mystery was declared by Paul: "That in the dispensation of the fulness of times he might *gather together in one all things in Christ*, both which are in heaven, and which are on earth; even in him." (Ephesians 1:10.) Christ, the Eternal Reconciler, will make of many, one, restoring all things to that harmonious order which prevailed when the Gods pronounced Creation "very good." All division will end, all alienation will cease; perfect unity will prevail throughout the earth in consequence of the restoration of all things both physical and spiritual. (See D&C 86:10 and Acts 3:21.)

The saints have been commanded to watch for that awesome revelation "when the *veil* of the covering of my temple, in my tabernacle which hideth the earth, shall be *taken off*, and all flesh shall see me together." (D&C 101:23. See D&C 124:8; 109:74.) Earth's Lord will pass through that veil and burst upon an unprepared, and therefore, terrified world. He will descend from the celestial regions—"the regions which are not known, clothed in his glorious apparel, traveling in the greatness of his strength"—to claim his rightful throne. (D&C 133:46.)

---

[6]From his poetic parallel of D&C 76:62, 63. (*Times and Seasons*, [February 1, 1843], pp. 82-85.)

[7]See JD, 1:331. The very fact that the earth has to be born *again* into the Lord's presence is good evidence that it was in his presence when it was first organized. As Son of Man, Jesus Christ is the God who ministers to the terrestrial kingdom. (See D&C 76:76.) The millennial earth was seen in vision by the ancient apostles, Peter, James, and John. They were shown "the pattern" by which the earth would receive its paradisiacal glory on the same occasion they beheld the transfiguration of Jesus. (See Mark 9:2, 3; 2 Peter 1:16-18; D&C 63:20, 21; HC, 1:283 and 10th Article of Faith.)

For the "curtain of Heaven" will part "and the face of the Lord shall be unveiled." (D&C 88:95; Revelation 6:14-17.) And when it is, the heavens will be bathed in a divine radiance of such transcending splendor as to swallow up the lesser light of Earth's fallen expanse. As God possesses more light and truth than that of the combined intelligences over which he reigns, (see Abraham 3:19-21; TPJS, p. 353, n.8) so will the glory eminating from the presence of Jesus Christ overwhelm and blot out the combined brilliance of sun, moon and stars!

> And so great shall be the glory of his presence that the sun shall hide his face in shame and the moon shall withhold its light, and the stars shall be hurled from their places.[8]

Reunion of the Continents

The division of the earth's primal land mass into the various continents during the lifetime of Peleg will be reversed in connection with the restitution of all things. For Jesus Christ is a perfectionist, he will not be satisfied until every jot and tittle of prophecy has been fulfilled. When he ministered to Israel in America, he expounded "all things which should come upon the face of the earth, even until the elements should melt with fervent heat, and the earth should be wrapt together as a scroll, and the heavens and the earth should pass away." (3 Nephi 26:3. See also JST Genesis 14;34, 35.) The prophet Mormon called upon the Gentiles of our day to repent, and he asked: "Know ye not that he hath all power, and at his great command the earth shall be rolled together as a scroll?" (Mormon 5:23. See also Mormon 9:2; Revelation 6:14 and 16:20.) In a modern revelation, the Lord spoke in plainness of the future union of the continents:

> He shall command the great deep, and it shall be driven back into the north countries, and the islands shall become one land;

---

[8]D&C 133:49. This phenomenon should not be confused with the latter-day obscuring of the heavenly bodies in consequence of the global unheavels which will fill the atmosphere with thick dust. (See 3 Nephi 8:19-22.)

And the land of Jerusalem and the land of Zion shall be turned back into their own place, and the earth shall be like as it was in the days before it was divided. (D&C 133:23, 24.)

Joseph Smith is quoted as saying, "yea, the Eternal God hath declared that the great deep shall roll back into the north countries and that the land of Zion and the land of Jerusalem shall be joined together, as they were before they were divided in the days of Peleg."[9]

Orson Pratt accepted the literalness of this amazing prophecy in saying that the "earth is now divided into continents and islands. We may ask, are these to change their location? The answer is, yes....Such islands as Great Britain will change their location, as well as those of the Pacific Ocean and all others in like manner; and I have no doubt there will be a vast change between the location of continents and the location of the great oceans and seas at that time. The earth will doubtless be rolled back to the position it formerly occupied." (JD, 18:315. See Isaiah 24: 1, 19, 20.)

The wedding of the land of Jerusalem and the land of Zion (America) will fulfill Isaiah's beautiful metaphor concerning those cities from which the law of the Lord shall issue forth:

Thou shalt also be a crown of glory in the hand of the Lord,
And a royal diadem in the hand of thy God.
Thou shalt no more be termed Forsaken;
Neither shall thy land any more be termed Desolate:
But thou shalt be called Hephzibah,
And thy land Beulah:
For the Lord delighteth in thee,
And thy land shall be married.
(Isaiah 62:3, 4; See HC, 1:275.)

The "welding together" of the continents will be another of Christ's miraculous acts in connection with his return. However, the final configuration of the earth's millennial land masses is a matter of speculation. Will there be one, vast island-continent surrounded by a global sea, or will a band of land girdle the globe with an ocean on either

---

[9]Lundwall, *Inspired Prophetic Warnings*, pp. 41, 42. The statement was made in about 1844.

side? We are uninformed. Nevertheless, "the earth shall be like it was in the days before it was divided."

The Great Deep

When the "mighty ocean" is driven back into the "north countries," the natural consequence will be that "the islands shall become one land."[10] How extensive this process will be is unrevealed, but it will almost certainly include those islands now located in the central and western Pacific. They will be absorbed into that vast land area now serving as the Pacific basin.[11] In all likelihood, the basin—with its valleys and mountains—will be raised to the level of the present islands, thereby making of many lands, "one land." (This, together with the other prophesied geologic changes, will greatly increase the planet's land area, thereby providing for a much larger population during the millennial period.)[12] This unprecedented phenomenon will necessarily displace the "great deep," causing it to be "driven" away into the "north countries" in a flood of incomprehensible magnitude.[13]

This vast quantity of water will be augmented by the melting of the polar ice caps when the earth undergoes its fiery baptism and its

---

[10] To say that "the islands shall become one land" is also another way of saying that the continents will be reunited and the earth restored to its pre-Peleg state. The terms "island" or "isles of the sea," can refer to entire continents as well as lesser land masses. For example, the Nephites in America spoke of themselves as being "upon an isle of the sea." (2 Nephi 10:20.) Satan's "mother of abominations" sits upon "the islands of the sea." (D&C 88:94 and Revelations 17:1-5.) The Pacific ocean is the deepest and the largest body of water on earth, averaging 14,000 feet in depth and covering some 70 million square miles, or one third of the planet's surface. It contains about 20,000 islands.

[11] The Atlantic ocean will be greatly reduced in area, and, in effect, driven south when North and South America rejoin Europe and Africa—the relationships which existed originally according to substantial geological evidence.

[12] The human population in the millennial period will probably exceed that of all previous generations combined.

[13] The fact that it will flood northward suggests that the highest elevations of the emerging Pacific basin will lie to the south.

millennial climate is terrestrialized. Even without the displacement of the planet's oceans, Such a melting would inundate the coastal areas of the present continents. However, the elevations of these regions will be changed when the continents are joined by the Lord who will also "break down the mountains, and the valleys shall not be found." (D&C 133:22.) This will serve to redistribute the globe's materials so as to prevent coastal flooding. Then too, if portions of the planet have been removed and are restored in connection with the return of the lost tribes and Enoch's city, its increased land mass will easily contain earth's seas and oceans.

Some of the "great deep" may be used to restore those "waters which encompassed the earth "above the firmament" beginning on the second day of creation. (See Moses 2:6-8.) Indeed, that region may be, at least in part, what is meant by "the north countries." In any event, it is quite likely that the restitution of all things will include these ancient "waters." The presence of such water vapor could serve as a canopy against the harmful cosmic radiation now bombarding the earth.[14] This would contribute to the promised longevity of mankind. However, such radiation is very unlikely when the earth is enveloped in terrestrial glory.

Finally, some of these waters will almost surely be channeled back into the bowels of the earth—"the fountains of the great deep" which were "broken up" in connection with the Deluge. (See Genesis 7:11; 8:2.) This will replenish the earth's aquifers which have been so badly depleted in the twentieth century. It might be objected that sea water would have to be desalinated before it could be used for agricultural purposes. True; and it will be—by heating and evaporation. The presence of the Lord will be "as the fire which causeth the waters to boil." (D&C 133:41.) The very seas will boil: "He maketh the deep to boil like a pot." (Job 41:31.) This will also rid the sea of those "corruptible" forms of marine life which are unfit to swim in terrestrial waters. (See D&C 101:24.)

---

[14]Many statistical studies have demonstrated the harmful somatic and genetic effects of excessive radiation. It has been shown to reduce longevity and to exacerbate, if not cause, such conditions as cancer and lukemia. (See *The Genesis Flood*, pp. 399-405. See also Isaiah 65:20; D&C 63:51 and 101:30.)

Humbling of the Mountains

When the whole earth becomes the mountain of the Lord—the dwelling place of God—there will be no need for any other high places. The Lord will be everywhere. "The earth shall be full of the knowledge of the Lord, as the waters cover the sea." (Isaiah 11:9. Compare Habakkuk 2:14.) This knowledge will be personal, not vicarious, because, as the Lord said, "all shall know me, who remain, even from the least unto the greatest, and shall be filled with the knowledge of the Lord, and shall see eye to eye." (D&C 84:98. Compare Jeremiah 31:34.) The temporal and spiritual equality which will characterize millennial society will have its counterpart in the very topography of the earth. The great mountain ranges will be no more. They, too, are symbols of this fallen world and will be brought low before their Creator even as men are to be humbled before him: "And the loftiness of man shall be bowed down, and the haughtiness of men shall be made low: and the Lord alone shall be exalted in that day." (Isaiah 2:17. See also D&C 104:16.) The high and mighty shall be brought down that the meek and lowly might be exalted.

Isaiah's prophecy became John's message: "Every valley shall be exalted, and every mountain and hill shall be made low: and the crooked shall be made straight, and the rough places plain." (Isaiah 40:4. Compare Luke 3:5; D&C 49:23.) The psalmist wrote: "The hills melted like wax at the presence of the Lord, at the presence of the Lord of the whole earth." (Psalm 97:5.) His fiery glory will envelop the earth as an oven and the mountains will become molten and flow down until they become one with the valleys. (See Isaiah 54:10; 64:1-3; Micah 1:4; Revelation 6:14; 16:20; 3 Nephi 22:10; D&C 109:74; 133:22, 40, 44: HC, 1:283, 444.) This, together with the planet-wide shifting of the ocean basins and continental land masses, will result in a millennial earth characterized by relatively level plains and low, rolling hills. As it was in the beginning, so will it be in the time of the restitution of *all* things. The physical barriers (oceans, mountains, deserts, continents) which the Lord established after the flood to divide the nations will be no more.[15] Both spiritual and physical unity will prevail.

---

[15]The leveling of the mountains is but a step toward the ultimate perfecting of the earth wherein it will become as flawless as a sea of glass.

Earth Healed

The fall of Adam together with the subsequent sins of his children down through the generations led to the earth being repeatedly cursed against mankind. However, the great Jehovah will come with "healing in his wings" (Malachi 4:2) in fulfillment of his ancient promise to "heal the land" when his people turned from their wicked ways. [16] No longer will the earth be burdened with sterile deserts and wastelands; the "river of God" will flow generously. (Psalm 65:9.) "And in the barren deserts there shall come forth pools of living water; and the parched ground shall no longer be a thirsty land." (D&C 133:29.) This modern revelation reflects the words of Isaiah: "I will open rivers in high places, and fountains in the midst of the valleys: I will make the wilderness a pool of water, and the dry land springs of water." (Isaiah 41:18. See also 35:6, 7.)

Isaiah further wrote that the "trees of the field shall clap their hands. Instead of the thorn shall come up the fir tree, and instead of the brier shall come up the myrtle tree." (Isaiah 55:12, 13 and JD, 24:210.) President Brigham Young put the burden of Earth's redemption partially on man himself:

As fast as we learn to conform our individual wills to his will, overcoming sin within ourselves, will we have power to subdue sin in those that surround us, and in this way the whole earth will be redeemed from wickedness. The curse which has been brought upon the earth through the Fall will be removed through the faith and virtues of the Saints. When we become sanctified in the truth, and our faith, through the Gospel of the Son of God, becomes sufficiently powerful we will be able to remove the thorns and thistles and obnoxious weeds that grow immediately around us, and to bless and sanctify our gardens and farms, so that they will bring forth spontaneously the fruits and flowers, the cereals and vegetables that sustain life; and upon this principle as righteousness extends will the whole earth eventually be redeemed and sanctified, when all things will be as they were in the beginning, when the Lord finished the earth and

---

[16]See 2 Chronicles 7:14. Orson Pratt noted: "When it rains upon the exalted valleys, it will wash down the rich soil upon the rocky mountains which have sunk beneath, making them fertile." (JD, 18:320.)

pronounced everything to be 'very good.' (JD, 19:4. See also JD, 1:203 and 10:301.)

The earth's longed-for season of rest from the "filthiness which [has] gone forth out of [her]" will be one long harvest time. In prophesying of Israel's redemption, Amos said: "Behold, the days come, saith the Lord, that the plowman shall overtake the reaper, and the treader of grapes him that soweth seed; and the mountains shall drop sweet wine, and all the hills shall melt." (Amos 9:13.) This blessing will extend to peoples everywhere in that day. Like a beloved wife and mother, the earth will yield of her strength—gladly, lavishly, continually:

> The earth hath travailed and brought forth her strength;
> And truth is established in her bowels;
> And the heavens have smiled upon her;
> And she is clothed with the glory of her God.
> For he stands in the midst of his people.
> (D&C 84:101. See also Psalm 67; Ezekiel 34:27 and HC, 5:61.)

The Zion of the latter-days—being both the pattern and the nucleus of terrestrial life in the millennium—will be the harbinger of better days for mankind. Isaiah tells us that in "that day shall the branch of the Lord be beautiful and glorious, and the fruit of the earth shall be excellent and comely for them that are escaped of Israel." (Isaiah 4:2.) The Lord has promised the righteous who dwell in the Zion "the good things of the earth, and it shall bring forth in its strength." (D&C 59:3.)

> "For the Lord shall comfort Zion: he will comfort all her waste places; and he will make her wilderness like Eden, and her desert like the garden of the Lord; joy and gladness shall be found therein, thanksgiving, and the voice of melody." (Isaiah 51:3.)

The Father delights in blessing his children with those things which make for joy—soul happiness. His message is one of glad tidings, of the more abundant life. His purpose is not to render his children sterile of all that makes them human, but to immortalize and sanctify their humanity so that it becomes everlastingly divine. Only then can they become one with him. For the true God is not passionless; he is a sensate being. His life is rich with sanctified sensory pleasures. He told Joseph Smith that "All things which come of the earth, in the season thereof, are made for the benefit and the use of man, both to please the eye and to gladden the heart. Yea, for food and for raiment, for taste and for smell, to strengthen the body and to enliven the soul."[17]

Universal Peace

The regeneration of the earth will be a major factor in fostering universal peace. For the tempering of the climate, together with the union of the continents and the elimination of the great mountain systems, deserts, and arid regions will transform the entire earth into one, vast, promised land. The Lord has said that "it is not given that one man should possess that which is above another, wherefore the world lies in sin." (D&C 49:20. See also Alma 28:13.) And James noted that "wars and fighting" stem from the lusts of men for things they do not have. (See James 4:1, 2.) Christ's millennial reign will correct all material imbalances so that the needs and wants of every soul will be met without respect of persons or their places of habitation. No longer will there be "have" and "have-not" nations. No longer will a few peoples enjoy an over-abundance of earth's natural resources while their equally worthy neighbors suffer privation for the want of the merest necessities of life. Paul's "middle wall of partition" (Ephesians 2:14) which divided Israel from the Gentiles will be totally destroyed so that the physical and political barriers which now separate the children of God from one another will be no more. The frontiers of justice will extend from horizon to horizon. There will be one land, one faith, and one God. All righteous peoples—being "equal in earthly things"—will become "equal in the bonds of heavenly things." (See D&C 78:5, 6.) Peace and happiness will prevail earth-wide for a season.

The great image of Nebuchandezzar's dream will have been smashed to pieces. (See Daniel 2:31-45.) The governments of men, with their attendant oppression and corruption and ineptitude, will have crumbled into chaos—"the consumption decreed hath made a full end of all nations." (D&C 87:6.) Satan will have been driven from the earth; his kingdom and his subjects will lie in the dust. In its place will rise the

---

[17]D&C 59:18, 19. See also D&C 49:19. Brigham Young remarked: "Our senses, if properly educated, are channels of endless felicity to us....Everything that is joyful, beautiful, glorious, comforting, consoling, lovely, pleasing to the eye, good to the taste, pleasant to the smell, and happifying in every respect is for the Saints....Every faculty and power of both body and mind is a gift from God." (JD, 9:244.)

kingdom of God; Daniel's vision will be fulfilled. Earth's Creator, Redeemer, and rightful King, having been sustained to his high and holy office by the priesthood of all ages,[18] will rule with wisdom, equity, and love over his saints and all mankind: "But, verily I say unto you that in time ye shall have no king nor ruler, for I will be your king and watch over you. Wherefore, hear my voice and follow me, and you shall be a free people, and ye shall have no laws but my laws when I come, for I am your lawgiver, and what can stay my hand?" (D&C 38:21-22. See also D&C 45:59 and 58:22.) The King will anticipate the every need of his people: "And it shall come to pass, that before they call, I will answer; and while they are yet speaking, I will hear." (Isaiah 65:24.)

Christ will declare a thousand year armistice in the war which began in the courts of heaven. "And he shall judge among the nations, and shall rebuke many people: and they shall beat their swords into plowshares, and their spears into pruninghooks: nation shall not lift up sword against nation, neither shall they learn war any more." (Isaiah 2:4.) When war is no more, and human energy is fully directed toward creation rather than destruction, Jesus' words, "ye have the poor always with you," will no longer apply to the pure in heart:

"For they shall see the kingdom of God coming in power and great glory unto their deliverance; for the fatness of the earth shall be theirs.
For behold, the Lord shall come, and his recompense shall be with him, and he shall reward every man, and the poor shall rejoice;
And their generations shall inherit the earth from generation to generation, forever and ever. (D&C 56:18-20. See also Isaiah 65:21-23.)

Earth's King will say, "Peace, peace, be still" to every living thing, and universal harmony will descend upon the earth as the dews distilling. This will bring to pass Isaiah's gentle prophecy:

The wolf also shall dwell with the lamb, and the leopard shall lie down with the kid; and the calf and the young lion and the fatling together; and a little child shall lead them.

---

[18]This will occur at the council to be held at Adam-ondi-Ahman prior to Christ's world coming. (See D&C 116; Daniel 7:9-10, 13, 14, 22 and HC, 3:386, 387.)

And the cow and the bear shall feed; their young ones
shall lie down together: and the lion shall eat straw like the ox.
  And the sucking child shall play on the hole of the asp, and
the weaned child shall put his hand on the cockatrice' den.
  They shall not hurt nor destroy in all my holy mountain:
for the earth shall be full of the knowledge of the Lord, as the
waters cover the sea.[19]

And Isaiah's words are confirmed in a modern revelation: "And in
that day the enmity of man, and the enmity of beasts, yea, the enmity of all
flesh, shall cease from before my face." (D&C 101;26. See Isaiah 2:4;
Ezekiel 34:25; Hosea 2:18 and JD, 19:175; 20:18; 21:203; 24:210.) Both
man and beast will be purged of their carniverous appetites; they will
become as they were in the beginning before they were exiled from the
Garden of Eden; their diet will be essentially vegetarian in nature.[20]
  What will bring about so remarkable a transformation of human and
animal natures? The Spirit of the Lord. That Spirit which wicked men had
all but driven from the face of the earth will return even as they depart.
The spiritual voids created over many centuries by the prince of darkness
will be filled with the light of Christ. The very atmosphere (heavens) will

-----

[19]Isaiah 11:6-9. Compare Isaiah 65:25. Orson Pratt suggested: "And
then the animal creation will manifest more intelligence and more knowledge than they do now, in their fallen condition....they will even know
how to praise God....What? The animal creation endowed with language?
Yes, a language of praise." (JD, 20:18.)

[20]One of the primary purposes of the modern revelation known as
the "Word of Wisdom" (D&C 89)—with its injunction to eat meat spar-
ingly and only in times of winter or famine—is, as Hyrum Smith wrote: "to
remove the beastly appetites, the murderous disposition and the vitiated
taste of man; to restore his body to health, and vigour, promote peace
between him and the brute creation, and as one of the little wheels in
God's designs, to help regulate the great machinery, which shall eventually revolutionize the earth, and bring about the restoration of all things,
and when they are restored he will plant 'the tree of life, whose leaves shall
be for the healing of the nations.'"(*Times and Seasons*, 3 [June 1, 1842], pp.
799, 800. See also JD, 20:18.)

become so charged with it that all living things will breathe it like air.[21] For the Lord will bring to pass his strange act that he may "pour out [his] Spirit upon all flesh." (D&C 95:4.) His Spirit is not only peace, it is also life. Consequently, those who live upon the earth in the millennium will enjoy a greater portion of his Spirit and much longer lives: "In that day an infant shall not die until he is old; and his life shall be as the age of a tree." (D&C 101:30. Compare Isaiah 65:20.22.) As it was in the beginning, so will it be at the end: man's lost longevity will be restored and he will count his days, not by years, but by decades. The sicknesses and diseases, the trials and sufferings—both physical and emotional—which now afflict humanity will be unknown in that far better land of promise. Thus will mankind enter upon a new life, a life that is so superior to ours in both duration and quality that it can only be described as a state of terrestrial mortality.

Earth's Hour

In discussing the creation of the earth, Joseph Smith referred to other "worlds which were created at the time." (HC, 6:307.) Christ is the Savior of those worlds as well as this one; it is through him that "the inhabitants thereof are begotten sons and daughters unto God." (D&C 76:24. See also JD, 18:290.) However, in becoming the foreordained setting for the atonement which encircles these worlds within the arms of divine mercy, the earth, like its Creator, has descended below all things. Consequently, as noted by Brigham Young, it is "capable of becoming one of the highest kingdoms that has ever had an exaltation in the eternities." (JD, 10:175.) Our earth is the keystone of this eternity, from it holy men have gone forth to serve the needs of peoples on other planets. The Prophet Joseph Smith taught that Enoch was ministering to terrestrial beings on those planets "who shall be heirs of salvation." (HC, 4:209.) This ministry reflects the universal labors of Christ and harmonizes with Presi-

---

[21]Lorenzo Snow wrote: "The whole earth is the Lord's. The time will come when it will be translated and be filled with the spirit and power of God. The atmosphere around it will be the spirit of the Almighty. We will breathe that Spirit instead of the atmosphere we now breathe." (*Millennial Star*, 61 [August, 1899], p. 546.)

dent John Taylor's declaration that the Father, Son and Holy Ghost constitute the "First Presidency of this system and this eternity."[22]

He further wrote that the "twelve kingdoms" mentioned in a parable in the *Doctrine and Covenants* (88:51-61) are under the direction of this "Presidency." In the parable, the Lord likens his kingdoms to "a man having a field" into which he sends twelve servants with the promise that he will visit each of them: "every man in his hour, and in his time, and in his season—Beginning at the first, and so on unto the last, and from the last unto the first, and from the first unto the last."[23] It is significant that three cycles of visitation are mentioned with the third one ending, not with the first kingdom, but with the last. Since the principle that the last shall be first in all things that God has created, is immutable, this earth, which "abideth the law of a celestial kingdom," may well be the "twelfth" kingdom of the parable—the last to be organized in this creative epoch, and the last to be visited by its Creator. Being the last which shall be first, it could, indeed, become "one of the highest kingdoms that ever had an exaltation in the eternities." And this, the dispensation of the fulness of times, being the last of all, is, likewise, the greatest of all—being the sum of all previous dispensations. It then follows that Joseph Smith, the eternal president of this dispensation is one of the greatest servants of God to be found in any of his kingdoms! In any event, earth's time with

---

[22]Taylor, *Mediation and Atonement*, p. 76. The paragraph from which this quote was taken first appeared in an editorial written by John Taylor for the *Times and Seasons* (February 15, 1845)—a response to W. W. Phelps' earlier editorial (January 1, 1845) in that newspaper.

[23]D&C 88:58, 59. Orson Pratt identified the twelve kingdoms with the other planets of our solar system which were also hidden from the Lord's presence. Hence, the need to visit them. (See JD, 19:293, 294.) Benjamin F. Johnson, a confidant of Joseph Smith, wrote of this concept to George Gibbs in 1911: "He [Joseph Smith] gave us to understand that the there were twelve kingdoms, or planets, revolving around our solar system, to which the Lord gave equal division of His time or ministry; and now was his time to again visit the earth." (Letter of Benjamin F. Johnson to George S. Gibbs, compiled by Chas. S. Sellers, July 1, 1911 at Mesa, Arizona.)

her Creator will come in fullfillment of the parable of the twelve kingdoms. Jesus Christ will spend an "hour" with this earth and its millennial inhabitants so that he might be glorified in them, and they in him—"that they *all* might be glorified." (D&C 88:60.)

The enveloping glory of the paradisaical earth will far exceed that of its former telestial state. Its millennial moon will equal the brilliance of the present sun, and its millennial sun will, in turn, be seven times brighter than it is now. (See Isaiah 30:26.) Only those living things which have been quickened by terrestrial powers will be able to abide or endure Earth's new environment. Like Nebuchadnezzar's fiery furnace (which presaged it), the earth will be heated "seven times more than it was wont to be heated." Being so, it would consume things telestial even as that ancient furnace consumed those who sought to destroy Shadrach, Meschach, and Abednego. (See Daniel 3:19-25.) But Earth's terrestrial inhabitants will be bathed in the enlivening glory of the fourth man, the Son of God, who will be in the midst of his people in that day even as he was in the midst of the three Hebrews so long ago!

While the millennial earth will enjoy a most glorious state of peace, rest, and abundance, it will not begin to equal the majesty with which it will be endowed when it realizes its true destiny. Having been the footstool of the Son, the earth must become the footstool of the Father as well.(See D&C 38:17 and 88:19.) Therefore, its terrestrialization will be followed by the final ordinances which will bring it back into the presence of the Most High. In time, it will leave this solar system, pass the stars—those symbols of that lesser kingdom to which it fell after the transgression of Adam— and assume its foreordained place near the throne of God. However, before it can actually "enter into life" and become infused with immortal glory it must, as must every living soul, pass through the veil of death. It must "flee away to make room for the city of God."[24]

---

[24]See HC, 1:283. The New Jerusalem in America and the renewed Jerusalem in Palestine will constitute, respectively, the Western and Eastern capitals of Christ's millennial government. Orson Pratt expressed the view that "both of these cities will be caught up, when the earth undergoes its final dissolution, and when made new, they will come back again, the New Jerusalem first, followed by the old Jerusalem." (JD, 18:347. See JD 14:236; 16:323.) Note that the primacy of the New Jerusalem over the old Jerusalem is based upon principle of the last being first.

CHAPTER TWELVE

Earth's Death and Resurrection

When the Gods planned the earth, they also determined the length of its existence from its birth to its death. Whereas we are uninformed as to how much time elapsed between its creation and fall, modern revelation is explicit in declaring its temporal lifespan to be seven thousand years. How will it die? The manner of its passing is a clue to the time of its passing. Earlier scientific thinking postulated that Earth would either be destroyed when the sun exploded or else become a frozen hulk when the sun's energy supply was exhausted and it sputtered and died like a candle flame. However, the current theory maintains that the sun, a middle-aged star, will increase in luminosity (and, hence temperature) until it becomes a "red giant."[1] It is then supposed to radiate enough energy to literally vaporize the earth. This is known as the "heat death;" it is expected to occur in four or five billion years.[2] While empirical research seems to

———————

[1]It is believed that following the "red giant" stage, the sun will become a "white dwarf" and after exhausting its nuclear energy supply, then become a dark burned-out voyager through space. It will have "lived" for about ten billion years.

[2]All life on earth will have been destroyed by the suns' increasing temperatures long before this takes place.

warrant this prognosis, the Creator has chosen to overrule in the matter; he foreordained Earth's death in something over another thousand years!

Following Christ's millennial reign and that subsequent, unspecified space of time called the "little season" (when Satan will be loosed to war against the saints for the last time), the earth—having lived out its appointed days—will pass away.

End of the Earth

The wages of Adam's transgression—the so-called "original sin"—was to be death for every living thing, including Mother Earth herself.[3] Because of Adam, *all* die. (See 1 Corinthians 15:22.) All things were born to die so that they might eventually live forever. The demise of this planet is spoken of in scripture as "the end of the earth." We read that the "end shall come, and the heaven and the earth shall be consumed and pass away."[4] It will cease to exist as an organized planet, having been atomized "so as by fire."[5] But it will not be cremated by blind circumstance in some future fire storm resulting from the magnification of the sun. The earth's passing will be far more than the bursting of an insignificant bubble in the cosmic cauldron of chance events. Christ, not chance, will bring about its death; it will vanish away "by the power of his almighty word." All that will

------

[3]Orson Pratt said: "This death, or dissolution of the earth is a penalty of the original sin. Infants and righteous men die, not as a penalty of their own sins, but because Adam sinned; so the earth dies, or undergoes a similar change, not because of the transgressions of the children of Adam, but because of the original transgression." (JD, 1:331.)

[4]D&C 29:23. See also Matthew 5:18; JS-Matthew 55; D&C 38:5; 43:31; 45:26; 88:26. The "end of the earth" should not be confused with the "end of the world" which refers to the destruction of the telestial order at Christ's coming. (See JS-Matthew 4, 31; D&C 45:22; 2 Nephi 27:7; Jacob 6:3; Mosiah 4:7 and 3 Nephi 27:16.)

[5]Orson Pratt said: "What is it that will make the earth die? It will be the withdrawing of the spiritual portion from it, that which gives it life—that which animates it, and causes it to bring forth fruit; that which quickens the earth is the Spirit of God." (JD, 21:201. See also JD, 2:340 and D&C 43:32.)

remain will be the disorganized matter from whence it came. The earth will have returned to native element.[6]

A New Heaven and Earth

However, death is no more the final fate of the earth than it is of the numerous varieties of physical life it has produced. Therefore, following its dissolution, the earth will experience its ultimate and most sublime transformation—its resurrection as an immortal, spiritual body endowed with the fulness of celestial glory: "Wherefore, it shall be sanctified; yea, notwithstanding it shall die, it shall be quickened again, and shall abide the power by which it is quickened, and the righteous shall inherit it." (D&C 88:25, 26.) At the command of its Creator it will rise from its grave complete and whole, its every particle restored—spirit and element being inseparably connected forever.

The Creator respects the material integrity of man and the earth. Their *essential* identities will never be lost, their unique components will

---

[6]The principle of the last being first applies even to Mother Earth. Her offspring—man, animals, and other appropriate life forms—will be resurrected before she is. Hence, before this planet is reduced to native element, every order of life destined for immortality will be removed from it. The fundamental principles taken from the earth to fashion their physical organisms will be reorganized and joined to their spiritual counterparts. Were this not the case, those principles would become intrinsic components of the earth itself when it is immortalized. This would frustrate the Redeemer's plan for a perfect resurrection of all things. (See D&C 29:24, 25.) Obviously, the resurrection of all life-forms will require that their spirits leave the spirit world before the earth's own spirit and body are separated by death. Thus the earth—spirit and body—will become as devoid of life at its death as it was at its birth. The earth, like man, brought nothing into this sphere of existence, and it will take nothing out of it. (See JD, 6:282 and 16:323.) Prior to the dissolution of the earth, the final judgment involving primarily the telestial dead who come forth in the second resurrection will take place. (See Revelation 20:10-15; D&C 19:3; 38:5 and JD, 16:322.)

never be used in the formation of other organisms.[7] Brigham Young said that "the elements will be burned and purified and be renewed; but not one atom of earth's organism will be lost; for that which is governed by law shall be preserved by law." (Conference Address, October 8, 1875. See D&C 88:34.) All that has been, will be again; nothing will be lost: "For all old things shall pass away, and all things shall become new, even the heaven and the earth, and all the fulness thereof, both men and beasts, the fowls of the air, and the fishes of the sea; And not one hair, neither mote, shall be lost, for it is the workmanship of mine hand." (D&C 29:24, 25. See Ether 13:8, 9.) The planet earth will be born again *physically* even as it had been born again spiritually. Through the power of the atonement and the resurrection wrought by Jesus Christ, the earth will be totally redeemed from both its spiritual and temporal falls. John the apostle beheld this celestialized earth in vision and he saw a *new* heaven and a *new* earth: "for the *first* heaven and the *first* earth were passed away; and there was no more sea." (Revelation 21:1.) The resurrected earth, although bathed in immortal glory, will not be a strange, unfamiliar creation. Like its resurrected inhabitants, it will be its old self made agelessly new. The new heaven and the new earth "shall be *like unto the old* save the old have passed away, and all things have become new." (Ether 13:9.)

The earth is a covenant world, it was designed from the beginning to become a great celestial sphere. (D&C 88:25.) The eternal "measure of its creation" is a celestial measure. It was never destined for a lesser glory; therefore, it was never placed under the law of a lesser kingdom. (See D&C 88:36-39.) In its primeval excellence, it was an immortal, physical realm worthy of the presence of God. Its fall to a telestial condition drove it from His presence and it became a temporal sphere with all of its present imperfections and limitations. However, like man, it was meant to grow from grace to grace until it regains and magnifies the glory it once possessed. "Therefore, it must needs be sanctified from all unrighteousness, that it may be prepared for the celestial glory; For after it hath filled the measure of its creation, it shall be crowned with glory, even with the presence of God the Father. (D&C 88:18, 19.)

Our Heavenly Father is a celestial deity; he is the crowning glory of celestial worlds. He cannot set foot upon lesser ones since, in eternity, like can only cleave to like. It was the Son of Man (the Lord, Jehovah) and *not*

---

[7]Joseph Smith taught that "no fundamental principle" of the human system "ever goes into another in this world or the world to come." (HC, 5:339.)

his exalted Father who spoke of the earth as "my footstool."[8] While Jesus in his humility walked upon it in its fallen state, he will not do so in his glory until the earth is cleansed in the sanctifying fire and made worthy of his presence: "And I have made the earth rich, and behold it is my footstool, wherefore, *again* I will stand upon it." (D&C 38:17.) Thereafter, when the earth becomes a celestial "mother," it will be crowned with the presence of our celestial Father. It will move in harmony with mighty Kolob once more.[9] It will flee this benighted solar system for the distant reaches of galactic space.

Return to Primeval Place
> And thou, O Earth, wilt leave the track
>   Thou hast been doom'd to trace—
> The Gods with shouts will bring thee back
>   To fill thy native place.[10]

No longer will Earth beg the borrowed light of lesser worlds. No longer will it be the slave of this sun, held captive by its gravitational powers and dependent upon its life-sustaining rays. The earth will be "free indeed." It will have returned to the presence of the Godhead who organized it in the beginning.

Joseph Smith confirmed this point when he said that this earth "will be rolled *back* into the presence of God, and crowned with celestial glory." (TPJS, p. 181. See also JD, 8:8, 200 and 9:292.) On several occasions, Brigham Young stated the same idea: "When [the earth] is celestialized it will go back into the presence of God, where it was *first* framed." (JD, 9:317. See also JD, 7:163 and 17:143.)

The cycle will be complete. Having begun its career "near the throne of our Father in Heaven" or, in other words, "near the planet Kolob," Earth will return to her "native place." However, she—like her celestial inhabitants—will be far more exalted and far more glorious in returning to the Father's presence than she had been when departing from it.

---

[8]See Isaiah 66:1; Matthew 5:35; Acts 7:49. The house of the Lord is also described as the Lord's footstool. (See 1 Chronicles 28:2 and Psalm 99:5; 132:7.)

[9]Brigham Young said that the resurrected earth "will take its place in the rank of the celestial ones." (JD, 14:136 and 17:117.)

[10]Snow, "Address to Earth."

Earth To Be Enlarged

While neither the original nor the final size of the earth is known, a few interesting comments on the subject have been made. The substance of them all is that the earth was considerably larger in the beginning than it is now and that, consequently, it will be considerably larger hereafter. Samuel Holister Rogers wrote that in the winter of 1840-41 he "attended a public meet held in Vincent Knight's house at which the Prophet Joseph Smith gave the following instruction: 'When this world was first made it was a tremendous big thing. The Lord concluded it was too big. We read in the Scriptures that in the days of Peleg the earth was divided so the Lord divided the earth. When the ten tribes of the children of Israel went into the north country he divided it again, so the earth has been divided and subdivided." (Journal of S. H. Rogers, p. 17.)

Eliza R. Snow confirms the Rogers' journal entry both in the previously quoted and following stanzas of her poem, "Address to Earth":

> But thy dimensions have been torn
>   Asunder, piece by piece,
> And each dismember'd fragment borne
>   Abroad to distant space.

                    ****

> And thus, from time to time, thy size
>   Has been diminished, till
> Thou seemst the law of sacrifice
>   Created to fulfill.

                    ****

> A 'restitution' yet must come,
>   That will to thee restore,
> By the grand law of worlds, thy sum
>   Of matter heretofore.[11]

---

[11]Eliza R. Snow reiterated these ideas in private conversations over a period of about thirty years. Charles L. Walker quoted her as saying that the earth was ninety times smaller than when first organized.

According to Charles L. Walker, Addison Everett testified to hearing Joseph Smith teach that "the earth had been divided and parts taken away but the time would come when all would be restored and the earth again would revolve in its original orbit next to Kolob and would be second in size to it." (Walker, 18 Oct. 1880, vol. 2, p. 505) If Joseph Smith was accurately quoted, the earth's dimensions will be materially increased when it becomes a star.[12] How much that increase will be is a matter of conjecture.

Animal Life Restored

Earth is patterned after the world from whence man came—a world of dazzling natural beauty where exquisite trees, flowers, and shrubbery of seemingly endless variety abound. Magnify all the lovely things of this planet a thousand times over and we would still fail to comprehend the splendor of the resurrected earth. Not only will the planet and its enveloping atmosphere be renewed, but all the worthy hosts that were organized in the beginning as well. They will fly through its heavens, swim in its waters, and move upon its breast again.

The natural beauty of the resurrected earth will be accented by the presence of resurrected animals and birds of every kind. In commenting on John the Revelator's vision, Joseph Smith said that John "saw every creature that was in heaven,—all the beasts, fowls and fish in heaven,—actually there, giving glory to God . . .

> I suppose John saw beings there of a thousand forms, that had been saved from ten thousand times ten thousand earths like this,—strange beasts of which we have no conception: all might be seen in heaven. The grand secret was to show John what there was in heaven. John learned that God glorified Himself by saving all that His hands had made, whether beasts, fowls, fishes or men; and He will glorify Himself with them.
>
> Says one, "I cannot believe in the salvation of beasts." Any man who would tell you that this could not be, would tell you that the revelations are not true. John heard the words of the beasts giving glory to God, and understood them. God who made the beasts could understand every language

---

[12]Interestingly, astonomer's maintain that no heavenly body could become a star unless its mass was at least 3,000 times that of Earth.

spoken by them. The four beasts were four of the most noble animals that had filled the measure of their creation, and had been saved from other worlds, because they were perfect: they were like angels in their sphere. We are not told where they came from, and I do not know; but they were seen and heard by John praising and glorifying God.[13]

The great oceans will not be found on the new earth for, according to the book of Revelation, "there was no more sea." (Revelation 21:1.) However, the earth will not be devoid of celestial waters. John's "fellow servant," the prophet-angel of his revelation, showed him "a pure river of water of life, clear as crystal, proceeding out of the throne of God and of the Lamb." (Revelation 22:2, 1.) Since marine life will also be resurrected (see D&C 29:24) and enjoy "eternal felicity," it is apparent that the earth's celestial waters will be the habitat of at least some of them, for, as Joseph Smith observed, there will be "fish in heaven." (HC, 5:343.)

A Sea of Glass

John the apostle beheld God sitting upon his throne with a "sea of glass like unto crystal" lying before him. (Revelation 4:6. See also Rev. 15:2; 21:18, 21.) Some eighteen centuries later, Joseph Smith learned that the sea of glass was "the earth, in its sanctified, immortal and eternal state."[14] It will be like unto the very heavenly body where God and his angels dwell, for they reside on a great Urim and Thummim—"a globe like a sea of glass and fire, where all things for their glory are manifest, past, present, and future, and are continually before the Lord." (D&C 130:7, 8.)

-----

[13]HC, 5:343. See also Revealtion 4:6-9; 5:6-14 and D&C 77:2-4. The ultimate progress of any organized intelligence lies in its willingness and ability to submit to and unite with a greater intelligence. (See D&C 88:40.) In this respect, the earth and many of her creatures, will be blessed in their "eternal felicity" above many a child of God. Is it not ironic that certain classes of animals will be found in the celestial kingdom while certain classes of men will not?

[14]D&C 77;1. See also JD, 8:200; 14:136 and 16;323. The glass industry maintains that silica, soda, lime, and potash are so plentiful that if the earth were melted down "you would end up with a ball of glass." See *Science Digest Special*, (July 1967), p. 45.

The resurrection will not only restore, but vastly improve upon the intellectual faculties of those who are raised with celestial powers. They will be prepared to receive and employ knowledge on a level incomprehensible to mortals.[15]

The earth will abet this metamorphosis of the human mind by endowing it with seer power on a divine scale. As a celestial orb, the earth will constitute a mighty Urim and Thummim, a revelator of all things pertaining to lesser worlds:

> This earth, in its sanctified and immortal state, will be made like unto crystal and will be a Urim and Thummim to the inhabitants who dwell thereon, whereby all things pertaining to an inferior kingdom, or all kingdoms of a lower order, will be manifest to those who dwell on it; and this earth will be Christ's.[16]

Joseph Smith taught that when the earth was celestialized "the Saints could *look in it* and see as they are seen." (HC, 5:279. See also 1 Corinthians 13:12.) Brigham Young expressed the same idea when he said that men will be able to "look *in* this earth and see all the eternities of God." (JD, 8:200.) He described the experience as rather like looking in a mirror: "You step up and you look and you see Adam as he was. You would like to see Jerusalem as it looked when the temple was finished, I walk up to this looking glass, and I look. Well [when] the whole earth becomes like that it will be a true mirror, or Urim and Thummim. And everything you desire to see or know is present before you; you look and it is there." (Discourse, March 17, 1861, Church Archives.) The earth and its enveloping heavens will be charged with those intrinsically glorious material principles of immortality associated with the Spirit of the Lord that can only be endured be beings who are capacitated to dwell in a totally sanctified atmosphere—"for, for this intent was it made and created, and for this intent are they sanctified." (D&C 88:20.)

---

[15]Orson Pratt discussed the future powers of man on a number of occasions. (See JD, 3:97-105; 19:177-178, 292-294 and 21:256-263, 328.)

[16]D&C 130:9. See JD, 14:136 and HC, 5:279. A personal Urim and Thummim will be given to the most exalted inhabitants of the celestialized earth "whereby things pertaining to a higher order of kingdoms will be made known." (D&C 130:10.)

The Holy Cities

When Earth is endowed with celestial glory, the two holy cities from which the law of the Lord issued forth to the nations in the millennium will return to their ordained places. The Revelator wrote that he saw the "new Jerusalem, coming down from God out of heaven prepared as a bride adorned for her husband." (Revelation 21:2.) Thereafter, an angel showed him the second city: "the holy Jerusalem, descending out of heaven from God." (Revelation 21:10. See JD, 18:346-348.) Ether, the last of the Jaredite prophets, had written of these cities centuries earlier:

> The earth shall pass away. And there shall be a new heaven and a new earth . . .And then cometh the New Jerusalem; and blessed are they who dwell therein, for it is they whose garments are white through the blood of the Lamb . . .And then also cometh the Jerusalem of old: and the inhabitants thereof, blessed are they, for they have been washed in the blood of the Lamb . . .And when these things come, bringeth to pass the scripture which saith, there are they who were first, who shall be last; and there are they who were last, who shall be first.[17]

The New Jerusalem, having been established last in point of time, will be given precedence over the Jerusalem of old—the last shall become the first to descend to the celestialized earth!

---

[17]Ether 13:10-12. In commenting on Ether's prophecy, Joseph Smith wrote: "Now we learn from the Book of Mormon the very identical continent and spot of land upon which the New Jerusalem is to stand, and it must be caught up according to the vision of John upon the isle of Patmos. Now many will feel disposed to say, that this New Jerusalem spoken of, is the Jerusalem that was built by the Jews on the eastern continent. But you will see, from Revelation xxi: 2, there was a New Jerusalem coming down from God out of heaven, adorned as a bride for her husband; that after this the Revelator was caught away in the Spirit, to a great and high mountain, and saw the great and holy city descending out of heaven from God. Now there are two cities spoken of here." (HC, 2:261, 262. See also JD, 1:332; 16:323 and 20:15.)

Beholding the holy Jerusalem as it descended to the eternal earth, the apostle John described it as being of "pure gold, like unto clear glass."[18] "The city had no need of the sun, neither of the moon, to shine in it: for the glory of God did lighten it, and the Lamb is the light thereof."[19] Neither the earth nor its inhabitants will be obliged to borrow light any longer, for they will be filled with the glory of God—they will be as those star-suns that never fade and never die. Both will be realms of pure spiritual light, the brilliance of which would cause a thousand temporal suns to fade into nothingness.

The Meek Shall Inherit the Earth

"Blessed are the meek: for they shall inherit the earth." (Matthew 5:5.) This was the promise of Jesus to his disciples some nineteen centuries ago. Cynical men continue to ridicule these words by pointing out that it is not the meek, but the mighty, who have dominated the earth since Cain murdered Abel. But they err, not knowing the scriptures nor the mind of the Lord. Jesus well understood the character of this world with its fawning obeisance to power—whatever its guise. He knew that might will continue to make for right as long as men and devils dictate human affairs.

Indeed, in his beautitude, Jesus was quoting an ancient psalmist who had written those words with the very problem of injustice in mind:

> But the meek shall inherit the earth; and shall delight them-
> selves in the abundance of peace . . .I have seen the wicked in
> great power, and spreading himself like a green bay tree. Yet
> he passed away, and, lo, he was not: yea, I sought him, but he
> could not be found. (Psalm 37:11, 35, 36.)

Neither Jesus nor the psalmist was alluding to the meek or to the earth in their fallen states. For the promise does not pertain to either of

---

[18]Revelation 21:18, 21. Joseph Smith described the streets of the celestial kingdom as having the "appearance of being paved with gold." (D&C 137:4.)

[19]Revelation 21:23. See also Ether 13:3, 10. Orson Hyde mistakenly assumed the sun would continue to give light to the earth. (See JD, 1:130.)

them as they are, but only as they shall be. Death precedes inheritance.
This is doubly true in this instance: the death of the meek and the death of
the earth. Both must be made glorious before the inheritance can be
claimed.

John Taylor said that "if you possess any portion of this earth by right
or title or authority, you will have to get it from God, and you will have to
get it when the earth shall be renewed." (JD, 22:220. See also JD, 1:293;
14:237, 238; 20:16, 17.) The immortal earth is the true and everlasting
land of promise of the saints of God in all ages. Lands which have been
designated as "promised lands" are but symbols of what is to be.

These promised lands can only be received by covenant, otherwise
there is no inheritance. Only those who are joint-heirs with Jesus Christ in
all that the Father possesses, have a legal claim to the earth after they are
dead. Orson Pratt spoke to this point:

> In the resurrection, the meek of all ages and nations will be
> restored to that portion of the earth previously promised to
> them. And thus, all the different portions of the earth have
> been and will be disposed of to the lawful heirs; while those
> who cannot prove their heirship to be legal, or who cannot
> prove that they have received any portion of the earth by
> promise, will be cast out into some other kingdom or world,
> where, if they ever get an inheritance, they will have to earn it
> by keeping the law of meekness during another probation.
> How great will be the disappointment to the rich, the high and
> the noble, who have rejected the messages of eternal truth,
> sent forth in different ages for the redemption of men, when
> they find that there is not a foot of the new earth that they can
> call their own; the whole of it having been lawfully disposed of
> to the poor and the meek.[20]

Brigham Young emphasized that the meek shall not enter into their
inheritances until the Lord Jesus Christ is crowned King of kings—King
over all those for whom he made exaltation possible: "[When] the Savior
has presented the earth to his Father, and it is *placed in the cluster of the
celestial kingdoms*, and the Son and all his faithful brethren and sisters have
received the welcome plaudit—'Enter ye into the joy of your Lord,' and

---

[20]JD, 1:332, 333. The possibility of "another probation" is purely
conjectural on his part.

the Savior is crowned, then and not till then, will the Saints receive their everlasting inheritances."[21]

No unholy thing will be able to approach, much less dwell in, the exalted city. Joseph Smith taught that "God Almighty Himself dwells in eternal fire" and "flesh and blood cannot go there, for all corruption is devoured by the fire." (HC, 6:366. See Deuteronomy 4:24; Hebrews 11:29, HC, 5:355 and JD, 14:236, 237.) The Prophet knew whereof he spoke, for he had beheld the celestial world on more than one occasion. In an 1836 vision of it he "saw the transcendent beauty of the gate through which the heirs of that kingdom will enter, which was like unto circling flames of fire; Also the blazing throne of God, whereon was seated the Father and the Son." (D&C 137:2, 3.) While such images may appear to be descriptive of a Dante's inferno for the divine, they are only meant to convey in human terms something of the wonder of those realms to be found at the pinnacle of all organized life.

The great gulf between God and man is corruption. Only those men and women who bridge that gulf through the redemptive merits of Jesus Christ and by their own obedience to his law will be capacitated to dwell in a celestial environment. Only the holy can abide the presence of the Man of Holiness.[22] (See Revelation 21:27; 22:14, 15; Moses 6:57, 59 and D&C 76:69, 70.)

How imperative it is for those who aspire to a celestial glory to know that salvation is far more than routine, mechanical conformity to a religious system; it is *becoming*. We must become *like* God to dwell *with* God. We must, as Joseph Smith taught, progress "from a small capacity to a great one . . .[being] able to dwell in everlasting burnings, and to sit in glory, as

----

[21]JD, 17:117. See also JD, 6:282. So literal is the promise of an inheritance that Joseph Smith told John Taylor that his, Joseph's, inheritance would be located near what is now Nauvoo, Illinois. (See Brigham Young's discourse of March 17, 1861; Church Archives, Salt Lake City, Utah.)

[22]The lake of fire and brimstone is not literal, the term is a metaphor for the exquisite spiritual and emotional pain of the wicked. (See Mormon 9:3-5.) Brigham Young declared that "were the wicked, in their sins, under the necessity of walking into the presence of the Father and Son, hand-in-hand with those who believe that all will be saved—that Jesus will leave none, their condition would be more excruciating and unendurable than to dwell in the lake that burns with fire and brimstone." (JD, 8:153, 154.)

do those who sit enthroned in everlasting power." (HC, 6:306.) Those who are "not able to abide the law of a celestial kingdom cannot abide a celestial glory." (D&C 88:22.) Consequently, they will be obliged to bid Mother Earth an everlasting farewell; their immortal mansions will lie elsewhere in the Father's house. While the meek—those who, through the redemptive power of Christ, were capacitated to dwell in celestial burnings—will inherit Earth forever and ever.

Epilogue

In claiming their inheritances on this resurrected earth, the sons and daughters of God will have entered into his immortal rest. (See D&C 121:32; Hebrews 4:9-11 and Alma 17:29.) The long quest will have ended; the perfect day will have begun.

> And I heard a great voice out of heaven saying, Behold, the tabernacle of God is with men, and he will dwell with them, and they shall be his people, and God himself shall be with them, and be their God. And God shall wipe away all tears from their eyes; and there shall be no more death, neither sorrow, nor crying, neither shall there be any more pain: for the former things are passed away. (Revelation 21:3, 4.)

The Prophet Joseph Smith summed up the grand objective of tne Father's labors when he wrote: "Happiness is the object and design of our existence; and will be the end thereof, if we pursue the path that leads to it; and this path is virtue, uprightness, faithfulness, holiness, and keeping all the commandments of God." (HC, 5:134, 135.) The earth is but a means to that end. While it will be a treasure house of wonders for the exalted sons and daughters of God, their "fulness of joy" will stem from the unity of Spirit which will seal them to their divine parents and to each other. Being filled to perfection with the Spirit of the Lord, the many will be as one—the One God. Earth and her chosen ones will have come full circle; having begun in spirit, they will have returned to spirit. However, in doing so, they will be richly added upon with the splendor of their once-corrupt, but now-sanctified physical bodies. They will possess divine creative powers which will enable them to enter into the most glorious enterprise of all.

The work of the Father—the immortality and eternal life of man—will become their work as well. For those endowed with eternal lives, the command to "multiply and replenish the earth" will never be revoked. They will increase forever.

In time, they will organize new earths out of eternity's infinite materials.[1] Their newly-begotten children will follow in their steps and make the long journey to another fallen world where they, too, will experience the essential realities of a mortal existence.[2] And when they go, they will take something of the celestial earth with them. For just as Mother Earth, in her fallen state, provided their once-mortal parents with physical bodies, so will Mother Earth, in her glory, provide the holy offspring of those parents with spirit bodies. In this way, an endless chain of life is formed, link by link, to bind the family of Man together from world to world and from eternity to eternity!

The "eternal round" of the Gods will have begun again. The curtain will rise on yet another production of the endless cosmic drama. Of course, there will be new players performing the old, familiar parts. Ancient actions will be repeated as ancient dialogue again falls from the lips of heroes and villians and wise men and fools. And when the final curtain comes down, love and mercy and sacrifice will again have triumphed over human frailty: the immortality and eternal life of another generation of the family of Man will be a reality. And a new realm of immortal glory will find its place among that galaxy of celestial worlds to which Earth will have long since ascended.

---

[1]Brigham Young cautioned: "We can have no other kingdom until we are prepared to inhabit this [earth] eternally." (JD, 3:372.)

[2]Orson Pratt said that the resurrected saints would "swarm out like bees from the old hive, and prepare new locations." (JD, 1:294. See also JD, 18:297; 19:289.)

Index

Abraham: shown endless worlds, 8, 10; wrote authorized account of creation, 54, 57; original knowledge of creation found on records of, 55; defined time in terms of Kolob, 69

Adam: is Michael, 61; subject to Kolob's time, 70; holds keys of universe, 90; immortal before fall, 80, 92; transgressed natural law, 92; exiled to Adam-ondi-Ahman, 94

Adam-Ondi-Ahman: Adam exiled to, 94; Adam met with posterity at, 111; seen in vision by Joseph Smith, 111

Agency: man given moral, 30, 112

Agrippa, Herod, on Israelites beyond the Euphrates, 148

Ahijah, prophesies fate of Israel, 148

Allegory, of Zenos, 158

Allen, Daniel, testimony of, on John the Revelator and the lost tribes, 161, 198

Alma: on relationship of faith to knowledge, 26; dead return to God, 53

America: site of Garden of Eden, 94; to come under judgment, 192; cities of, inhabited by lost tribes, 192

Amos, on bounty of millennial earth, 214

Amulek, explanation of teaching of, on state of dead, 48

Angel, Enoch a ministering, 140

Animals: benign before fall, 89, 101; herbiverous before fall, 101; destroyed in flood, 117; enmity between man and, to cease, 217; on celestial Earth, 227; to be resurrected, 227

Apostasy, rampant in America, 172

Aquifers: Earth's, being depleted, 181; to be replenished, 213

Ararat, ark landed on mountains of, 121

Arctic: identified with lost tribes, 156; regions mapped extensively, 159

Ark: design of, given by revelation, 115; dimensions of, 115; size of, precludes local flood, 121; symbolic of baptism, 126; Zion, a spiritual, 136

Armageddon, wicked gathered to, 196

Assyria, Israel conquered by, 146

Astronomy, data on, 3

Astrophysicists: concerned with origin of universe, 9; purposes of, 21

Atmosphere: altered by flood, 133; formed on second day of creation, 81; of earth in millennium, 218

Atomic holocaust: world not to end in, 205; possible description of, 184

Atonement, Christ's sufferings in, 168

Babel, tower of, 143

Babylonian, Gilgamesh Epic of flood, 120

Bacon, Francis, advanced theory of unified continents, 143

Ballard, Melvin J., all spirits tested in pre-existence, 46

Baptism: of earth, foreordained, 120, 126; a witness for flood, 126; dual ordinance, 126; by immersion essential to symbolism, 127; Earth's, completed at Christ's coming, 134; Earth's, of the Spirit, 205

Blood: replaced spirit, 100; men hate own, 113; God free of man's, 115; not to be shed wantonly, 132; moon bathed in, 194

Body, physical, not duplicate of spirit, 38

Born again, earth to be, 205

Brown, Benjamin, hearsay statements of, on lost tribes, 163

Cain, 102

Calamities: manmade, 180; cause of latter-day, 186

Canaan, people of, cursed, 103

Cannon, George Q., accepted geologist's views as compatable with scripture, 67

Capacities, spirits of different, 40

Catastrophism, characterizes earth's history, 17, 75, 125

Celestial earth: Father is God of, 224; described, 233

Chance: creation not by, 19; end of Earth not by, 222

Chaos: would prevail without Spirit of Lord, 24; earth formed out of, 75

Chiasmus, Earth's history plotted as, 72

Children: little, saved in celestial kingdom, 43; not tried after death, 43; some, too pure to live, 43; not tempted by Satan, 43; spiritually alive in Christ, 43; have eternal life, 44; fate of, unclear, 44

Christ: spirit body of, 52; creator of all things, 60; appointed in Grand Council, 62; limits ministry to gathered Israel, 153; is morning star, 167; judgments at death

Star: lost tribes journeyed toward polar, 151; lost tribes on, 159, 163; theory, taught by Joseph Smith, 160-164; new, at birth of Christ, 167

Stars: origin of, 9; eternal, 10; not meteorites, 195; to fall, 195, 208

Suicide, men would commit, to gain spirit world, 53

Sun: and moon stood still, 31; became light source after fall, 84; earth brought near the, 84; not celestial world, 96; to be darkened, 194, 196; to be blotted out, 208; millennial, to be brighter, 220; theories as to end of, 221

Talmage, James E., portion of ten tribes in distinct body, 154

Taylor, John: on God controlling law, 14; righteous men exalted to godhead, 61; Earth organized near Kolob, 66; harmony of Abraham's creation account with geological facts, 68; elaborated on statement of W. W. Phelps, 74; heard Joseph Smith identify Adam with Daviess County, 94; defends God's moral integrity, 113; Enoch's city translated, 138; explanation of Enoch's extra-terrestrial mission, 141; vision of latter-day judgments, 184; First presidency of this eternity, 219; inherit only renewed earth, 232; Joseph Smith's eternal inheritance, 232

Teleological argument, defined, 18

Temple: veil of, in Jerusalem torn, 170; gathering for purpose of building, 193

Ten tribes: origin of, 146; led away by Father, 150; location known to Ancient, 150; repentance of, 151; not in Europe, 152; visited by Christ, 152, 192; a distinct body, 152; views on location of, 155-164; return will cause earth to reel, 161, 164; first to return to earth, 162; reconciliation of theories on, 164; to return prior to Christ's coming, 187; keys for leading, 187; modern revelation on return of, 191; enemies a prey of, 191; records of, 193

Time: reckoning of, 57; involved in earth's organization, 67; use of, by Abraham, 68; meridian of, 72; Gods ended labors on seventh, 78; earth fell from celestial, 95; Saturday evening of, 177

Translated: Enoch's city, 138; nature of, beings, 140; beings minister to other planets, 140, 189, 218

Translation, Enoch learned doctrine of, 138

Treasures, of lost tribes, 192

Trials, need for, to be exalted, 49

Tribes: remnants of scattered, 154; of earth to mourn, 200

Twelve, proclamation of the, 193

Uniformitarianism: working hypothesis of science, 16; defined, 16; prophesied by Peter, 17; opposed by catastrophism, 75

Universe: extent of, known, 3; origin of, 4-8; age of, 8; energy flows through, 11; witness for God, 19

Urim and Thummim: Noah had, 115; Earth to be a a great, 228; home of the sanctified, 229

Vegetarian: man and beast, before fall, 101; man and beast to be, in millennium, 217

Vegetation: corrupted by fall, 99

Veil: physical body is a, 48, 204; of temple torn, 170; earth passed through, 203; fell from Christ, 204; Earth hidden behind, 207; Earth must pass through, 220

Vision: of redemption of dead, 40; of John Taylor, 184

Walker, Charles L.: Joseph Smith on desireability of spirit world, 53; Brigham Young on Earth's original location, 97; Addison Everett and Jacob Gates on lost tribes, 161; testimony of a Mrs. Green on lost tribes, 163; testimony of Eliza R. Snow on lost tribes, 163, 164, 226; Addison Everett on Earth's division and restoration, 227

War: first, followed cursings, 107; atomic, in last days, 184; prophesied by George Albert Smith, 185

Waters: above and beneath earth, 116; source of flood, 118; essential to earth's rebirth, 120; covered highest mountains, 121; receded from America, 121; reduced cosmic radiation, 133; of earth, polluted, 181; ancient, to be replaced, 211

Wegener, Alfred, on continental drift, 143

Week, earth's temporal, 177

Whitney, Orson F.: God punishes men to